It's Not Only
Rock 'n' Roll

Praise for *It's Not Only Rock 'n' Roll*:

'My friend David Crosby said it best . . . Those moments just before you go to sleep are like the elves taking over the workshop. I like the elves to be present every moment in my life. There is so much to see, to experience and comment on. Creativity is all around you. Open up and let it rip.'
Graham Nash

'What most astounded me when I read Jenny's book again (it's been many years since the first time!) . . . is what an interesting read it is, and as relevant today as it was twenty years ago.

'It seems I had a very naive and joyful approach to writing and performing, a feeling I believe is still there in me somewhere. Over the years, after I retired, I gradually wrote less and less, whether that was lack of belief, motivation, or simply that I had nothing more in me to offer, I don't know.

'I'm seeking help to restore that childlike pleasure I found in creating music. Someone dear to me told me recently that the gift never goes away, it only needs to be woken up – to get those juices active again.

'So this I am doing, and rediscovering the joys of songwriting, because there's no doubt that when I write something good, it's with some kind of stunned disbelief that it came from me. I would love to feel that again.'
Christine McVie

'The substance and revelations that are garnered in this book are second to none. Speaking for myself the journey Jenny took me on was an example of her innate skill to set a stage on which the story of the creative process can unfold.

'So many of my fellow musician artists in this book have clearly allowed their inner hearts to show – and thus have become part of the author's quest to bring the true magic of the creative to its rightful place – a place that, if allowed, is for ALL to revel in!

'In the words of William Shakespeare, "If music be the food of love, PLAY ON."'
Mick Fleetwood

Jenny Boyd Ph.D.

with Holly George-Warren

It's Not Only Rock 'n' Roll

Iconic musicians reveal the source of their creativity

JOHN BLAKE

Published by John Blake Publishing Ltd,
3 Bramber Court, 2 Bramber Road,
London W14 9PB, England

www.johnblakepublishing.co.uk

www.facebook.com/Johnblakepub facebook
twitter.com/johnblakepub twitter

First published as *Musicians in Tune* by Fireside in 1992
This edition published in paperback in 2013

ISBN: 978-1-78219-462-0

British Library Cataloguing-in-Publication Data:

A catalogue record for this book is available from the British Library.

Design by www.envydesign.co.uk

Printed in Great Britain by CPI Group (UK) Ltd

1 3 5 7 9 10 8 6 4 2

Papers used by John Blake Publishing are natural, recyclable products made from wood grown in sustainable forests. The manufacturing processes conform to the environmental regulations of the country of origin.

Every attempt has been made to contact the relevant copyright-holders, but some were unobtainable. We would be grateful if the appropriate people could contact us.

Dedicated with love and gratitude to the
memory of George Harrison

CONTENTS

IN SEARCH OF CREATIVITY

'IF I LIVED MY LIFE LIKE I PLAY THE DRUMS,
I WOULDN'T HAVE ANY PROBLEMS.'

TONY WILLIAMS

It's funny how you can look back and pinpoint the exact moment an idea is born. I can remember the conception of this project, though I never imagined a book as the outcome. I came across an example, an artist, someone I had known for years, an eminent musician considered a genius by many. I began to imagine what it must be like for him, having such an incredible talent on one hand and yet seemingly so tormented on the other. What a weight to carry, I thought. I had seen him play and heard his music numerous times. There were moments during his performance where his music bordered on the sublime. I felt he was so gifted, as if in touch with another world.

I wondered if it was possible that the responsibility of such a gift was too much for this artist. Did he ever long to ignore it and head in another direction? Was it in hope of defusing his awareness and his feeling of being special that he turned to alcohol and drugs? I had heard him say he wanted to be like the man on the street – the man who, in his eyes, was not burdened with such a great talent or a mission to fulfil.

And so – on the surface – drink seemed to help him escape. In reality, though, he suffered unbearable loneliness, and there was no real escape for him. There was only one thing he could do and that was to acknowledge his God-given talent and accept that he had a purpose in life. He could contribute to society through his music, spread the word, and bring people together.

This is what he eventually did. He now had the strength and the humility to realise this was his life's work, his destiny. He had become aware of something that was stronger than his will, and so he had no choice but to bow to that power and obey it.

This image touched me deeply. It made me wonder, not only about this particular artist but also about other musicians I knew. While creating, were they aware of something greater than themselves? Did they consider their talent a gift? Did they have a sense of destiny? If artists are acutely aware of their gift and sense of destiny, do they feel more in tune with their inner voice?

These questions arose in my mind after having spent the past 20 years living in a world populated by musicians. I came of age during the tumultuous sixties, a time of great social and artistic upheaval, and along the way I developed friendships with some of the world's most innovative performers. My British family lived in Kenya, East Africa, during the first six years of my life, but we returned to

London in the mid-fifties. My love of rock 'n' roll started with Fats Domino, Duane Eddy, the Everly Brothers and Buddy Holly. At the age of 16, when 'Love Me Do' crept into the charts, my elder sister, Pattie, met and later married George Harrison. I left school aged 17 and became a model. London was bubbling over with excitement at that time; innovations were occurring in every aspect of culture: art, fashion, film and especially music.

Being a model for trend-setting Carnaby Street designers put me right in the centre of the 'zeitgeist'. In 1965 I started going out with drummer Mick Fleetwood who was then performing with a band called the Bo Street Runners. Mick and I spent many days and nights caught up in the whirlwind of London life, going to nightclubs and socialising with other musicians.

In 1967, I moved to San Francisco and immersed myself in the psychedelic sounds of Haight-Ashbury, as well as attending the Monterey Pop Festival, the first of its kind. On my return to England, George asked me to accompany him and Pattie, along with the other Beatles, to India where we studied Transcendental Meditation with Maharishi Mahesh Yogi. During that time I was able to witness the creative process at work as I watched John, Paul and George playing bits of new songs to each other, sitting on the rooftop of our bungalows and strumming their guitars. These songs were later to be heard on *The White Album*. Before going back to England I travelled with Pattie and George to join sitar master Ravi Shankar on a tour in South India.

Not long after our return to London, I renewed my relationship with Mick Fleetwood, who had been recording and touring successfully with his group Fleetwood Mac, at that time one of England's major blues bands. We eventually began living together, and I spent much of my time with the members of the band.

Particularly impressive was the group's co-founder, songwriter and guitarist Peter Green. He had an intensity that seemed to radiate from his body when he played. Peter knew that I had been on a retreat in India and confided to me that he'd had a spiritual awakening. When I travelled with Fleetwood Mac for part of their 1970 American tour, Peter was high with this new awareness. Somehow, though, his great creativity seemed to gradually overwhelm him. He donned robes, grew a beard and long hair, and looked very much like a biblical figure. A powerful person at the pinnacle of his career, Peter keenly felt the audience's adoration and began to envision himself as a kind of saviour. He thought that the band should give up their homes and tour around the world like gypsies – at the height of his artistic prowess he was no longer fulfilled doing the circuit for fame, money and possessions. Unfortunately, after his dream got squashed Peter left the band and seemed to retreat within himself. This was the first time I had ever seen creativity become a disruptive force.

Fleetwood Mac limped along, adding new members, one of whom was bassist John McVie's wife, Christine, who was already an established singer, songwriter and keyboardist. Mick and I were married while the entire band was living in a large house in the country. The band toured constantly and managed to survive a virtual revolving door of musicians. After the birth of our two daughters, Mick and I moved with the rest of the band to Los Angeles in 1974.

When American musicians Stevie Nicks and Lindsey

Buckingham joined Fleetwood Mac, it was a creative shot in the arm for the band. From the beginning there was an almost magical chemistry among the new members and Mick, John and Chris. Together they recorded a vibrant album, *Fleetwood Mac*, and more endless touring followed.

Eventually the constant touring and its effect over the years had a negative impact on our marriage. We filed for divorce and in 1978, I moved back to England with our two daughters. We lived in a cottage in the country close to Pattie and her new husband, Eric Clapton. It was while visiting friends in Los Angeles, over Christmas 1982, that I met and later married Ian Wallace, a British drummer who'd been in King Crimson and had relocated to California to play with Bob Dylan. Back in L.A., I went on tour with Ian while he played for Crosby, Stills and Nash, Bonnie Raitt, Bob Dylan, and other American musicians.

After many years of being involved in everything that went along with the rock 'n' roll world, I decided to go to college and study psychology. After working for my Bachelors degree, I continued with a Masters in Counselling Psychology and then began my PhD.

While contemplating this topic for my dissertation it became obvious to me that the subject of creativity was something I'd always been fascinated with. Being surrounded by talented musicians for over 20 years was inspiring to me, but at the same time had often left me questioning my own sense of creativity. Although I completed my dissertation on the subject and received my PhD in 1989, my investigation and interviews continued. *It's Not Only Rock 'n' Roll* is the result of the information and ideas gathered from 75 interviews that took place between 1987 and 1991.

About the Authors

Jenny Boyd is a research psychologist and author with a Ph.D. in Human Behaviour. For the last 20 years she has lived in England and worked as an addictions consultant. She is founder and director of Spring Workshops, organising psychotherapeutic groups for people in need of personal development. She lives in London with her husband.

Holly George-Warren is the award-winning author of more than a dozen books, including *Public Cowboy No. 1: The Life and Times of Gene Autry*. She has contributed to numerous publications, including *Rolling Stone*, *MOJO*, the *New York Times*, and the *Village Voice*. She resides in New York with her husband, Robert Burke Warren, and their son, Jack.

Chapter 1

NURTURING CREATIVITY

'MY CREATIVE LIFE IS A CONSTANT STRUGGLE TO ACHIEVE A
BALANCE BETWEEN LETTING THINGS FLOW IN AND LETTING
THINGS FLOW OUT.'
DON HENLEY

What exactly does the word *creativity* mean? I have struggled with that question and its ramifications for many years. In the past I considered creativeness and talent as going hand in hand, talent being a natural ability or aptitude, which perhaps was inherited genetically. It was my belief that only those special people who were born with a great gift could create something novel and extraordinary. I have since come to see that talent and creativeness are two entirely different things. Simply having talent does not always guarantee that one is creative; conversely, one does not require an exceptional gift to be creative.

In its most basic form, creativity is a universal, innate quality. Its prerequisites are traits we as human beings naturally possess: curiosity and a sense of wonder. These inborn characteristics are essential for exploring our

1

surroundings and thinking intuitively and imaginatively, fundamental aspects of creativeness.

Creativity can also be used in another sense, to describe the creation of artistic and highly specialised pursuits. In addition to that basic sense of wonder and curiosity, creative people also have a prodigiously developed interest in something. The root of this interest could be hereditary: for example, a strong capacity for understanding or feeling music, an innate gift for painting or drawing. This kind of special talent, coupled with the natural instinct for discovery, draws a person to explore a particular area. Such a person has a fixedness of purpose, a complete absorption and passion in doing the things that make up the creative process.

Although we will be concentrating our discussion on professional musicians, whose creativity belongs in the latter category, we will see that there are several elements common to both types of creativeness. In a few cases the artists may even fall into the first group, as do most people. The overwhelming difference is that all of those I have interviewed for this book fit the description given by psychologist Frank Barron, a pioneer in creativity research, who wrote: 'Creative individuals are persons whose dedication is nothing less than a quest for ultimate meaning. Or perhaps it is not so much that they are dedicated as that they understand themselves to have been elected and have accepted the office. What is enjoined upon them is to listen to the voice within and to speak out.'

Barron's 'voice within' is that deepest part of our being, labelled the 'unconscious' by Sigmund Freud and Carl Jung, the fathers of modern psychiatry and psychology, respectively. The unconscious is the part of our psyche that does not normally enter our awareness but that – in my opinion – can be reached through the creative act.

Creativity is more than just *producing* something, though. The much greater meaning to creativeness was aptly described by psychiatrist and author Silvano Arieti: 'Creative work ... may be seen to have a dual role: at the same time as it enlarges the universe by adding or uncovering new dimensions, it also enriches and expands man, who will be able to experience these new dimensions inwardly.' This latter aspect of creativity was termed 'self-actualisation creativeness' by Abraham Maslow, a psychologist who has studied and written extensively on the creative process.

The 75 musicians here range greatly in their degrees of talent, yet each is remarkably creative. How have those whose talent is not as brilliant come to lead creative lives equal to those who are musical geniuses? What is it about their psyches and their lives that have made their careers possible? I sought out musicians from the complete spectrum of popular music – rock, jazz, blues, soul, funk, hip-hop, pop, folk, country – to ensure a variety of artistic backgrounds.

Equally important, I wanted to find out if and how their ability to create enriched their lives. Has it enabled them to know themselves and therefore be more fulfilled? Have they undergone what Maslow considered the climax of self-actualising creativeness, the *peak experience*? If so, what is such an experience like, and what has been its effect on their lives?

I chose to study musicians because I believe their gift is very special. More pervasive and accessible than any other art form, music touches almost everyone. Musicians are the torchbearers, the spokespersons of our time. Their songs express not only the feelings and ideas of the individual but of his or her generation and its culture. I also hoped that the artists' answers to these difficult questions could help those of us who do not feel particularly gifted in one area but who have the capacity for self-actualising creativeness. (The complete list of interview questions, as well as a brief description of each musician interviewed, can be found in the Appendix.)

How Nurturing Fosters Creativity

To look at drawings and listen to stories created by children, it is obvious that they are naturally imaginative and inventive. In fact, Maslow described a childlike nature as being an element of creativity, writing: '... Self-actualisation creativeness [is] in many respects like the creativeness of all happy and secure children. It [is] spontaneous, effortless, innocent, easy, a kind of freedom from stereotypes and clichés ... It seem[s] to be made up largely of "innocent" freedom of perception, and "innocent" uninhibited spontaneity and expressiveness.'

What happens, then, to these qualities, along with the vivid imagination and the instinctive creative urge that are so apparent in the young? It seems that in order to thrive, creativeness must be nurtured and encouraged. Unfortunately, many of us find our creative inclinations crushed by our parents, the school system, and society in general, whose intentions are to enforce the status quo.

I asked musicians what their childhoods had been like.

Had their musical talent been recognised at an early age, and if so, had it been encouraged? Was their environment conducive to an interest in music? Were they given inspiration and motivation to play music at an early age? I have come to the conclusion that although the majority of them had musical parents, this was not a prerequisite of their being creative. Regarding the age-old psychological question of nature versus nurture, 95 per cent of those interviewed told of the nurturance and encouragement they received while growing up. I believe that these were the vital components needed that gave the musicians the courage and faith in themselves needed to pursue their creative yearnings.

Psychologist Dean Keith Simonton, who has researched the genesis of creativity, emphasised: 'On the whole, environment seems to play a much larger role than heredity in the emergence of genius. Though intelligence is to some measurable degree subject to genetic inheritance, environmental family and intergenerational influences appear far more important in the development of a potential creator.' Certainly, almost everyone knows talented people who do not use their gifts. Could it be they were inhibited during childhood from expressing themselves freely?

Indeed, the vast majority of artists I interviewed were encouraged by parents or grandparents to develop their innate artistic talents, regardless of the parents' own musical skills. Of those given encouragement, the only slight difference I could find between the ones with musical parents and the ones without was that children with musical ancestors tended to become aware of their special talents at an earlier age than those whose parents had no musical knowledge. Most of the artists described their parents as music lovers who made music an important part of their family life. Their childhood stories convinced me overwhelmingly that a nurturing environment can foster creativeness.

Encouragement from Grandparents

Some musicians recalled first finding inspiration and encouragement from an enthusiastic musical grandparent. Years ago, when I accompanied my sister Pattie and Eric Clapton to his grandmother Rose's house, the first thing I noticed in her sitting room was a large upright piano. Eric later told me that his grandmother, who had raised him because his mother was young and unmarried, had instilled in him a love for music that she herself shared: 'I think I wanted to be a musician from the minute I was born. I wanted to play anything my grandparents would get for me, which included violin and drums. When I was really young, my grandmother used to encourage me "to do a turn". It was a big thing that everyone would have their own song. My gran would have a certain song if it was Christmas or if people had come round to visit. As a tiny tot, I was inevitably put up in the big bay window, they would pull the curtains, and I would sing "I Belong to Glasgow". That was before I was aware of show biz. It was a very musical family background. Rose played the piano very well.

'When my mother came back [to the Clapton household], she introduced jazz into the house. She was a big jazz fanatic – things like Benny Goodman, Harry James, or swing and big-band jazz. This was all very prevalent in my home when I was nine or ten. I clicked on that, especially Glenn Miller.'

Keith Richards, guitarist and songwriter for the Rolling Stones, fondly described his grandfather's early influence on him: 'I first started holding guitars and bashing away on pianos when I was a little kid. My grandfather used to run a dance band, and he turned me on to the playing of music. We were very close to each other. He had seven daughters and lived off the Seven Sisters Road in London, which was pretty ironic. He had this incredible sense of humour – for one guy to live in a house full of eight women, you've got to have a laugh!

'When I used to visit him, a guitar would be on top of the piano, and I thought that's where the guitar lived. Just a few years ago I found out that he used to put the guitar there especially for my visits. He'd take the guitar out of its case, polish it up, and leave it there. He never asked, "Do you want to play?" He would just let me look at it, and slowly I would ask if I could touch it.'

Another well-known British guitarist and songwriter, Peter Frampton, vividly remembered his grandmother's role in introducing him to music: 'My father's mother had a piano – with the candlesticks on it and everything – on which she used to play vaudeville music. One day when I was five or six, we went for a visit, and she produced a ukulele. I thought it was marvellous, so she gave it to my father for me to play later on, when my hands were big enough. A couple of years later I ran across the dusty case in our attic and asked my dad what it was. He reminded me of the ukulele, and so I asked him to show me a few chords. My father played guitar in a college dance band before the war, so he knew the basic chords and how to tune it.

'I was about seven-and-a-half when I started playing, and I became obsessive about it at a very early age. When I was eight or nine my grandmother took me up to Shaftesbury Avenue and showed me all of Tin Pan Alley [the music centre of London]. She also took me to Selmer's [a famous music shop], where I remember seeing [early British rock 'n' roll guitarist] Hank B Marvin's guitar in a glass case. She encouraged me more than my parents [did] at the very early stage.'

Singer and songwriter Stevie Nicks was encouraged musically by her parents, but her ultimate inspiration was her grandfather, whose songwriting ability greatly influenced her. She fondly recalled her early years: 'My mom said that I started singing when I was very young. They always had music going for me because I seemed to have such a love for it. Even as a baby in a crib, I wanted music. My dad's father was a country and western singer, so he brought music into my life as soon as I was able to understand music at all. I was singing duets with my grandfather when I was four. My grandfather rode the railway trains across the country and played in different places. He played harmonica, fiddle and guitar. He wasn't a great musician, but he was a really good songwriter. I'm kind of the same way. I consider myself a good songwriter, but I don't consider myself a very good musician.'

Musical Encouragement in Working-Class Families

Many musicians I interviewed came from backgrounds where money and luxuries were in short supply. Fortunately for these artists, though, their parents managed to provide them with a guitar or other instrument and, most important, the encouragement to play music. This proved true when the parents were not musically inclined themselves. I'd first met the late George Harrison's parents back when the Beatles were at their peak. I thought how wonderful it must be for them to witness their son's achievements.

When I interviewed George for this project, he explained that his parents' love of music had ignited his desire to play guitar: 'Neither of my parents were musicians, but they did have an upright piano in the house, and my dad, who was a merchant seaman, bought a lot of records and a wind-up gramophone from the States. There was always music about the house, and they also liked to dance. My mum was often singing. Since they really appreciated music, they encouraged me. When I was 12, I wanted to buy a friend's guitar, and my mother gave me the 3 pounds and 10 shillings to buy it. My mum really liked the idea of me playing, because Dad was always out working at night or doing shift work.

'There was a friend of my father's who, he remembered, used to play guitar when they were on the ships together. My father had sold his guitar because he needed the money, but this guy had continued playing. So my father called him up and asked him if he would show me a few things. This guy owned a liquor store, and whichever evening of the week he closed the shop, I'd go down there and he would show me how to play the guitar. I'm sure that set a certain pattern in my music, because he taught me all those old songs. He taught me all the chords to what you would call "dance band music", and that stayed with me until this day. He was a great help to me, showing me where to put my fingers and how different chords follow each other, just by playing songs, really. In retrospect, I think he had an enormous influence on me.'

As a founding member of The Hollies, Graham Nash was also part of the new sound that emerged from northern England in the early sixties. He, like George, was encouraged by his parents to follow his dreams – something that was rare for most kids whose hardworking parents feared the economic instability of a musical career. Graham said of his early years: 'My father was an engineer, a foreman in a moulding company in Blackpool, England, and my mother took care of the family. I had friends who played guitar and seemed to have talent, but they were dissuaded from their destiny by their parents who said, "You've got to get a real job; this will never last. Go to the factory like your grandfather did and his father and your father and get a gold watch at 65."

'I think my parents recognised something in me that they encouraged instead of deflated, and I'll always be grateful to them for that. I was always encouraged as a boy to follow my natural instincts; my mother and father instilled in me that if I followed my heart, I'd come to no harm. Neither of them were musicians, although I found out about six months before my mother died that she was living her life [vicariously] through me. She had ambitions when she was a young woman of going on the stage and performing.

'At 13, I was given the choice of either a bicycle or a guitar; fortunately I chose the guitar. There was no doubt in my mind I would be a rock 'n' roll star. I would practise my autograph at school and draw the latest Fender guitars and drum kits and stuff. I had no fear of audiences, and I could always sing. When I first met Allan Clarke, who later joined The Hollies with me, we were five years old and would sing in the school choir. We would stand up in front of the school and sing hymns in harmony. It was no big deal at all; in fact, it was a kind of a thrill. I continued to perform with Allan, and from the age of 13, I knew that I would be a hit. I don't know why; I don't know what that was based on. I knew that Allan and I had something that pleased audiences, and we obviously translated that to mean that we could make it out there. I think that was also seen by our parents, which was the reason why they encouraged us.'

Blues guitarist B. B. King grew up in the poverty-stricken Mississippi Delta. While most middle- and working-class Americans of the day viewed a guitar as a luxury, music was integral to the rural African-American culture from which B. B. King emerged. He described his first encounters with the stringed instrument: 'For some reason I was always crazy about the guitar, and most families in the area had some type of old guitar – that's the one thing families in the area I grew up in could afford. When we went to church, the preacher, who was my uncle's brother-in-law, played the guitar.

'After church the preacher would come to our house, and all the adults would have dinner, and the kids would have to wait until the adults had finished before we could eat. Usually when the preacher would visit, he would lay his guitar on the bed. He always had a nice guitar; the electric guitar was coming in then, and he had a guitar that was amplified with pickups. So when he laid his guitar on the bed and then went in for dinner, I would crawl up on the bed and start playing with that guitar. One time they caught me, and I thought I'd surely get it. But the preacher didn't scold me; he showed me three chords, which I still use today.

'That was my first experience, but I had an aunt who collected records all the time. Some of the artists on the records she had were Blind Lemon Jefferson, one of my favourites, and Lonnie Johnson, another of my favourites. She had many others that included Robert Johnson, but Robert Johnson never did get to me like Lonnie Johnson did. Plus I had a cousin I was crazy about named Bukka White [a seminal blues player and songwriter]. I was crazy about Bukka, his personality ... I liked his playing but his personality was beautiful. Then as a teenager I sang gospel and played guitar with several quartets.'

Music as Family Entertainment

Musicians who grew up in musical households – even when the performing was more amateur than professional – seemed to get a positive dose of parental encouragement along with an early love of music. Many of these artists spent their childhoods during the fifties, before television took centre stage in family life. In that era playing music was an activity that parents and children could participate in together.

David Crosby, a founding member of the Byrds and Crosby, Stills and Nash, reminisced about family musical endeavours during his childhood: 'My dad, who was a Hollywood movie cinematographer, could play mandolin; my mother was quite musical. She didn't play an instrument but sang in choirs and loved music dearly. There was music in our house a lot. We had one of the earliest long-playing record players ever made; even before that, she used to have a big old 78 player to play symphonies. She played a ton of classical music around the house, so that naturally inclined me towards music. My brother also played, and we actually used to sing as a family. My parents were very anti-TV, and my mother had this idea that we should stick to older values, so we used to sit and sing around the fire. We'd sing folk songs from a book called *The Fireside Book of Folk Songs*. The story is that I started singing harmony when I was five or six years old.'

Keith Strickland started his musical career as the drummer in the B-52s, then became the band's guitarist. These talents, along with his songwriting ability, he partially attributes to the musical encouragement he received as a child: 'Neither one of my parents played music professionally, but there was a lot of music around the house. We had a piano, and my mom was very good at improvising on it; she'd just make up songs. Thinking back, that had a very profound influence on me and the way I write. My sister took piano lessons, my brother played trumpet in a band, so there was always music in my house. Plus I had a cousin who lived in New Orleans, so through the fifties and early sixties, whenever she would come and visit, she would bring all these fifties rock 'n' roll records, like Little Richard, Fats Domino, the Everly Brothers, Elvis Presley. So at a very early age I was exposed to rock 'n' roll, and I just loved it. My mother was my first inspiration, but rock 'n' roll, that was it! I was around five or six and I would just beat on things. Since I was always pounding on things, my parents bought me a snare drum. I never took lessons. The drums came very naturally; I was always rhythmically inclined. I also played piano. Because the piano is very percussive, I immediately related to it in that way. So I would sit at the piano and write out little melodies and things.'

The Wilson household was also musical, with sisters Ann and Nancy, who later formed the band Heart, both getting incentive to play. Guitarist Nancy Wilson recalled a variety of music being played in their home: 'Both of our parents were musical. Our mother was a college-level concert pianist and our dad was a baritone in a barbershop quartet, so we had all sorts of musical influences. We always had a hi-fi, as they called it then, and listened to everything from opera to Ray Charles to Judy Garland to Aretha Franklin. Our parents have been really amazingly encouraging all along. I think it's much more conducive if your parents aren't throwing your records out the window! [My sister Ann and I] were given piano lessons with teachers, and also our mom would sit down with us a lot, and we'd just pick up things by ear. We always sang as a family and harmonised. It was a fun way to grow up, with music all around.'

The late jazz drummer and composer Tony Williams offered another example of the enormous impact that an encouraging musical family has on the budding musician: 'My dad played saxophone, but he was more of an amateur musician. When I was a kid, he worked for the post office. He liked to play saxophone, but I don't think he ever had the desire or the talent to be a full-time musician and support a family and make all of his money from music. My mother liked listening to a lot of music. Through her, I grew to have an appreciation of classical music, because she had those kind of records that you buy in the supermarket of Tchaikovsky, Rachmaninoff and Wagner, things like that. So she would play those around the house, and my dad would be playing Count Basie and Gene Ammons and things like that. My friends and I were always listening to Frankie Lymon and the Teenagers, and the Clovers, and groups like that. There were a lot of different kinds of music around the house.

'I was nine when I first started playing the drums, but there are stories and pictures of me as a toddler – around two or three years old – performing. My dad could get me to sing little songs. When I first started playing I used to go out in front of my dad's band and sing and do a little tap dance. In fact, the first time I played a set of drums was in front of an audience. I had never played the drums before. I asked my dad if I could play with his group, and he said yeah. We were at this club, so the next set I went up and played for the first time. After about four years of playing, my mom thought it would be good if I took lessons, but they were basically for reading music.'

Like Tony, singer-songwriter and former Doobie Brother Michael McDonald grew up with a father who was an amateur musician. Michael recalled the profound effect his dad's love of singing had on him, beginning when he was just a wee lad: 'My father was a singer. He wasn't really professional, though it seemed to be such a big part of his life. He was an Irish tenor, coming from a first-generation American family. We have a big Irish family, and they're all nuts about music. All our social functions were centred on somebody singing, my dad usually, with a lot of music in the house.

'My father was welcome in every bar in St Louis because he could sing, but he didn't drink. He's probably been to more bars than any drunk you'd ever meet in your life, but he just loved to sing there. I remember the first time he put me up on a bar. I was four years old and I sang some ridiculous song for a four-year-old, like "Love Is a Many-Splendored Thing". Everybody got a big kick out of it and laughed. I'm sure it was horrible, but I remember thinking I'd never done anything up until that point to solicit such a response from people. It made a big impression on me.

'I always followed my father around. Every Saturday afternoon we spent in bars, meeting different friends – that was his social life. The story he tells me is that one day I pulled on his pants leg and said, "When can I sing?" Then we became a dynamic duo: every place he went, I went with him, if I could and it wasn't too late. I always got to sing a few numbers. It kind of fused itself in my brain somewhere then that [making music] is what I'd do. My social life with my dad was an overriding factor in my life. He was my biggest musical influence at a very early age. I think there's a part of me in the back of my brain that is doing this for my dad, for his attention.'

Like Michael McDonald, the singer-songwriter Jackson Browne was blessed with an enthusiastic musical father who demonstrated to his young son the pleasures of playing an instrument. Jackson vividly recalled those early years: 'My father was a real good piano player and grew up playing a pipe organ. He liked Dixieland but could play a number of things. He also got jobs playing for the silent movies. When my father had a party, the whole house would fill up with people, the loudest people you'd ever heard – he and his friends were great revellers – and there'd be four or five guys playing. My dad would say to me, "If you want to have fun, play an instrument because you always go to parties and you're always indispensable." He wanted me to play the trumpet, and I played it for two or three years when I was a kid. I loved the trumpet, but then when I was 10 or 11, I realised that I wasn't going to whip out a trumpet at a party. It would be cooler to sit down at the piano so people could come around and sing.'

Throughout our interview, drummer Steve Gadd, who has performed with such artists as Paul Simon and Aretha Franklin, returned to his assertion that his family's support had enabled him to develop artistically: 'My family were music appreciators, but my uncle, who lived with us, was a drummer. He wasn't playing professionally but had played as a kid in high school. I remember coming downstairs and seeing a red parade drum that belonged to my uncle. I was two or three. That was the first time I ever saw a drum, and I'll never forget it. I guess I must have fallen in love with it. They say I always used to bang on things, pick up the silverware and play it on the table or hit on something. So my uncle got me this little round piece of wood and gave me a pair of drumsticks and showed me how to hold them. He had a little round piece of wood and sticks too. At night when everyone was home from work, the whole family would sit in the living room listening to records, and my uncle and I would play along with the music. Sometimes my father would do it; sometimes my brother would play.

'During the day when my parents were working, I'd be with my grandmother and I would listen to music and play along with records for hours. There was always a lot of encouragement. When I was six years old, I started taking lessons. My grandmother used to take me to my drum lessons. My drums were set up in the living room with the record player right behind. My parents let me play whenever I wanted to. They never ever told me not to play. The first thing I'd do in the morning, even before I ate breakfast, was to sit down and play the drums. I'd come home from school for lunch and sit down and play a little bit, and the first thing after school, sit down and play. The people around me paid a lot of attention to what I was doing. I had a natural love of the instrument, but [it was added to by] the encouragement I got from my parents, the happiness they got seeing me do what I was doing while I was playing. They got a lot of enjoyment out of it.'

Singer and songwriter Stephen Stills, a founding member of Buffalo Springfield and Crosby, Stills and Nash, described how his father indulged not only his musical whims but those of his playmates: 'My dad had a tremendous collection of old jazz records; he was an agent when he was in college. My mom used to sing in the church choir and had a beautiful contralto voice. I started playing drums, then piano, then bass, and a little trombone. Guitar was later in the game; I'd already been playing music since I was about six, [but] didn't get a guitar until I was 14. My dad bought me a set of drums when I was eight, because I was going to tear up the furniture. He even bought a guitar for this kid I wanted to form a band with.'

Like Stephen Stills, blues artist John Mayall was inspired as a kid by his father's love of music: 'My father was a musician, and I was exposed to all his record collection at an early age. He had guitars around the house, so when I was big enough I started to get the rudiments together. [My parents] split up when I was about 11, but I did see him. His record collection was really what started all my musical interest.'

British guitarist and songwriter Richard Thompson spoke of the lasting effect of early reinforcement on an artist's means of expression: 'My father was a music fan; he's a great jazz fan and played a little guitar in a police dance band. So there was a guitar in the house, plus his record collection – 50 per cent Jimmy Shand and 50 per cent Duke Ellington and Django Reinhardt. My musical taste is still 50 per cent Jimmy Shand and 50 per cent Duke Ellington and Django Reinhardt. I think childhood is a big influence on life: what you hear when you're three or four years old really tends to stay with you. About 10 years ago I did a version of a Duke Ellington song, and I did all the parts on the guitar. I realised I hadn't heard this song since I was eight years old, but I'd remembered every single part, got the whole arrangement completely down. Amazing.'

Singer Patty Smyth was also inspired by a parent's record collection. Patty remembered how her mother's lifestyle and love for music influenced her: 'My mother was a circus performer – she ran away to the circus when she was 16 – a trapeze artist and a dancer. When I was growing up she was a club owner in the [Greenwich] Village [in New York], so I spent a lot of time around music. She was a singer, but I don't think it was her gift; her dancing was.

'When I was about six, I remember that my mother had all these records. I played them over and over and had them memorised. I sang with them and amused myself for hours. My mother had some big plants, and I vividly remember crawling through the plants and singing Barbra Streisand

and Frank Sinatra songs. It brought a lot of joy. That's my earliest memory of being taken out of myself. Later on there were the Beatles; I got turned on to rock 'n' roll. I just listened to music all the time. My mother bought me a guitar when I was 12. So when I was 15, I put together a band. I had always written poetry and prose and lyrics since I was a child. But I really started writing songs that I performed and later recorded when I was 24.'

Singer and songwriter Huey Lewis got his musical cues from his dad, who was an amateur musician, and his first experiences with poetry from his mother: 'My father was an amateur jazz drummer for a number of years and flirted with being a professional musician but finally ... went back to school and became a radiologist. I always listened to music around the house. Dad played in different bands, and he always played music loudly – he was a nut for music. Always jazz, very, very loud, 24 hours a day, so I always listened, but since he only played big-band jazz that never had a singer, I gravitated in my early teens to listening to singers. I think it was sort of my way of rebelling.

'My parents split up in '62 or '63, and my mother, who was an artist, started hanging out with the San Francisco beatnik set, so there were a lot of poets over. My house was pretty wild in the creative sense, and when the sixties thing exploded in San Francisco my mother was well into it. I first went to the Fillmore Auditorium with my mother when I was 13 years old. She liked the early San Francisco bands – the Grateful Dead, the Jefferson Airplane. I had to rebel somehow, so I always liked blues and R&B music. I got a harmonica from someone and that was it.'

Singer-songwriter Robert Burke Warren, formerly of the

Fleshtones and now a solo artist, is another who found encouragement through his bohemian mother and musical father: 'My earliest memories are of music, mostly the Beatles. My mother was a big Beatles fan. She was very open-minded, and my father was an amateur musician, a guitar player and singer. In college he played in coffeehouses; he was a big Peter, Paul and Mary fan, a folkie. He had taught himself how to play. I can remember him singing and playing. He died when I was seven. Everyone I've met who knew him said he was a natural musician, could just pick out a song.

'I remember when I was really young hearing music in my head, songs. It wasn't until later on that I tried to reach out and put it into another form, to try and communicate it to someone. I started playing bass when I was 14. My family encouraged my creativity from the outset. Although when I was 17 and they saw I was serious about pursuing music as a career, they tried to convince me to put it on the back burner, but they never told me to give it up altogether. Even the other things they encouraged me to do were creative. They said that music was a rough business. My grandfather was a writer for [the trade magazine] *Variety*, and they knew about show business and how it could be. I was a sensitive soul, and they were afraid all my ideals would be smashed – but they haven't been yet.'

Music was an essential part of her childhood, recalled songwriter, singer and pianist Christine McVie: 'There was always a piano in the house, and I started playing it when I was about five years old. My dad wanted both my brother, John, and me to play. His father had played the organ in Westminster Abbey, but when he died, Dad had to become chief breadwinner. He had wanted to go to college to pursue his musical studies, but he couldn't. Instead, he had to get a job playing in the orchestra pits during pantomimes and things like that. Later on he ... finished his studies and became a music teacher. I learned to play the cello at school when I was 11, and my dad also used to give me lessons. Our family had a string quartet playing in the house at Christmas time: my dad and John on violin, my mum on viola, and me on cello. It was fun.'

Singer and songwriter Steve Winwood, who started his career at age 15 as vocalist in his brother's jazz band, was surrounded by musical influences as a child: 'My father played several different instruments, and my mother was musical, although she never actually exploited it. My grandfather on my mother's side was a musician, a church organist and a fiddle player. All my father's brothers were musicians, and my father's mother played piano. My older brother was also a musician, and there were always instruments around the house. I was gently encouraged towards music, though I was never forced to learn. But I felt sure I was going to be a musician too.'

Rolling Stones guitarist Ron Wood, whose first creative endeavours were in art – a medium to which he's returned in recent years – followed a pattern set by his father and brothers: 'My dad had a 24-piece harmonica band that toured the racetracks of England, and he used to play a kind of barrelhouse piano. My two brothers had already set the mould both musically and artistically. They both went to Ealing Art College, where I followed them, and they both had bands. Art, my older brother, introduced me via jazz to the first 78s of "I'm Walkin" by Fats Domino and "Great

Balls of Fire" by Jerry Lee Lewis. Mum and Dad knew I wanted to follow that course, and they were very good about it. They just said, "As long as you don't get into any trouble with the law, you can do whatever you want!"'

Ringo Starr had an unusual childhood in that he was plagued with serious illness, which frequently rendered him bedridden. His family, extremely worried about his health, agreed to all of the ailing child's whims, the strongest of which was tapping away on any surface available. That attention and indulgence set him on the path to become one of the world's most famous drummers. He colourfully described his early musical obsession: 'My grandma played mandolin, and my grandfather played banjo. This always sounds like a sob story, but when I was seven I was very ill with peritonitis, and in the hospital they told my mother three times that I would be dead in the morning. I don't remember this, but I was later told that in my delirium I called out, "Mouth organ!" And so my grandfather tramped the bombed-out streets of Liverpool – it was just after the war in 1947 – looking for a harmonica. I believe he found me one, but I had no interest in it! We also had a piano in which I had no interest either. I used to walk on it as a kid, being a spoiled brat!

'When I was 13, I was back in the hospital again, with TB. To keep you busy, they would get you to knit or make things or do some lessons for schooling. But then every so often they brought in instruments for the kids to play. There were drums, triangles, tambourines and maracas – percussion instruments. I got to play the snare drum. There was a big easel, and if the nurse pointed to the red dot, I hit the drum, and if it was yellow [the other children would] hit the triangles. Well, after that I wouldn't play in the band unless I got the drum. That was my first real madness for drums. I even used to play on the little cupboard next to my bed, where they kept the bedpan. I used to tap on that. Then I got out of the hospital and started making kits out of biscuit tins, and putting little bits of metal on it to make it sound like a snare drum. I would cut down pieces of firewood for sticks.'

Vocalist Dolette McDonald, who has sung backup with Sting and Don Henley, found inspiration through her mother's itinerant preaching, of which gospel singing was an integral part: 'My father had an incredible voice. My mother could sing, but my dad has the most wonderful bass voice. I discovered [music] at such a young age, it's natural for me. It was like a family thing; everybody in my family did it.

'My mother was an evangelist and used to travel and preach in many different churches. She taught me a song when I was five years old, and I sang it in front of the church. I used to travel with her and sing first [before the preaching] and warm up the audience. When I saw the reaction of the crowd, it was "I kinda like this!" – being a natural ham and always on. I don't know if that was because my brothers and sisters would egg me on all the time to do stuff, but I just loved performing.

'A singer in my church also inspired me musically. She was beautiful with long flowing hair and had an amazing operatic voice. I just admired her. I was a little girl and would follow her around and try to sing like her. Out of all my musical influences, if I ever had any, this was the person who I could say was my hero.'

The great blues songwriter Willie Dixon was inspired by his mother's love for sacred music and his father's penchant for the blues. This foundation fostered his own form of self-expression: 'My mother sang in church and so did my dad, but never in the choir or nothin' like that. My father sung in the fields in Mississippi, and he sung just about some of everything and anything his mind came upon, like most of the blues artists and most of the people around that time.

'I've been writing practically all my life to a certain extent, because my mother used to write poems, mostly about spiritual things. I learned how to write poems, and I was thinking as a youngster I would get a chance to make poem books and sell them, but after I made so many, nobody was interested in them until I started to make songs out of them, kind of popular songs. I couldn't get them sold or nothing done with them, so I began to turn them into blues. My mother was a devoted Christian [and so thought the blues were profane], but my father – they called him a kind of an outlaw – he didn't care because he felt that Christianity and all those things was a lot of baloney and brainwash. So he would sing the blues, and she would sing spirituals, and I began to weigh the both of them. Eventually I decided with the blues.

'When I was about 12 or 13, I was taught a lot about harmony from a fellow named Theo Phelps, who had a group called the Union Jubilee Singers. I joined the group and we would practise singing and go to all the little country churches and city churches and have singing contests all over everywhere. I sang bass all the time, so it taught me a lot about the bass lines. We rehearsed at his house, and in learning how to sing the various parts of harmony, it did me a lot of good because I could always use it in arranging things as I became older. Our group finally got a chance to sing on [radio station] WQBC in Vicksburg [in the 1930s]. That's when radio first came out. We sang every Friday evening, and that was a big event in our life.'

Most artists whose childhood homes were filled with music recalled gaining from that a sense of the joy and fun inherent in the art form. Conversely, Irish singer and songwriter Sinéad O'Connor discovered through her musical father the powerful emotions that could be conveyed in a song. She described the bittersweet impact of this revelation: 'Both of my parents were musical. They both came from very old Dublin families, and Dublin people are very musical. My mother used to sing opera when she was a teenager. I think my father attempted to play the piano, but he wasn't very good. When I was very small, my family used to sing songs all the time. My father was always singing to us; each of us had our own special song that he would sing to us before we went to bed. Mine was "Scarlet Ribbons", which is a very upsetting, very disturbing song. So right from a young age I understood songs could get over very strong emotions. When I was about 12, I started writing songs. I wrote in my head, but I didn't think of it as writing. I sort of sang to myself as I walked along to school.'

Growing Up with Professional Musicians

I interviewed several artists whose parent or parents were working musicians. In their homes, music and creativeness were a way of life. In addition to possibly inheriting their parents' musical talent, these fledgling musicians grew up with a great deal of incentive to be creative. Their childhood stories illustrate how the early recognition and support of talent can enhance artistic potential. I met with a musical parent and child, jazz and new-age flutist Paul Horn, and his son Robin, a drummer who often plays in his father's band.

Paul, who I first met in India in 1968, told me about his own musical family: 'My mother played piano and recorded music in the twenties. She worked for Irving Berlin's publishing house, as the staff person who played the songwriters' music when they came in. In those days they didn't have tape recorders, so if you were a songwriter and wanted your song to be published by Irving Berlin Music or anyone else, you had to go in and sing the song yourself or bring someone along to sing it. Many times they didn't have their own accompanist, so my mother would sight-read and sing too, if necessary. She had her own radio show and made records, but she stopped all that when she got married.

'My parents were pretty hip for their generation. They really laid no trips on me and didn't push me in any direction. Their attitude was, whatever I wanted to do was cool and they'd support it. So if I wanted to be a musician, that was fine, even if I wanted to be a jazz musician, which was not looked upon from the majority of the people with too much respect in those days. I started taking piano lessons when I was four. My mother decided not to teach me herself, which was probably a good decision, since we were of like temperament. But she'd be there to support and help me if I didn't understand something with my lesson.'

Paul's son Robin came of age during the sixties and was exposed to music early on, through his father's career as well as the musical environment of that time. He remembered how exciting the sounds were for him: 'I grew up in Laurel Canyon, where lots of L.A. musicians lived. As a boy, whenever I heard live music coming from a house, I would go up and knock on their door and introduce myself. I'd say, "I'm a drummer" and then just walk in. I was eight years old and didn't even think about the social consequences. At that time the climate was very open to do such a thing. Mickey Dolenz from the Monkees lived right across the street, and the Turtles lived down the block.

'It all seemed to happen automatically: I knew I wanted to play, and within two weeks I heard this guy playing drums, knocked on his door and convinced him to give me lessons. If it's an inner drive at that age, it's in all innocence, though. I wasn't even aware of it. Nurturing it and seeking out a teacher wasn't something I was forcing; it just happened. It took over, and I now think that part of the creative process is nurturing itself.'

I first met Julian Lennon when he was a little boy. Twenty-odd years later, we got together again for an interview. I was curious to find out how his creativeness had been affected by having such an artistic but frequently absent father. Julian, who is now a songwriter and singer, told me he'd been encouraged by his father, John, and his mother, Cynthia: 'At 11, I got my first guitar from Dad after I told him that I used to play an acoustic at school. The gym teacher had been teaching us how to play guitar when there was a break between lessons, and he had spare guitars. Mum never pushed me in either direction, but I started to have a great interest in playing piano all of a sudden. When I was around 14 or 15, she bought me a piano for my birthday, and I've stuck with it ever since. She didn't push me in that direction but helped me along with it.'

The late British songwriter and singer Kirsty MacColl

grew up as the daughter of a well-known folksinger and songwriter, Ewan MacColl. She told me that in their household, creativeness was a way of life: '[After my parents' divorce] I used to see my father on Sundays and visits, and he was fairly encouraging because he was a songwriter and a playwright before that. It wasn't like I was the only one in the family who was creative. It was the norm; everyone in the family was expected to be creative.'

Randy Newman, a songwriter, singer and pianist, came from a family of professional musicians. His uncles, who composed film scores, inspired him, but it was their mother – his grandmother – who actually encouraged him. Randy, who scores films himself, described that creative environment: 'My uncles were musicians, film composers; Uncle Alfred did pictures like *How Green Is My Valley* and *Wuthering Heights*. He won nine Academy Awards. Two other uncles did motion picture music. One used to conduct all the Danny Kaye pictures. He was musical director. My Uncle Lionel was head of music for 20th Century-Fox for 45 years. All of them were very good conductors. My father was a doctor, and he played the saxophone a little.

'Unfortunately, no one made me practise [playing piano]. It was something I was good at and would get praised for at an early age. I'd play for my grandmother, and she would like it. She was encouraging but died when I was 11. My uncles thought I was sort of good; it wasn't much, but it was enough. I was seven, and it was always work for me. It was like the family business in some ways.'

Terri Lyne Carrington, who has been performing as a jazz drummer since her teens, was nurtured along musically not only by her parents but also by their friends, well-known jazz artists. She fondly recalled her early influences: 'My father's a musician; my grandfather was a musician; and my mother is musically inclined – she studied piano. My grandfather passed away before I was born, but his drums were in the house; my father plays saxophone. I started playing saxophone first, and when I was seven I switched to drums. I'm an only child, and my father wanted a son to carry on the musical tradition in our family, so when I decided to play, he was really happy. I started taking lesson when I was eight.

'My dad and his musician friends – [jazz stars] Illinois Jacquet, Roland Kirk and Clark Terry – encouraged me to play. Jazz drummers would come into Boston, where we lived, and ask me to sit in with them: Elvin Jones, Art Blakey, Buddy Rich. Beginning when I was 10, I was a special guest in Clark Terry's band with Louie Bellson, George Duvivier, Jimmy Rawls, Eddie "Lockjaw" Davis, Garnett Brown and Al Cohn.'

Another jazz artist who grew up in a musical family, saxophonist Branford Marsalis described how his approach to music was inspired by but differed from his father's, the jazz pianist Ellis Marsalis: 'My father is a piano player; my mother is musical but she doesn't play anything. I was always aware of [music]. It was different for me; my dad lived music, but I just liked playing with things. I was very mechanically gifted, fixing things. The piano was like a machine; clarinet, saxophone – they were all like little machines that you had to learn to manipulate. The love for music came later, when I was about 14. The piano was my first instrument; I was five or six. Then the clarinet when I was between seven and eight, then sax when I was 15. The first two records I ever bought in my life were Elton John's "Goodbye Yellow Brick Road" and Cheech and Chong's "Big Bambu", and I learned [to play] everything off both albums.'

Guitarist and songwriter Billy Burnette, a one-time member of Fleetwood Mac, also came from a family of career musicians. His father and uncle were rock 'n' roll pioneers in the fifties, and Billy followed in their footsteps, beginning at a very young age. He described the impact this had on his life: 'My dad, Dorsey, and my Uncle Johnny had a group called Johnny Burnette and the Rock 'n' Roll Trio. They started off by writing a lot of the really big Rick Nelson hits. They also had some success on their own; my dad had a couple of big hits, and my uncle had five or six in the early sixties.

'I was real young when I started getting into it and singing professionally. I did my first record, a Christmas song, in 1960, when I was about seven. I would sing, because I didn't start playing guitar until I was in my teens. When I was eight years old, I did a lot of stuff like Dr Seuss records; Herb Alpert used to produce some of them, so it was fun. I also did some children's shows. I was about 11 or 12 when I sang with Brenda Lee, and we toured the world. I loved it. I had it in my mind a long time before I actually learned to play guitar, that that was what I wanted to do because of the excitement of touring. I can remember being on the road with Brenda and wanting to go out after the gig, but I was too young, so they locked me in my room. At that age I made my mind up that this was what I wanted to do forever.

'My dad was always pushing me. When I wasn't in studying my songs and was out playing baseball, he would tell me to make up my mind which one I wanted to do. I was real young and I wanted to do it, but he gave me that extra little push that I needed at the time.

'I started playing guitar a couple of years after I got back from touring. Guitars were always around the house. It was the next thing for me to do – to pick up a guitar and say, "Dad, show me a few chords." I learned a few, and there were always people coming by and teaching me stuff. I was one of those kids that bugged everybody and asked a lot of questions. Later on, when I was in my twenties, I got to play in my father's band. It was great; he was my best friend.'

The parents of Rod Stewart's long-time guitarist Robin Le Mesurier, who had played with French icon Johnny Hallyday, were famed comic actors and TV personalities in England during the fifties and sixties. Hattie Jacques and John Le Mesurier instilled in their son a love of performing. Robin recalled how that love, coupled with the presence of music around the house, became the catalyst to his pursuing a musical career: 'Growing up was a lot of fun, especially the people who I met because of [my parents'] industry; it was like *Carry On Christmas* [one of a series of *Carry On* films John and Hattie starred in] 'round our house. My dad was a great pianist; he always said he would much prefer to earn his money playing the piano rather than acting. My mum first started out as a singer in music halls; she had a very good voice. They always used to be playing music. In fact, I remember, when I was about four or five, there used to be lots of noise, lots of parties, and funny-smelling cigarettes. And people like Peter Sellers and Spike Milligan used to be there jamming at three or five in the morning. I didn't really appreciate it until I was about five or six, then I really started listening to music a lot. One day my godfather brought back a guitar from Spain, and I just sort of got attached to it. I taught myself to play.'

One of the most extraordinary childhood stories I heard was that of the late sitar maestro Ravi Shankar, who as a young boy began touring the world with his family's music and dance troupe. Encouragement came from all around, as he spent his early years immersed in a glamorous world populated by creative people: 'When I was 10, my eldest brother, who was a dancer, formed a group of musicians and dancers made up of my mother, two brothers, cousin, uncle, two family friends and myself. I was the youngest. So we all went from Benares, India, to Paris, which became our headquarters.

'I was awestruck. I was thrown into this whole atmosphere of dance, music, and millions of miles of brocade and costumes being sewn and ornaments being made for our troupe. We copied the costumes from the old temple sculptures of all the mythological subjects such as Shiva and Krishna.

'It was a prime time, for Paris was the centre of the art world. All the great musicians, painters and writers were in Paris – Cole Porter, Gertrude Stein, Henry Miller, Toscanini, Jascha Heifetz – and a number of ballet dancers. I remember them so well in different salons that I used to visit. Segovia used to live near us and would come to visit us, and I used to sit on his lap. When we first came to the States in 1932, I heard jazz – Cab Calloway, Duke Ellington, Satchmo and Count Basie. Then we went to Hollywood – Joan Crawford here, Greta Garbo there, Gary Cooper. This is all the glitter and glamour we were with, and I was learning dance at that time. I also had the freedom to pick up the sitar and play.

No one stopped me, but unfortunately no one taught me properly, so what I was doing was watching and copying and playing by ear. I was very good at that; I was playing in the background all the dance pieces, and then I would dance also. So that's how the years went by.'

Igniting the Creative Spark

In addition to the musical inspiration their families provided, most of these artists also recalled a general feeling of acceptance and encouragement. Their childhoods seem to characterise certain elements that psychologist Carl Rogers identified as being external prerequisites to fostering creativity. Rogers emphasised the importance of 'psychological safety', wherein an individual is accepted as having unconditional value and is given understanding rather than criticism. Equally essential, theorised Rogers, is 'psychological freedom', which can be found in environments where one is allowed to think and feel what is true for oneself.

Among the many musicians whose childhood stories illustrate Rogers' concept is Living Colour guitarist and songwriter Vernon Reid: 'I grew up in an open environment, where I was allowed to have different kinds of thoughts than my parents. My parents were very strict on one level; on another level they were very open. I was never told not to read this or not to read that. I was an avid fan of science fiction and comic books, and I was allowed to read that. If I had an imaginative idea, I was never told, "That's stupid". They may have looked at me funny and said, "That's interesting", but I never felt like my imagination was stupid. My imagination was allowed to grow.'

Jason Farrar, a composer, singer and instrumentalist, overcame his blindness and began learning to play music when he was only three years old. At 12, he had already realised how important the belief in oneself is to being an artist, something he credits his parents with instilling in him: 'When I was young, I was in a church, and people didn't know I could play until I copied on the piano the song they had been singing. They gave me money for piano lessons, but at that time my family didn't have a piano. We had an organ, though, so a man would come over and give me organ lessons. Later I got an old upright piano, and I got piano lessons, then singing lessons. [At 15] I got my synthesizer and drum machine, and I've been doing performances with them ever since. My mom told me when I was little that I could do anything, so as soon as I realised what I could do – with my mom and dad encouraging me – I decided to be an entertainer.'

Jazz drummer Peter Erskine was allowed free rein to express himself from a young age. He described how his parents appreciated and supported his musical awareness and sensitivity: 'My mother told me stories that when I was a little kid I'd talk about hearing music; I'd say, "Did you hear that?" and look around. My dad fashioned a little drum kit for me out of Chinese tom-toms, with a tiny sizzle symbol out of paper clips. I remember asking my dad for lessons when I turned five, and he drove me down to the music shop and just by chance the guy who taught was there. He was a very patient guy and very enthusiastic. My parents were extremely encouraging. My father's psychiatry practice was connected to the house, [but] he never once complained when I used to play drums, even though his patients were there. At about 10 or 11, I remember how shocked I was when I was talking about one piece of music to my friend, describing how I got the chills when I was listening to it, and my friend had no idea what I was talking about. I was amazed that not everybody responded the same way.'

Red Hot Chili Peppers singer and songwriter Anthony Kiedis was also encouraged by his parents to be himself. He followed the example of his father, a rebellious non-conformist, who was a major influence on him: 'Both my parents were very encouraging towards my creative talents. I moved in with my [divorced] father when I was 11; it was an incredible change for me, because I went from a very backwards mid-western culture, where they're not really aware of what's around them, to Hollywood. There, it was much more the epicentre of culture, and there were a lot more things happening.

'My dad was very crazy: he was concerned that I become well educated, and he always gave me great books to read, as well as little vocabulary tests and things like that. At the same time, he was very much a hippie/gangster/playboy/over-the-edge party maniac on the Sunset Strip, and I wanted to be just like him, so I followed his every footstep. He was a graduate of UCLA film school; he was very together as far as that was concerned. He led the wild, unrestrained, reckless life, but he encouraged me to do creative things. When I would write a paper, he would always want to read it, and he really enjoyed my writing. And that's pretty much all I did until I started acting – when he started acting, I decided I would do what he was doing. There was never any suppression from my parents.'

Like Anthony, songwriter, singer and guitarist Lindsey

Buckingham got positive signals from his family to follow his heart: 'In general, my parents were supportive of everything; they were supportive of me as a person. When I first started playing music at age six, I didn't take lessons; I just learned to play by ear and by listening to my brother's records. It was a hobby, something ingrained in me at a very young age, so the guitar has always been there. I never felt like I had to sit down and learn to play the guitar. It was something that excited me, that animated me; that charged me up. It meant a great deal to me. I would just play along to songs and learn chords, and my style just sort of evolved. I don't think my mother was of a mind that music would be something that I should pursue professionally. I think she knew the entertainment business was a rough one, and that there are a lot of pitfalls and a heavy lack of stability. So she didn't encourage me to seek that out, but she certainly encouraged me to play.'

Fortunately for Lindsey and all the other musicians included in this chapter, they got the emotional support they needed to pursue their artistic dreams. But what of those who did not receive such nurturing yet managed to progress in their musical endeavours anyway? How did they persist through the difficult learning process? What gave them the drive to seek out teachers or learn to play on their own? How did they maintain the determination and willpower to keep practising and not give up? For example, when I was a child, I loved music but didn't have that sense of 'this is it' when I strummed my guitar.

After discussing these questions with musicians, I have concluded that some people have certain qualities which motivate them to passionately pursue creative lives. These forces are so strong that even those discouraged from being creative can rise above a hostile environment and fan the creative flame. As we will see, numerous artists' stories bear this out.

Chapter 2

THE DRIVE TO CREATE

'MUSIC IS A MEANS OF EXPRESSION THAT RINGS
TRUER AND IS MORE CONNECTED TO THINGS INSIDE
THAN SPEECH.'
LINDSEY BUCKINGHAM

When I first began this book, I came across a quote by Goethe which I kept pinned up above my writing table: 'The first and last task required of genius is love of truth.' It is the vocation of artists to seek their own truth and then express it in their art. But to be a seeker of truth also demands certain qualities: drive, courage and motivation.

A creative person's drive determines whether or not he will be able to express himself, no matter how much talent he has. What is the nature of this drive? Is it the need to make oneself whole, to complete the process of fulfilling one's potential?

Some psychologists, such as Abraham Maslow, Carl Jung and Rollo May, have theorised that everyone has an inherent desire to actualise their true nature. Why are some people more able to self-actualise and to do so earlier and throughout their lives than others? From my interviews I discovered that this drive may in part be linked to an artist's strong feeling of his own destiny, his call in life, as well as the fulfilment of his actual potential. Psychologist Frank Barron told me that the drive to create is fuelled by the need to express oneself artistically and to discover one's own meaning in the universe.

For some artists, having found at an early age their natural means of expression, music became an easier way to communicate than any other. I remember when I first met Mick Fleetwood, he was extremely shy and found it difficult to carry on a conversation. He used to telephone me, say hello, then put down the phone receiver next to his drum kit, which he would then begin to play, while I listened for the next 45 minutes.

Mick exemplified how artists who discover themselves through their creativeness can more easily communicate their essence via their art form. Maslow described this quality: 'Artists are in touch with their intrinsic nature and are continually in the process of becoming more of who they really are.' Being closer to the core of their being, they allow this basic elemental nature to guide their lives, which in turn results in their feeling more fulfilled and whole.

The Courage to Create

Courage also plays an important part in creativeness. It takes courage to be different, to go against the status quo, which creative people invariably must do. Artists have long been considered society's 'outlaws'. As Maslow wrote: 'Every one of our great creators … has testified to the element of courage that is needed in the lonely moment of creation, affirming something new (contradictory to the old). This is a kind of daring, a going out in front all alone, a defiance, a challenge.'

Courage is essential for one to truly believe in oneself. This is another reason acceptance plays such an important role in the musician's childhood. When that courage is mixed with faith in oneself, the artist gains a firm grounding from which to pursue his or her talent as a means of self-expression. By trusting themselves first rather than relying on the approval or consent of exterior societal forces, artists tend to reject tradition. They are not afraid to break down the old to make way for the new. Because of this feeling of intrepidation, the artists can look into the depth of their imagination – into the world of chaos – fearless of being overwhelmed by the unknown. This courage and faith enables them to delve into disorder and stay there until they find meaning. As Rollo May says: 'They knock on silence for answering music. They pursue meaninglessness until they can force it to mean.'

This fearlessness makes artists better able to integrate their inner world with the outside world. Whether this courage is innate or derived through a nurtured self-confidence during childhood is not clear. While most of the musicians I interviewed received encouragement during their early years, some did not. What gave this latter group the stamina to withstand the pressure to conform?

Some of them experienced the intense frustration of not fitting in with their environment or their peer group, particularly during adolescence. This led to an underlying feeling of having to struggle through typical social situations, yet they persevered as if they knew in the back of their minds that there was something much bigger on the horizon.

Whereas through socialisation most adolescents lose their childhood belief that literally anything is possible for them, many creative individuals never lose faith that whatever they dream will actually come to pass. This goes hand in hand with their sense of destiny, of being true to their inner voice. When I was first introduced to Mick Fleetwood, we were both 16, and though I was still a schoolgirl, he had already left his home in Salisbury, in south-west England, to make his way all alone to London. As a child he had discovered the drums, and it was an intense revelation for him: he knew without a doubt that he wanted to be a drummer. This was much, much more than a childhood whim. From that moment on, he lived and breathed the drums, much to the dismay of his schoolteachers, whose classes he failed, and his parents, who worried what would become of their wayward son. They needn't have worried: Mick had more motivation and drive – to become a professional drummer – in his little finger than most studious schoolboys have in their entire being. Mick knew deep inside that his destiny awaited him 'out there' and that he was only biding time until the day came when he could begin his journey into musicianship.

In our interview Mick vividly described his childhood, his drive, courage and determination, as if the day he discovered the drums were only yesterday: 'I was obsessed with wanting to be a drummer; I didn't drool over a musician and think, I've got to be like that player. It simply happened. That was it: I wanted to be a drummer, and I can't remember why. It had to be from my dad. He would play the bottles or even play rhythms with the change in his pocket.

'I remember one time when my family was driving through Europe, we stopped in a small German village. There were cows underneath the inn we stayed in and these old yogurt-eating guys who live to be 120, sitting around downstairs in the inn. They were all sitting around a 12-volt battery with a wire attached, getting a buzz out of it. That was the setting. Before going to bed that night, I crept downstairs and saw Dad in the bar with all these elderly guys, playing the bottles, having a great time.

'At boarding school I became obsessed with playing drums. I never had a kit, never played, it just started to happen. I had this dream: I wanted to be playing in London at a club. I had it all planned out. All I did at school was to send away for drum catalogues. The only other thing I enjoyed was the little bit of acting I did. I had a drum catalogue that was literally eight inches thick; I had taped them all together. I used to drool over these drums; it was my dream to have a Premier drum kit.

'I remember going out on my own and sitting underneath a tree. I had my catalogues with me, and I just made a secret pact then and there with myself that I was going to play drums. I remember tears pouring down my face – and that was it. That was the moment I knew I wanted to do this. I ran away from school because I had this vision. I knew what I wanted to do, that was the commitment I made to myself. I made a private pledge, and I prayed to God, and then that was it.

'I didn't practise or work at being a drummer – I just did it. There were a few [drum styles] I mimicked, but that stopped after I started playing with other people. Apart from learning the songs, my practice was my playing. My dad was wondering what the hell I was going to do; he wanted to take me to an unemployment counsellor. But not long after that I started playing drums in London at the Mandrake Club.'

Mick's experience illustrates characteristics of creative adolescents described by psychiatrist and author Silvano Arieti: 'A few adolescents start to think that their own personal growth will continue if they reach beyond the limits of what seems to them a restrained and small reality.' Arieti pointed to the difficulty the creative individual encounters when he or she becomes aware of the 'vast discrepancy between the human condition and his [or her] own ideals'.

As a child, blues guitarist Buddy Guy also had an active imagination, which took him far away from his tiny, rural hamlet. He grew up to live out his most vivid dreams: 'I used to lay and dream a lot of times that I was onstage in front of an audience. It crosses my mind now every time I look out at a huge audience. Every time I look out there I remember those dreams, when I'd wake up and I didn't even know what a guitar was.'

What happened to Buddy occurred to other musicians I talked to as well. Keyboardist Greg Phillinganes described the young imagination and ambitious dreams that prefigured his career: 'I used to daydream about playing in front of massive crowds, getting the kind of reaction that the Beatles got. When I was in high school I grew strongly attracted to Stevie Wonder, musically speaking; I put posters of him all over my bedroom. I used to dream a lot about playing with him, and I told my friends that I would play with him one day. And then it happened. I'd seen him only twice in concert. I was introduced to him by a friend of mine who was asked to audition for him. The friend gave him a tape of my playing, so Stevie had me come out to New York from Detroit. I did that and was with him for almost four years. The childhood dream had been very strong – and that's what happened. I was pretty amazed.'

Graham Nash also pursued his childhood dream of being a musician, against the odds. 'If something hadn't made me strive towards what I believed in, I could have ended up in Manchester in the mill. It was through parental encouragement and my taking advantage of opportunities that enabled me to do it. All my life I knew I would be doing this, though I must confess it's gone on a little longer than I thought it would. I still have an insane drive to create and express myself, and it'll never stop because I don't know how to stop it.'

The Young Outsider

Several musicians recalled feeling strongly out of place during childhood. They sought ways to express themselves, '[to reach] beyond the limits of a small and restrained reality'. Because they found it difficult to communicate with others, they became more introspective than the average child. They learned to maintain and trust their own inner world, which most children leave behind once they blend in with others, largely out of the desire to be like everybody else. Singer, songwriter and drummer Don Henley, a founding member of the Eagles, described feeling like an outsider in the rough and tough Texas town where he spent his childhood: 'The older I got, the more different

I felt from the other kids. I felt I didn't really belong in the town where I'd grown up, that the other kids were very different from me and I didn't have anything in common with many of them. A lot of them were violent and insensitive, and I was a very sensitive little kid. I was rather small in stature, so I got picked on and beat up a lot. This is all very typical, and the older I got, the more I realised it was alright to be different, and that it was, in fact, a good thing.

'In the beginning, when you're young, you think that if you're different, that's not good. What Nietzsche speaks of as "the voice of the herd" is very strong in you. Then, the older you become, your confidence grows, and you realise that it's alright to be different. Maybe they're wrong and you're right. But for a while, you think they perhaps know something that you don't know. I had a reversal of that in my late teens, thank goodness.

'After I got into junior high school, the thing to do, of course, where I was brought up in Texas, was to play football. That was the heroic natural thing for a male to do – and I only weighed about 98 pounds. So when I was 15, I tried to play football, and that was a miserable failure. The coaches were sadistic, it was very brutal, and I got pounded royally, so I quit that.

'After I failed at football, I joined the high school marching band at the behest of a friend of mine. My first instrument after I joined the [high school] band was trombone. For a year another kid, who also quit football, and I had to practise by ourselves with very little instruction. Neither of us were progressing very well. We both used to go around beating on our textbooks with our fingers and with pencils – it just annoyed the hell out of everybody. One day someone said, "Why don't you try playing drums instead of the trombone?" So we both switched to drums, and we were both naturals at it.

'I taught myself and spent the next two-and-a-half years in the high school marching band playing drums. My mother bought me my first real set of drums when I was 17 and didn't tell my father until she'd actually done it. We both sprang it on him that evening, but he was good-natured about it. A group consisting of myself and three other high school mates gradually evolved out of a Dixieland band, which included a lot of older gentlemen. We broke away and became a rock 'n' roll band doing instrumentals. Then around 1964–65, after the Beatles were becoming the rage, we decided that we were going to have to sing, so that's when I started singing. I had to learn to play drums and sing at the same time; I had mastered it pretty well after about a year.

'[I think the choice to create] goes back to childhood. Take, for instance, a reasonably bright and sensitive little kid, a kid growing up in an environment that's antagonistic towards sensitivity. I grew up with a lot of very rough people. I think that kind of environment drives you inside and makes you introspective. I was simply too young to have an insight regarding human nature or the human condition. I didn't understand why people were the way they were. I felt like an alien. I believe that being exposed to that kind of adverse outer environment at such a tender age drives one towards a richer inner life, a life of dreams and fantasy, a life of yearning and creativity.'

Sinéad O'Connor described how she has followed her heart since childhood even though it meant being treated as a renegade by her peers and a problem by authority figures. Although hers is a lonely path, she has always valued her own sense of truth over society's expectations: 'I felt very much different [from the other kids], and they contributed to making me feel different. I *still* feel different. I always got in trouble all my life for saying things, saying what I thought, expressing myself. It just never occurred to me to be any different; I wasn't trying to cause trouble. I'm not aggressive at all, but I'm very emotional. We're brought up to not be emotional. It's so hard, especially since I'm young. It's difficult because you're up against everyone, you're on your own, you're up against a wall of fucking trouble, because everyone's telling you that you're bad and you're awful and you're horrible, and you begin to ask yourself if you are. You begin to think it. It's so hard to actually retain what your purpose is – or to even realise what it is – and think it doesn't matter if they think you're a bastard.'

Michael McDonald explained that he, too, felt outside the mainstream as a child, but that the benefits of this 'forced' introspection far outweighed the disadvantages. 'I think a lot of creative people are emotionally handicapped in some ways, usually through experience. Therefore, the creative process is a thing that is developed *because* of those deficiencies, as a way of dealing with the world around them. I've noticed that with a lot of people that urge to be creative, that urge to find that experience over and over again, comes from a feeling of not belonging in this world, always feeling out of place. That kind of forces them to be observers because people who feel that a lot tend to observe other people. I know that's how I was when I was growing up – always comparing everything around you to yourself. I think for people who write, their talent is born out of that constant questioning of themselves versus the environment.'

Jackson Browne described how he didn't fit in with the surfer culture that dominated the southern California town where he grew up. Unlike the other guys he knew, who wanted to spend their spare time in wetsuits, Jackson was drawn to music: 'I was 13 when I started playing the guitar. It was something I could do by myself when everyone else was surfing. I used to take the guitar when a group of us would go surfing at Huntington Beach, I would eventually end up sitting on the beach, playing guitar because I was so skinny, so little. My friends were all bigger than I was. In those days, wetsuits were very rudimentary big things that the water went sloshing through, and it was cold in the winter time. I would wind up sitting there, just having been washed up on the beach exhausted. Eventually someone said, "Hey, if you're not going to surf, if you're going to sit there and play the guitar, I know a lot of guys who would want this spot in the van." So I decided to just stay home and play guitar; inevitably one thing takes over from another. So music became my big interest when I was 14.'

Julian Lennon told me he spent much time playing music as a child. Perhaps part of his need to express himself stemmed from his circumstances: The son of a Beatle, he was considered a curiosity by his schoolmates. Julian recalled the impact this had on his life: 'I had a mad childhood, because having a famous father meant having fans outside your gate every morning before you walked to school. There would be hundreds of them. A lot of Americans used to stand outside and give me presents. After coming home from school, there would be a new toy every day. It was exciting.

'But when I got older and was in school, I suddenly realised people were acting differently towards me. I couldn't understand the reason why at first – then it dawned on me. A lot of aggression towards me was built on rumours started by one person. Just one of them was, "Julian has 10- and 20-pound notes stuck on his wall to impress people when they walk in." That gets around a town and everybody looks at you like you're … you know. It was either because Dad was famous or maybe you could get something from me or from being associated with me. It was very bizarre. I started getting interested in playing music about then, when I was nine or 10.'

Eric Clapton's family situation resulted in his feeling different from most other kids in his small village who were raised by the then-traditional mother-father unit: 'I was born in Ripley, in Surrey, in 1945, near the end of the war. I was brought up by my grandparents; I was illegitimate, and my mother was too young to bring me up. She was 15 when I was born. My father had been transferred back to Canada, being a Canadian Airman, and I don't really know if she left me in terms of abandonment or was told to go. It's not very clear. I was brought up in the Church of England; it was a fairly religious society in the village. When I was nine, my mother came back to see if I was alright. That's when I found out that things were not as they appeared to be.

'From then on, I had a very confused childhood. I felt different from most of the other kids, but there was a little gang of about four or five that all seemed to have something in common in terms of being maladjusted. Most of these kids had moved to Ripley from outside the area. At the age of about five or six, they had been uprooted from their original village or town and placed in this little village. They weren't at all happy with their situation, and so we seemed to have something in common. These were the kids I hung out with, and we were the first ones to start smoking and listening to rock 'n' roll. I wanted to be different from everyone else. I sensed that I was, so I developed the philosophy of flaunting it, but that wasn't in an outgoing way. Instead it was very introverted. I wanted to be a beatnik before beatniks were even heard of in Ripley. I was the village beatnik.

'I was 13 when I started playing the guitar. I then stopped for a while when I became interested in art. I was very good at art and got a scholarship to go to a school in Kingston. I travelled from Ripley to Kingston every morning, half training to become an artist and half interested in music. The music got the better of me in the end, and I was thrown out of art school. At 17 I started to work professionally in a band. I was pretty much a loner in terms of what I believed in to be musical for myself and was very defensive about it; I was very serious and protective towards my musical ambitions. I don't think I really knew that playing music was what I wanted to do for life until I was 20. I think I was probably quite serious about it though, so there must have been an inkling.'

Musical Rebels

Traditional social conventions were not the only things Eric and some others described overcoming. Many artists resisted the limitations imposed by formal music or art lessons as well, feeling the need to break free of all limitations. Julian Lennon, for example, found piano lessons detrimental to his own self-expression: 'I had one piano lesson, but I hit the wrong chord and got whacked over the hand with a ruler, so I thought, this isn't the way to learn music. At about 11 or 12, I started writing bizarre sorts of songs. By teaching yourself, you can find things that people who are taught wouldn't normally find, like playing inversions of chords, which normally people wouldn't play. I guess that's how I came along with my own style. I just stuck to the weird stuff that people don't usually play, and they'd say, "How do you play that?" Then they realised it's the same chord just played a totally different way, because I have no knowledge. I still don't know what I'm playing, but as long as it sounds right, that's all that matters. Finding the weirdest chords and trying to make a song out of them gave me the drive to keep playing music.'

Steve Winwood extricated himself from a stifling and uninspiring music education: 'Shortly after I turned five or six, I had some [music] lessons, but I fooled the teacher by doing things by ear instead of reading. That didn't last long, and I didn't really have any training until I was 14. Then I got into the Birmingham and Midland Institute of Music as a part-time music student while I was still at school. I did that for about a year and a half before I got kicked out for playing rock 'n' roll and jazz, which, of course, was not acceptable. They made me make the choice – so they kicked me out.'

Singer and songwriter Peter Gabriel also broke loose from the restrictions of lessons – both musically and educationally: 'I used to sing in the choir when I was very little and always loved music. My parents bought me a couple of records, and I started listening to the radio and taping things off the broadcast, and then dancing. I stopped piano classes when I was young because I hated all my lessons. Then I started relearning it when I was 12 or 13, picking out a note one finger at a time. At school there was a sense that I could cut through the repression, just letting my hair down and dancing and screaming. It was physical and emotional and intellectual all at once.'

Beginning in childhood, singer, songwriter and Genesis drummer Phil Collins did not follow a traditional path, preferring his drum kit to toys. During adolescence he became dissatisfied with his successful career on the British stage when he discovered he could not express himself honestly through drama. Phil's musical drive was so great that he gave up acting to play music professionally although it meant disappointing his parents, who had encouraged him in the theatre. He recalled: 'I had a pretty normal upbringing. My dad used to have a little boat, and he belonged to the yacht club with about one hundred other people who had boats. Because of that, they used to put on dinners and dances, and a couple of times a year they'd put on pantomimes, and I would play in them, usually as Humpty Dumpty. Apparently I was given a little drum when I was three and took to it. When I was five, my uncle made me a small drum kit that fit in a suitcase. I would play these shows, and so I was exposed to that kind of thing from very early on until I was 11 or 12. My mum started an agency to book kids for commercials and TV, so I started going to auditions. When I was 14, I got the part of the

Artful Dodger in *Oliver!* That's when I moved from my grammar school to stage school.

'All along, though, I didn't want to do anything else but play the drums. I'd bypassed all the train sets and stuff. I knew from a very early age that I didn't want to do anything but that. I used to come home from school and just practise and play, although I realised I couldn't do that professionally until I was grown up. Other kids would be playing football more than I did. All I wanted to do was sit at the drum kit upstairs and play along with my records.

'At the time, that was a lot different from my friends, who had no interest in music at all. I used to be in my own little world. I always used to play in front of the mirror because I had read that it was good to watch yourself play so you don't look down at what you are doing. I would put the record player on as loud as it would go and play along with it. It must have sounded terrible downstairs where they were trying to watch television. I remember sitting in the living room and playing along with the television while everyone else was trying to watch it. When I was 14, I started drum lessons – I'd taught myself from the age of five – thinking that as this was what I wanted to do in my life, I should try and do it properly. I decided I'd do the pop group thing when I was old enough, then after that finished, I'd probably do sessions or go into a big band – that seemed like the kind of thing to do in your late twenties, early thirties – and then I'd end my days in a pit band, like an orchestra pit.

'I used to go home with all the orchestra musicians in *Oliver!* I was in the show on the West End for seven months, then I started being asked to do other things. At the point when I was 16 or 17, I told them I didn't want to do any more acting. I just wanted to play the drums and I was finally old enough to get into a professional band. My mum and dad weren't very happy about that, especially my dad, because he liked showing me off at the office – "My son's in the West End stage!" as opposed to being in a rock group. There was deathly silence around the house for a couple of weeks.'

Singer-songwriter Joni Mitchell was also encouraged by her parents to be creative, until they no longer approved of her means of expression and withdrew their support. By this time, Joni, like Phil, trusted her inner resolve enough that she was undaunted by her family's disapproval, and she continued to follow her creative path. Ostracised by her peers since her early years, she was already accustomed to being different from what people expected and to heeding her inner voice. Joni described her youth in a small Canadian village: 'In my early childhood because I was creative – I was a painter always – I had difficulty playing with the other children in the neighbourhood, just because they couldn't get in on my games. The town I lived in was a small third-world town; the mail still came at Christmas on open wagons drawn by horses with sleigh runners. There were a lot of music lessons taking place in the town. Since mainly the kids were athletic, they were sticks- and stone-throwers; they were hardy, robust, physical, not very creative. The creative people in the town generally studied classical piano or classical voice, so I had a lot of friends who were considered the singers. I was always considered the painter, but I was in association with child musicians. I spent a little time in the church choir.

'At seven, I begged for a piano – I used to have dreams

that I could play an instrument – so I was given piano lessons. The lessons used to coincide with the television broadcast of *Wild Bill Hickok*; this was bad timing [since it was a favourite show], plus the piano teacher used to rap my knuckles because I could memorise and play by ear quicker than I could read. So she made the education process extremely unpleasant. So I quit, but I still used to sit down and compose my own little melodies; that's what I wanted to do, to compose. In that town, it was unheard of, considered inferior. The thing was to learn the masters and play them. I thought I was going to be a painter when I grew up, but I knew I could make up music; I heard it in my head. I always could do it, but it was discouraged. So when I quit piano lessons in my teens, my parents weren't supportive about my wanting to buy a guitar. Since they weren't really supportive, I had to buy my first instrument myself.'

Joni managed to overcome the disapproval of her peers, her teacher and her parents to pursue her own creative dreams. She seems the perfect example of the intrepid creative person, unafraid of what others think, as described by Maslow: 'Perhaps more important, however, [is] their lack of fear of their own insides, of their own impulses, emotions, thoughts. They [are] more self-accepting than the average. This approval and acceptance of their deeper selves then [makes] it more possible to perceive bravely the real nature of the world and also [makes] their behaviour more spontaneous.' Maslow pointed out that these people are less afraid of their own thoughts, considered by others as 'nutty or silly or crazy. They [are] less afraid of being laughed at or of being disapproved of.'

Rich Inner Lives

Science cannot tell us whether some people are simply born with a more vivid imagination or whether certain individuals are more adept at maintaining it and tapping into it. What is certain, though, is that imagination is important in motivating artistic individuals to create. Many musicians described having extraordinary fantasy lives as children and/or teenagers. Graham Nash, for example, spoke of realistic recurring dreams and 'hallucinations': 'I once saw a golden city in the clouds from my bedroom window. I remember sitting at the window that faced the street – it was a stormy day – the clouds opened, and I saw what I thought was a golden city. It was very fleeting. I used to hallucinate a lot when I was a child: the cracks in the ceiling would turn into railroad tracks, ocean liners. I would make animals out of the folds in the bedspread, for instance. I always saw faces in shadows, crocodiles in the clouds. But the golden city struck very deep – it must have been a five-second thing – and I often wonder what it was.

'Whenever I was ill as a child and had a fever, I had two recurring dreams that I must have had a dozen times. One, I'm floating above my classroom watching myself being taught, observing this whole scene. The other one is of a huge truck, and on the back of it is a roll of brown paper that is 20 feet in diameter. The truck pulls forward and the brown paper rolls off, starts rolling towards me, which I start running away from, and it gets faster and faster. And it's unrolling as it's moving so it gets smaller, but it never gets small enough to stop rolling. All my life, I've been chased by this roll of brown paper.'

The extra sensitivity that is often characteristic of a creative person leaves an individual more open for the experience of such phenomena as Graham described. Of course, along with this added dimension to one's life comes the fear of being 'strange' or different from others. In the case of singer-songwriter Rosanne Cash, these experiences transcended simple imagination: 'I've had psychic experiences from the time I was a baby. I saw people that weren't there. They call those "imaginary friends" but they were very real to me. I had dreams that came true continuously. Some of this sounds pretty weird – it kind of makes me sound like I was a total looney! I've never told anybody this except my husband and a few close friends. I always did have dreams that came true and saw and heard people and knew that there was another world just beyond what I could see. And sometimes I could see through the veil. It still happens; it's not stopped. It frightened me for a while. It didn't frighten me when I was a child, but then it started frightening me when I was a teenager and in my twenties. Now it doesn't frighten me anymore.'

This did have an effect on Rosanne's feelings about herself, adding to her sense of aloneness. During her childhood, Rosanne's father, Johnny Cash, was always on the road, and then he and Rosanne's mother split up. Rosanne explained how she discovered her creativeness herself without anyone's help nurturing it along. 'I wasn't encouraged as a child to be artistic. In fact, I got angry about that [later in life] as I realised it. Nobody recognised it, that I had artistic tendencies or that I was the creative type. I don't feel like I was encouraged at all. There was no room for it at school; outside of school, it just wasn't focused. I felt

I was very strange. The kind of forums I wanted to work in were unacceptable or unexplainable. So, I became very passionate about music. It inspired me continuously. I listened to music all the time. I was very passionate about what I listened to, beginning with the Beatles. I wanted to be a writer, and I always wrote. I always kept journals and wrote really bad poetry. Then I started writing songs when I was 18.'

Silvano Arieti described the effect an active inner life coupled with a lack of creative outlets can have on a child: 'Whereas the average person very early in life learns to check his own imagination and to pay more attention to the requirements of reality than to his inner experiences, the creative person follows a different course. He feels himself to be in a state of turmoil, restlessness, deprivation, emptiness, and unbearable frustration unless he expresses his inner life in one or another creative way.' Such seems to have been the case with Rosanne.

This also appears to have been a motivating factor in the early life of Pink Floyd founding member Roger Waters, now a solo artist. Like Rosanne Cash, Roger did not recall having his creativeness nurtured at home. His very active imagination enabled him, however, to thwart his mother's expectations of normalcy, as well as those of other authority figures. Although he didn't start playing music seriously until college, he sustained his individuality throughout childhood and adolescence, chiefly through his inventive rebelliousness. Roger's description of his school illustrates how the traditional educational process seems designed to squash creativeness, a theme that he later explored artistically in his work *The Wall:* 'My father was killed in the war when I was three months old, and I was brought up in Cambridge by my mother, a schoolteacher. She didn't encourage my creativity. She claimed to be tone deaf – whatever that means – and had no interest in music and art or anything like that, and was only interested in politics. I didn't really have a happy childhood.

'I loathed school, particularly after I went to grammar school. Apart from games, which I loved, I loathed every single second of it. Maybe towards the end when I was a teenager, going to school was just an "us and them" confrontation between me and a few friends who formed a rather violent and revolutionary clique. That was alright, and I enjoyed the violence of smashing up the school property. The grammar school mentality at that time had very much lagged behind the way young people's minds were working in the late fifties, and it took them a long time to catch up. In a way, grammar schools were still being run on prewar lines, where you bloody well did as you were told and kept your mouth shut, and we weren't prepared for any of that. It erupted into a very organised clandestine property violence against the school, with bombs, though nobody ever got hurt.

'I remember one night about 10 of us went out, because we had decided that one guy – the man in charge of gardening – needed a lesson. He had one particular tree of Golden Delicious apples that was his pride and joy, which he would protect at all costs. We went into the orchard with stepladders and ate every single apple on the tree without removing any. So the next morning there were just apple cores. That morning was just wonderful; we were terribly tired but filled with a real sense of achievement.

'Syd Barrett [the cofounder of Pink Floyd with Roger], who was a couple of years younger, and I first became friends in Cambridge. We both had similar interests – rock 'n' roll, danger, and sex, and drugs, probably in that order. I had a motorbike before I left home, and we used to go on mad rides out into the country. We would have races at night, incredibly dangerous, which we survived somehow. Those days – 1959 to 1960 – were heady times. There was a lot of flirtation with Allen Ginsberg and the Beat Generation of the American poets. Because Cambridge was a university town, there was a very strong pseudo-intellectual but Beat vibe. It was just when the depression of the postwar was beginning to wear off and we were beginning to go into some kind of economic upgrade. And just at the beginning of the sixties there was a real flirtation with prewar romanticism, which I got involved with in a way, and it was that feeling that pushed me towards being in a band. I used to go with friends on journeys around Europe and the Middle East, which in those days was a reasonably safe place. How much all that experience had to do with my eventually starting to write, I've no idea.

'The encouragement to play my guitar came from a man who was head of my first year at architecture school at Regent Street Polytechnic, in London. He encouraged me to bring the guitar into the classroom. If I wanted to sit in the corner and play guitar during periods that were set aside for design work and architecture, he thought that was perfectly alright. It was my first feeling of encouragement. Earlier, I had made one or two feeble attempts to learn to play the guitar when I was around 14 but gave up because it was so difficult. It hurt my fingers, and I found it much too hard. I couldn't handle it. At the Polytechnic I got involved with people who played in bands, although I couldn't play very well. I sang a little and played the harmonica and guitar a bit. Syd and I had always vowed that when he came up to art school – which he inevitably would do, being a very good painter – he and I would start a band in London. In fact, I was already in a band, so he joined that.'

Creativity Spawned by Loneliness

The sense of aloneness and alienation in childhood was a common thread in many interviews. In some cases it was caused by events beyond the child's control; in others it was self-imposed. In both situations this sense was partially responsible for pushing the young musicians to find something within themselves to bring pleasure to their lives, since it could not be found externally. Rather than sublimating their vivid imaginations during adolescence, as most young people do, they held on to theirs and nurtured them. It became their companion.

American singer-songwriter Stephen Bishop had a childhood that aptly illustrates this concept. Like Rosanne Cash and Roger Waters, Stephen received little encouragement at home to be creative or to pursue his passion – rock 'n' roll music. Unlike Roger, Stephen had no partners in creative crime and thus depended on his own ingenuity to keep himself company: 'When I was five my father and mother broke up. My mother was very much into religion; she was an orthodox Christian Scientist. I was about eight when she remarried. Stephen described his stepfather as someone who inadvertently spurred on his creativity. 'He became very strong in the story of my life because I guess he was the catalyst in an inverted way: I was almost *forced* into being creative. He moved our family away from San Diego, where I had tons of friends and where things were always going on and I could walk to anywhere, to an area near the freeway.

'Ironically enough, our new home was right next to Kiddieland, an amusement park where I'd always wanted to stop but had been told by my folks that it was too far out of the way. I was 10 and had already been thinking of getting into music, wanting to play an instrument. Before that, I'd never thought of music; my brain cells were on a lounge chair watching *Gilligan's Island*. My stepfather bought me a clarinet, of all things. I started to learn to play it, and in a short time I could play it on my own. But I was very sad. I was forced into creativity because I didn't have any friends and I was very lonely. I would make a sword out of orange crates and have sword fights with a tree – that was the big highlight. I wound up being really resourceful; my loneliness and the situation made me creative.

'I started to make my own little comic books to amuse myself. My name at that point was Earl – I changed it in fifth grade to Stephen – and everybody at school called me Earl the Squirl. So I made Earl the Squirl the character in my comic books. I'd make up his adventures one after the other. Right in front of our house was the freeway off ramp, so next to it I built a shack out of orange crates, with a little roof and a bench. I would sit out there every day after school and wait for somebody to stop and buy my Earl the Squirl magazines. As well as playing the clarinet, I began to write little poems. I started being creative at that time, but it came out of loneliness. I don't think people realise that creativity can be your best friend, because it's a part of you.

'The advent of the Beatles really helped me creatively. They inspired me like no one else. I started playing Beatle melodies on my clarinet. My stepfather didn't dig this; he just hated the Beatles, and he hated rock 'n' roll and long hair. He hated change – it scared him. He wanted me to keep playing the clarinet, but I was on to bigger and better things. Pretty soon I begged my brother, who's nine years older, to get me a guitar, and he did. He got me an electric guitar and made an amplifier out of a stereo. It was exciting creating then because it was such a no-no. It was like having Mamie Van Doren in my closet.

'My stepfather's hatred of it all fuelled my desire, fired my creativity. I'd hear him talking to my mom, "He's playing that damned rock music." I was allowed to watch the Beatles on *Ed Sullivan* only if I cleaned up the yard every day for a year. They represented an energy my stepfather didn't want to look at. He was very discouraging. When I got two Ds in junior high, my mom wouldn't let me play my guitar for six months. That was pretty heavy because I was totally in love with my guitar. I would take it into my bedroom closet, which was quiet, to write songs. I would be in there working on an idea for the verse, really into it, and then all of a sudden the door would jerk open and there he'd be: "Look at you! You're just banging on that thing, look at you!" I'd be scared because he was very forceful. He would never let up. My creativity was just bubbling; in some ways it was kept down, but in others it was just fuelled by him. Writing songs really became exciting to me; I'd have to hurry up and write a song before he came home from work. This went on for years until I finally started a band, which he was always putting down. I had to keep it under cover.'

After spending the afternoon with Stephen, I realised that the childlike part of his nature is still very much alive. Stephen seems to relish devising inventive ways of amusing himself. That day, for example, he showed me his music room, his toys, and then had me listen to his telephone answering machine message. He loved concocting different personalities and imitating the voices of film stars to produce a scenario on his answering machine. He also enjoyed putting together eclectic mix tapes. While I was there, he pulled out numerous photo albums filled with pictures from long ago, as well as everything he had ever written, including his very first song, childhood stories he'd penned, and comic strips he'd drawn. Stephen reminded me of a creative little boy, making up games, skipping from one to the other with such enthusiasm.

Robert Burke Warren explained that part of his youth he has kept alive is his solitary nature: 'When I was around 12, I used to stay up all night. When everyone else went to sleep and the world shut down, I was able to hear things and commune with things without distraction – just walk around and not have a goal. I'd get on my bicycle and ride through the night on deserted streets; I was very content doing that. I spent an inordinate amount of time alone as a kid, and I got to know myself better. The core of everything is just to know yourself, to know who you are. The only way to do that is to spend time alone and experiment with your environment. I did that a lot.'

Richard Thompson said he was also a loner as a child and spent his time listening to records and learning to play guitar. Richard was one of many musicians who told me of their childhood affinity for early rockers like Buddy Holly and Elvis Presley: 'I found rock 'n' roll very exciting, even at the age of seven or eight. I wanted to play the guitar as long as I can remember, because Elvis had a guitar and Buddy Holly had a guitar. I actually got my hands on one when I was 10.

'I was very introverted and shy, so often instead of having friends, I'd sit at home and play guitar. I felt like a social misfit all through school. Guitar might have been a kind of revenge: "Well, at least I can do this; they think I'm nothing." I was going to show them. It wasn't the whole thing, but there was some element of trying to acquire acceptance and respectability by playing the guitar.'

Initial Inspirations

A strong admiration of other artists inspired many young musicians to learn to play their instruments. In fact, for some it seems as though their guitar or drum kit gave them the companionship they lacked, as well as giving them a means of expression. Albert Lee, the guitarist who has played with Eric Clapton and Emmylou Harris, among others, described how he came under his guitar's spell: 'When I was about 13 or 14, a friend's brother lent me his guitar. I learned to play the basics on it, and from then on the piano [which I'd been learning to play] took a backseat. I was really crazy about the guitar. I used to borrow guitars from various friends; in fact I played for two years before I actually owned one. I taught myself just listening to records – Lonnie Donegan, then all the early rock 'n' roll that came along, Elvis, Buddy Holly and the Crickets. As far as guitar players go, I guess it was the guitar player with Gene Vincent [Cliff Gallup] that really made me want to play, to really learn about guitar. I learned a lot from him, just copying his solos. They were very intricate and jazzy and had a lot of scales. It was a good way to practise, learning the scales.

'I left school when I was 15, and all I wanted to do was play music. I wasn't sure what I was going to do, but I wanted to do something with music. When I left school I wasn't quite good enough to go professional, but a year later I was. At 16, I did my first tour, and I've been on the road ever since. Once I discovered the guitar, I really didn't have any other interests.'

The late blues singer Koko Taylor, who spent her youth in Memphis and Chicago, found her heart's desire in the music of those cities. 'I grew up listening to older blues singers like Muddy Waters, Memphis Minnie, Bessie Smith, Howlin' Wolf – people like that – and that's where I got my greatest influence from. Of course, back in those days, singing the blues was really all we knew. Also gospel. So during that time I was singing gospel and I was also singing blues. I was not getting paid to sing; I was singing for my own enjoyment, and this was all I knew to do at that time.'

The late blues guitarist, songwriter and singer John Lee Hooker was greatly inspired by his stepfather and other musicians from the Mississippi Delta where he grew up: 'I was aware of my music when I was about 12. My stepfather [Will Moore] was a musician and he taught me how to play guitar in the style he played in. He played stuff that I'm playing now. My stepfather was playing with people like

Blind Blake, Charlie Patton and Leroy Cobb. He would go out and play in these house parties that I couldn't go to; I heard the records. My stepfather had one of those old machines that you wind up. I heard their music and I really liked what they did. I knew I wanted to be a musician and I was determined not to be a farmer.'

Steve Jordan, who has played drums with such artists as Keith Richards and Neil Young, was one of the many musicians who named the Beatles as a major influence on his musical life: 'My parents started giving me records really young. Before I could read, they had given me an extensive record collection. I used to identify them by the label. I heard a lot of Miles Davis: I was very inspired by Tony Williams and Art Blakey. I remember dancing in 1962, when I was six years old, to the original "Twist and Shout" by the Isley Brothers at my aunt and uncle's house. I was always dancing.

'My favourite artists were James Brown and the Beatles. They really are the essence of all the things that I think are important to me musically – everything else is an offshoot from that. The Stones have been very influential, Al Green, as well as Sly and the Family Stone, but that was a little later. The Motown sound: James Jamerson – hearing the sound of that bass – and Benny Benjamin, the drums on that, it's a part of the way I breathe. Listening to [Donald] 'Duck' Dunn and Al Jackson play together – their Memphis sound was very important. Those things inspired me the most.'

Peter Frampton explained that his initial drive to perfect his musicianship was his desire to emulate the playing style of Hank B Marvin, leader of the Shadows, a popular band of the late fifties and early sixties. 'It was really exciting learning to play. It was something I did very well, very quickly. It came easily, and so I worked long hours at it. It was my hobby, and I was obsessed with being as good as Hank Marvin.

'I have always had a challenge to meet, whether it was to be successful and recognised for my craft or to maintain the success, or just to please myself and grow as a musician, which is the most important thing to me. In my home studio I still go and enjoy myself, and if I play or write something new, it fuels the drive that I have always had to break new ground. There's nothing like coming up with a new piece of music to spur you on to do more.'

The Intense Drive to Create

Peter Frampton described the fulfilment he attains by playing music, almost as if he has no choice. It reminded me of something Jung wrote: 'True productivity is a spring that can never be stopped up … Creative power is mightier than its possessor.' This was reiterated by jazz drummer Robin Horn: 'If you are a creative person, you must have an outlet. I've had the experience of not letting it out, like not practising for a week, and I start to become a real uptight son of a bitch. Now I clearly see that the artistry has to come out, and if you don't let it, it starts screaming at you. It has to be satisfied and nurtured. I have a really strong inner drive. It's like an inner voice that nags at me. When I've finished playing, after about an hour, I feel a thousand times better.'

Similarly, American singer and songwriter Edie Brickell

observed, 'You feel like a prisoner if you don't create; you're jailed up inside of yourself. You've got to let that out. It's there and it just needs to come out. It's freedom, the desire for freedom.'

Bluesman Buddy Guy talked about slipping away from other activities to fulfil a demanding need – to make music: 'I've been aware of my love of music ever since I was big enough to know I could take rubber bands and put two nails in the wall and just stretch them. The sound the rubber bands gave was exciting to me. I was doing something like that as far back as I can remember. I recall I was just a normal kid like anybody else, only I would always wander off from the crowd and wind up trying to get some kind of sound out of something.'

Keith Strickland, too, was powerfully drawn to creative expression beginning at an early age, and this force has stayed with him throughout his life: 'I've always had a very strong drive to create, even before it became a career. I started very early, just experimenting, by expressing myself in creative ways. I've always drawn and painted. I have a very strong urge to create, but I'm not quite sure where that comes from. I've always played instruments, dabbled with anything. If there's an instrument around, even a saxophone, I'd be inclined to pick it up and see what I can do with it and not be afraid of it. I think a lot of it is just stating your intention to yourself like, "Okay, I'm going to play it." That's a large percentage of doing it. The whole creative process for me is just discovery – discovering what the instrument does, and what you can do, too.'

For some artists, musical role models triggered their drive to create; for others, their first contact with a certain instrument sparked their desire to play. My late husband Ian Wallace initially found inspiration through seeing a drum kit in all its glory during a concert. From that moment on, nothing could derail his determination to play the drums: 'I didn't know what I was going to be until I was 14. I was really into music then; I got a guitar, but I didn't know how to tune it. When I was about 15, I joined the school jazz society, and they had a local outing to the cinema where Acker Bilk was playing. We sat in the back, the stage was all set up, then the ice cream lady came up the aisle. I went down to get an ice cream and as I stood in line, I looked up at the drum kit and it was like the heavens opened and choirs started singing, and Jesus' rays came down on the drum kit. I knew then what I wanted to do. The next day I got all my albums and my guitar – without telling my mother – and took them to the local music store and traded them in for a little snare drum. I used to sit at home with cardboard boxes and things and a pair of sticks and play to old jazz records. I knew I wanted to play the drums. After that, that's all I ever wanted to do.'

Dedicated Hard Work

Like Ian, many musicians told me that the drive to create led to their immersing themselves completely in learning to play their instrument. What for some would have been hard work became a joy to these fledgling artists. Maslow described this aspect of creative people's attitude towards working at their art form: 'Duty [becomes] pleasure, and pleasure merge[s] with duty. The distinction between work and play [becomes] shadowy.' Several artists described intensive learning periods, in which they pushed themselves to master their instrument, either despite or mindless of the physical pain. Producer Jeff Lynne, founder of Electric Light Orchestra and a member of the Travelling Wilburys, discussed overcoming 'technical difficulties' while learning to play: 'I started out with my friend who had a plastic guitar, and it had only one string on it, and I said "Ooh, can I borrow that?" I borrowed it, and I learned "Guitar Tango" by the Shadows, by playing on one string. That's how I learned. Then one day, my dad bought me a secondhand Spanish guitar for two quid, and then I got some strings. Someone taught me how to tune up, but they taught me wrong. I didn't know that, so when I used a book to learn to form chords, it sounded terrible. I thought I was useless, and then a few weeks later someone told me about the real tuning. I was about 14. I didn't like school very much, and so when this guitar thing came about, even the one string, I realised I'd found something I'd like to do. And once I got the Spanish guitar, that's all I did – just played it for five or six hours a day. I loved it so much I didn't need anything else at all. I was good at it, fortunately. I could pick it up quickly, so I thought, maybe I'm good at this.'

The hard work and determination Jeff put into learning to play his guitar has been a constant throughout his career as a successful songwriter and producer. His tenacity at overcoming a challenge has remained an intricate part of his craft: 'Sometimes you can just work on a tune forever. You work it to death. You still don't like it, but you won't give up on it – you just keep trying and trying. Even on some of my big hits, it's been butchered in the end. I know it's there, but I can't find it. So I'll try a thousand alternatives to make it a bit better. And I won't give up on it, because if I've got a feeling that there's something there in the first place, it must still be right really. I don't give up very easily. You can get the first few chords as an inspiration and you don't know where they come from. The hard bit then, is making the verse and chorus and nice words. There's a million people who can come up with little bits and that's all it is – it's a bit. The hard work is making it into something that is a performance. When you come up with an original riff, you can suddenly hear if it's good. You can hear it going into a verse or a chorus. You can imagine it. Then you've got to *find* what you can imagine.'

Ron Wood started performing when he was just a kid and through his immense drive has continued to perfect his musicianship throughout his life: 'I first went onstage at the age of nine, playing washboard at the local cinema with my two brothers in a skiffle group. But even before that, I was lent a guitar, and a couple of members of the band – the guitarist and the banjo player – used to give me chord sheets. They used to write out easy chords for me to learn when I was about seven or eight. Then I took it a bit more seriously up to the age of 10. The guy who lent me the guitar took it back, so I had a gap of a couple of years. Then my brother saved up and bought me my own guitar. I was about 12 then.

'I didn't ever see any reason to stop playing just because my fingers hurt. I was never impaired by the physical side of it. I thought it was something I had to do. It still goes for today. You can never sit back and rest on your laurels, because the moment that feeling hits you – if you stop playing, then it's all over. You have to keep playing and get better. I'm playing for someone higher than me. Maybe it's that person in the crowd, God, or Eric Clapton! I never lose my ambitious drive; I'm always striving.'

Vernon Reid described how the difficulties of learning to play almost prevented him from continuing with the guitar, but his drive to create enabled him to overcome these stumbling blocks: 'I stopped playing for about six months because my first guitar was an acoustic, an old Gibson with a very high action and thick strings. I was skinny, so it was really painful to hold down the strings. At the end of six months, I said to myself that I'm really going to hang with this and not let it defeat me. I remember having that feeling.'

George Harrison's desire to play the guitar was so great that he literally did nothing else but master his playing skills and seek out fellow musicians. 'I put a lot of time into playing the guitar, learning how to clamp down on those strings while my fingers were hurting and how to change the chords, moving my fingers without the music stopping. I played a lot, even though it was just simple stuff, labouring on until I got it, even if just to play a skiffle tune or "Peggy Sue". It was something I didn't think about; I just did it. It was something that I liked. I just liked music and I loved guitars, so it was a labor of love, really.

'When I was 11, we moved from our neighbourhood into one of the new housing estates on the outskirts of Liverpool, and just after that, I also moved to the new grammar school. That was a big change in my life, because it was around the time I got my new guitar, and that's the school where Paul McCartney came into my life. There were also other people I met who were guitarists. I would hang out with anybody who had a guitar in those days, either they would come to my house or I would go to theirs. The guitar and music were the first things I was interested in. I didn't like school most of the time; it was much too serious. I didn't have a clue of what I wanted to be. I didn't want to be anything. The only thing that held my interest was music and the guitar and how to get out of getting a proper job. If it hadn't been for the band, I would have just been a bum.'

Drummer Steve Jordan also discovered his creative impulse as a young child. He told me how he persevered through the learning process even though his initial impressions of learning to play were a far cry from reality: 'When I was little I banged on everything. I used to get the coffee cans with plastic lids – that was my kit. It sounded good. I got my first drum when I was eight, with the provision that I take lessons at the local music store. The first time I went, the guy sat me behind this great set of Gretsch drums – blue sparkle. I felt just fantastic sitting behind this kit. The guy said, "Do you really want to practise and put the time in? It isn't going to be easy." I said, "Yeah, yeah!" I couldn't wait to get down and play. They didn't give me any sticks or anything, just let me sit behind it and said, "Come back next week." I couldn't wait, every night I was dreaming about the kit. So the next week I walked in the same room and there was this piece of wood with a slab of rubber on it, and there were no drums in the room at all. It was a practice pad! I was crushed, but I had to start there.'

Striving Against the Odds

Choosing to be a professional musician certainly could not be described as a 'safe' choice. It is characteristic, though, of another of Maslow's descriptions of creative people: '[They] do not cling to the familiar, nor is their quest for the truth a catastrophic need for certainty, safety, definiteness, and order.'

As I listened to the various stories of how these musicians struggled to succeed in their careers, I was struck by the amount of courage and determination necessary to surmount the uncertainties. I remembered when Fleetwood Mac first met Stevie Nicks and Lindsey Buckingham. Although the two had recorded an album together, they were still struggling to make ends meet. Stevie was waitressing long hours to cover her expenses as a musician. In our interview, she recalled those tough times, along with the obsession she had to be a musician: 'I wrote my first song on my sixteenth birthday. I finished that song hysterically crying, and I was hooked. From that day forward when I was in my room playing my guitar, nobody would come in without knocking, nobody disturbed me. My parents were very supportive and wouldn't let anyone disturb me until I came out. They'd even let me miss dinner if necessary, it was that important. They could hear that I was working, at 16 years old, and they would leave me alone. I started singing in assemblies at school and in folk groups. I sang whenever I could, for whatever I could possibly find to do; if it had anything to do with singing or music I did it.

'There were times when I was between 20 and 27 – before I joined Fleetwood Mac – that my dad would say, "How long are you going to do this? You have no money, you're not happy, you work constantly, you work at restaurants, you clean houses, you get sick very easily, you're living in Los Angeles, you don't have any friends, why are you doing this?" And I would just say, "Because it's just what I came here to do."'

Ravi Shankar also sacrificed many things while he worked towards becoming a sitar master, including his glamorous life touring Europe and America with the family's performing company. 'In 1935 my brother hired one of the greatest musicians in India as a soloist in our troupe. When he joined, I had never seen such a great musician; I was bowled over. He looked very ordinary, but there was some inner fire in him that felt like a volcano.

'I became his guide because I could speak French, German and Italian. He liked me because he missed his son, so he took me as his son and loved me very much. He stayed with the troupe only about 10-and-a-half months, but within that period he changed the course of my life. I was so spoiled by then. I was more of a dancer [than a musician], wearing the best clothes, staying in five-star hotels. I was having a lot of fun, singing, writing poetry, painting. Everything I did, people would say "Wonderful!" but he was the first one who said to me, "You are nothing; you can never do anything like this; you are like a butterfly; you are like a jack-of-all-trades; you have to do one thing properly, and I will teach you if you leave everything and come with me." I couldn't decide what to do, for at that time I was well known for my dancing. I choreographed a solo myself, which was a great success. Becoming a young man, I was really having a lot of fun with the glitter and glamour of the whole thing.

'It took me a year and a half, but finally I decided to go to him. He lived in a small town in India, near Benares. He couldn't believe it when he saw me – I was now 18 – his eyes almost popped out. I had shaved my head; I wanted to please him, and I did. That's how it started, and I stayed with him for seven-and-a-half years, living the life of a hermit almost, which was very difficult for me. I lived in the house next door to him, a very creaky old house with flies, scorpions, snakes, and even wolves at night. It was so uncomfortable, and I suffered very much. But he was my inspiration and was the one man I saw in my life who lived whatever way he preached.

'And so I learned the sitar. After seven years he told me to give programmes, perform at different festivals and on the radio. I was earning a little bit, but not very much. With his permission I went to Bombay, and then I really got into giving programmes and writing music for films, ballet and opera. Very quickly I became well known, in three or four years.'

Guitarist Rick Vito, formerly with Fleetwood Mac and now a solo artist, pursued his musical dreams, which required him to pull up stakes and move across the country. He explained where he thought his drive originated: 'In regard to playing, I could never *not* do it. I don't know what has made me stick this out through lean years when nothing much was happening. I think there's a little voice that tells you if you're special in some way, a little voice that reminds you not to forget about it. A certain amount of drive comes from being inspired by other people's work and wanting to achieve something that you're proud of and that other people will be respectful of.

'When I was about 16 or 17, I started thinking that I would play music professionally, not just on weekends in bars around Philadelphia, near where I lived. But I never made a firm stand on that until I was 20, when I heard the early Delaney and Bonnie records. I thought they were really saying something in a rock 'n' roll way that nobody else was at the time. I was determined to introduce myself to these people, and somehow I got backstage at one of their shows and met them. They were very encouraging, and so the second time they came back they invited me to play with them onstage, so I sat in with them. It was one of those things that brought the house down; it was amazing. Delaney told me that if I really wanted to get in the business I should move to L.A. From then on I made up my mind that nothing was going to be more important than that, so I moved to the West Coast.'

Like Rick Vito, several musicians feel that a strong belief in their self-worth is related to their own intense drive to create. This seems to verify the high degree of self-acceptance found in creative people. As Koko Taylor explained: 'The drive comes from you. You're the one that motivates the drive; it has to be in you. You have to have that spark to say, "I feel good about myself. I feel good about what I'm doing." And that keeps the energy up, that keeps the drive going.'

Don Henley also mentioned the importance of drive and the belief in oneself to attain creative success: 'I don't want to discount talent and ability, but I still maintain that a lot of it is just sheer desire. You've got to want it more than anything else in the world and be able to do whatever it takes. Most of all, you must believe in yourself – believe you can do it.'

I found Don's thoughts on artistic drive inspirational. To

prevail against the many societal forces that can shatter one's convictions, there must be a powerful faith in one's self. That belief in oneself is truly the core essence of the creative drive. And it is their innermost essence, that part of the psyche known as the unconscious, to which artists truly connect through the creative act.

Chapter 3

THE UNCONSCIOUS

'YOU'VE GOT TO KEEP THE CHILD ALIVE;
YOU CAN'T CREATE WITHOUT IT.'
JONI MITCHELL

From what source does creativity spring? Like many psychologists, I believe that it comes from the innermost part of us, the unconscious, defined by Jung as: 'Everything of which I know but of which I'm not at the moment thinking; everything of which I was once conscious but have now forgotten; everything perceived by my senses but not noted by my conscious mind; everything of which involuntarily and without paying attention to it, I feel, think, remember, want and do; all future things that are taking shape in me and will sometimes come to consciousness. All this is the content of the unconscious.'

Because its contents are derived from one's own life, the personal unconscious is unique to each individual. I have become increasingly aware of the treasure trove the unconscious holds and how it is linked to the creative process. I agree with Jung that it is a place of all-knowing, full of everything possible to imagine, and a world filled with chaotic powers. The conscious mind acts towards the unconscious as a filtering system, bringing order and preventing an overwhelming feeling of the unknown. The unconscious is raw and communicates through images, as in dreams, and through feelings, insights and flashes of inspiration.

According to Jung, the centre of the total personality lies midway between the unconscious and the conscious. It is up to us to try to reach this place, since it can allow us to bring some of the knowledge from the unconscious into the conscious mind. Where does creativity fit into all of this? The creative act enables one to reach the midway point. Artistry can give form to a whirling dervish of ideas, where the unconscious and conscious meet and chaos is given over to form and order.

While seeking a subject for my doctoral dissertation – the seedling that grew into this book – I fell into what I thought at the time was a deep depression. It was a feeling of being cut off from the day-to-day world of the conscious mind. Only once I'd conducted these interviews did I discover the feeling of being cut off I had experienced was similar to the description given by these musicians. It was a journey into the unconscious, which can sometimes be a difficult and often uncomfortable descent. After resisting the urge to escape, I accepted where I was and embarked on the journey that lay ahead. When I finally re-emerged from this germination process, I brought with me an idea, a creative seed from the unconscious that came with all the excitement and relief of giving birth.

This feeling was described beautifully by the German poet Rainer Maria Rilke in *Letters to a Young Poet*, a book Don Henley recommended to me: 'Everything is gestation and then birthing. To let each impression and each embryo of a feeling come to completion, entirely in itself, in the dark, in the unsayable – the unconscious – beyond the reach of one's own understanding, and with deep humility and patience to wait for the hour when new clarity is born; this alone is what it means to live as an artist: in understanding as in creating.'

Keyboardist Greg Phillinganes used similar images to describe an experience that occurs sometimes when he's writing: 'It's from my gut; you can definitely feel it, it's amazing – it's like birthing a child.'

The Childlike Nature of the Unconscious

Musicians seem to have no fear of the unknown world that is the unconscious. It is a place they frequent, many of them continuously since childhood. In fact, children visit that mysterious realm quite often, since they have not yet learned to fear it and are not compelled to adhere to the enforced status quo. 'A characteristic of childhood,' Carl Jung wrote, 'is that, thanks to its naiveté and unconsciousness, it sketches a more complete picture of the self, of the whole man in his pure individuality, than adulthood.' In their interviews, numerous musicians emphasised that throughout their lives they have tried to keep alive the childlike part of their nature. As guitarist Rick Vito told me: 'A lot of that purity and sweetness of life takes place in your childhood, when everything was innocent and totally creative. Children feel really free, and when I'm playing my best, I feel free.'

People who block out this childlike element within themselves are perhaps afraid of losing control or being different. As long as I have known Mick Fleetwood, I've found him to have the childlike spontaneity and enthusiasm most people shed after childhood. When we talked about this, he said: 'You have to work at it in some way, preserving that precious childlike part of you. There is some part in me that turns my back on bringing in too much information. I think it can be a little detrimental. It's more important to preserve that innocence that you have, the open book. As long as the whole book doesn't go yellow when you get older – if it's just the edges – then it means you're doing alright. And that's like a child: You come in and all you are is an open book, just waiting to absorb.'

Keith Strickland has also managed to retain a childlike nature, which has positively affected his creativity: 'Being in touch with the child in you is part of the whole creative process. I don't feel that I write songs as much as I make them up; it's playing the way you do in your childhood. It takes a little disciplined work to get back to that state of mind. It's a very open, non-judgmental state of mind, where you just simply play. [The B-52s] do that as a band: We go through the improvisational process; we jam, allowing anything to happen. It's just like playing, it's just like making it up, let's make up a song. Maybe that's why I create to this day – I still like playing, and I did it as a child. It was one of the ways I played – with music – so maybe that's why I still do it.'

The Unconscious at Work

Many of the musicians I spoke to were quite eloquent in describing this mysterious place, the unconscious, which is the source of their creative spring. Although few actually used the word *unconscious*, they spoke reverently of the process by which it becomes the crucial link to their creativeness. David Crosby explained the necessity of eliminating the rational mind to free the unconscious, which he labelled the 'jet pilot': 'I very often write something all in a blurt; it comes out pretty much finished, and it consists of thoughts that I have never consciously thought. They did not ever take place in the verbal personalised level of my mind. Your mind has many levels: intuitive and imaginative are the intelligent ones and the ones where the creative process takes place. They are not necessarily articulate in the way that normal speech is. You have to get the half-calculator mind out of the way for that other mind to really function.

'I've been amazed when that has happened to me repeatedly. Many of my best songs come out all in one blurt, and at those times I have the distinct feeling that this level of me is just a vehicle for some other level of me that has been sitting there cooking this thing up. It often happens when I'm in between waking and sleeping. I'll be going to sleep, and I'll be sort of drowsy and this motormouth mind – the one that's talking to you right now – will kind of shut down, and then BAM! This stuff will start to come, and I'll turn on the light quickly and write, write, write, and play, play, write, and then "Fantastic!" And about that time my other mind is starting to kick back in and say, "David, you're cool! *Whoaa*, buddy!"

'It happens best when I get a lot of the other stuff out of the way; that's when my most imaginative and creative mind levels work. It's as if your mind has many levels and only one can have the steering wheel at any one time. All of them get a vote on your behaviour, from the lowest baby levels to the most evolved ones you have. It's when the customary driver kind of nods off that the jet pilot can take over.'

Almost every musician I interviewed spoke of this feeling that sometimes occurs while creating, in which words or music seem to have been 'given' to them or are coming through them effortlessly. They were all too aware of how the rational mind can hinder creativity by getting in the way of the free flowing unconscious. Although the conscious mind is often referred to as an obstruction, it is required once the unconscious has been tapped, because it gives form to the chaos.

The experience of tapping into the unconscious can be indescribable, even for those with the gift for putting feelings into words. It is similar to the sensation one has upon awakening and remembering a vivid dream, and being unable to recall its specific contents. Don Henley articulated the exhilaration of reaching the unconscious, which, for him, has resulted in such songs as 'The Boys of Summer': 'There have been a couple of times in my life when I've had those experiences that people talk about, where you feel like something is being given to you from somewhere else, or it's coming through you. It always amazes me. Songwriters, at least in my own case and a few other people I know, are like actors. Every time actors do a movie they think they're never going to work again. Well, every time I'd write a good song, I used to feel like I probably couldn't do that again. But "it" always comes back, and every time it returns, it's like birds coming back for the summer. I'm always totally amazed. I'm so pleased that my brain cells are still working! I'm so thankful that there is still water in the well.

'This happened when I wrote "The Boys of Summer". It was incredible. It was just coming to me, and I don't know where it was coming from. I was in the car, driving up the Pacific Coast Highway. I was listening to the track, and the music inspired me tremendously. It helps when the music really inspires you. It gives me vision, and I see colours, I feel emotions, and I hear melodies and words. The music gives that to me. Inside my head I have a pool of subject matter, and the music dictates to me which subject belongs to which particular part. I make a marriage in my head out of the file of subjects and words that go to different pieces of music. A piece of music will unlock a set of images in my head, and those will come out and marry with the particular music.

'It doesn't matter who wrote the music if it inspires me. In this case, [guitarist] Mike Campbell [a member of Tom Petty's Heartbreakers] had written that particular music. It had a sound and texture that struck a chord in me. The lyrics weren't about things that I'd previously thought of – not consciously anyway. They were coming from my subconscious or coming through me. They seem to come out of thin air sometimes. When you get in a positive frame of mind like that – usually the further you get into the album – the more songs you write, the more ideas come to you and the more you get given. I had so much momentum at that point, that everywhere I looked there was something I could see that could be put into a song. I mean, every direction I turned, things are being given to me, or rather, I could see them. Maybe they were there all the time, I don't know. The part about the Cadillac happened when I was stuck for a last verse. I was driving down the San Diego Freeway when suddenly it was like somebody said, "Okay, here's some irony for you. Here's this unlikely, late-model car and here's this Dead Head sticker on it, and you can have this for the last verse if you want it." The symbolism was wonderful. It was as if somebody just shoved it in front of me and simultaneously gave me the ability to see it.

'Those are great times when that happens. It doesn't always happen that way, though small parts of songs sometimes do. This, however, was an entire piece. I always get some kind of inspiration on every song. I'll get a little bit of it, and then I'll have to sweat for the rest. I'll have to sit down and work tediously on it. Sometimes you sit down to write a song – you take the tape and you take a legal pad – and you just scribble. You write down a lot of crap and then narrow that down until one or two lines will be pretty good. Then you combine a couple of lines and then a couple more. It's busy work, manual labour, just sitting there.

'But this one all came together: verses, choruses, melody, everything – all right off the top of my head. This phenomenon has happened only once or twice before. I can remember parts of "Hotel California" came about that way. "Lyin' Eyes" also materialised very quickly, and more recently "The End of the Innocence". It's funny, but the best songs seem to occur that way. They just flow out of you, but your antennae must be up.'

THE UNCONSCIOUS

Jungian psychologist Jolande Jacobi wrote of the dynamic relationship between the conscious and the unconscious: 'Out of the unconscious rise contents and images, and they show themselves to the conscious mind as though secretly asking to be grasped and understood.' Jacobi quoted Jung's protégée, psychologist Aniela Jaffe, to describe the end result: '…"birth" may be accomplished and "being" created. If consciousness fails, the images sink back into the dark, into nothingness and everything remains as if unhappened.'

Jackson Browne articulated how he prevented the loss of such images, which for him become part of songs: 'There was an experience when I was trying to write. I hadn't written in a while; I was about 19. I did at one point kind of surrender. I thought, *Okay, I know it's not me that writes this stuff, so I'm at your service.* It was like a little prayer. I then wrote something that I felt was my first song that was very good. If you have a flash of inspiration, it comes from within you.

'I think there is something like a current. To tell you the truth, it's something I believe without spending too much time thinking about it. Mainly I spend a lot of time standing in line trying to get a little of it, trying to tap into it. I guess you could sum it up that it's like a current of electricity outside of you that also exists inside of you, and it's something you can direct in a clever way. It's not something you can consciously do, but if you were blocked, you would have to unblock. There are always creative people who are just plugged in; they have their finger in that big socket.'

Reaching 'No Mind'

Many musicians referred to a kind of mental 'stillness' that is necessary for the unconscious to make itself known through creative expression. In contrast, during day-to-day activities, we utilise the 'busy mind'. Some philosophies, such as Zen Buddhism, teach that during meditation the busy mind is to be replaced by 'no mind'. I think that is the same place many artists described reaching during their creative work.

Graham Nash explained this feeling as being similar to a 'void' that he experiences during creative moments. 'There are times when I don't believe where it's all coming from. I've had this ability all my life to observe a situation, internalise it, and then externalise it. In my later life it has come out musically. With some of my best songs, I can't remember the state I was in when I wrote them. It's kind of like I go into a void: it's very still. Time goes very quickly. It's like a suspension where one moment will last for an hour. But when I come out of that moment, it feels like it's only seconds long. I don't feel warm, I don't feel as if there's light around. I have no memory of writing the songs, but it's in my handwriting so I know I wrote them – as to where that comes from, I have no idea.

'When I'm taking a photograph, there's no doubt in my mind when to push the button, it all comes together – the composition, the light, the moment, all come together. What I do as a creative artist – whether it be photographs or art or sculpture or music – is centred in something inside me that is different from [what's inside] most people. It's all tapped from the same source – I can't really explain where that source is – which makes me believe in an external power that I'm tapping into, that a channel is opening up.'

Paul Horn, who has practised meditation for decades, also spoke of displacing the busy mind in order to create: 'In playing, what I have transcended is my self-consciousness, my mind drifting onto other things. I'm unaware of myself, I'm totally absorbed in the music, and as I get more absorbed in the music, then more can happen. I turn out to be a channel; my mind doesn't say, "Me, I'm playing good tonight" or "I'm not playing good". It's not judgmental, it's a happening that's taking place and that's enough, and it's exciting to be caught up in that.'

Joni Mitchell, who has been a student of Zen, described the concept of no mind and its role in her painting as well as her songwriting: 'When I paint for long hours, my mind stills. If you hooked me up to a meter, I don't know what you'd find, but maybe it's like a dream state. It goes very abstract. The dialogue is absolutely still, it's like Zen no mind. You hear electrical synapses, which could be cosmic electricity, snapping, and occasionally up into that void, in the Zen no mind, comes a command, "Red in the upper-left-hand corner." There's no afterthought, because ego is the afterthought; you paint red in the upper-left-hand corner, and then it all goes back into the zone again. You achieve that sometimes in music. I think I achieve it in the loneliness of the night just playing my guitar repetitiously. The mantra of it, the drone of it will get you there. In performance you're going down deep within and then you're coming back out to receive your applause. There's a more self-conscious art form in performance – people are applauding you.

'With writing, you have to plumb into the subconscious, and there's a lot of scary things down there, like a bad dream sometimes. If you can extricate yourself from it and face up to it, you come back with a lot of self-knowledge, which then gives you greater human knowledge, and that helps. To know yourself is to know the world; everything, good, bad and indifferent is in each one of us to varying degrees, so the more you know about that, the more you know about that which is external. So in that way, the writing process is fantastic psychotherapy – if you can survive. But it is tricky.

'With one particular song I wrote, when it came time to write about my experience, it was so dense with imagery that for me it was thrilling. It was hard for me to sift through it. There came one line, though, that was like a gift. It flowed out. I drew back and said "thank you" to the room. It just came out and said so much, I felt, so economically. I'd been grinding the gray matter trying to get this thing to come and maybe I then just relaxed or something. Whatever it was, when it poured out, it did seem like it was a gift. There are pieces in a song that just seem to pour out in spite of you. I mean, you're the witness, but the language does seem to come from someplace else.'

Michael McDonald described the struggle he must undergo sometimes to rid himself of the rational mind: 'The real source of inspiration is such an intangible thing, and I don't know what it is. With songwriting, which is probably the focus for me, and even with singing and playing, there's an intangible element to it that I can't describe. When we're really playing and singing well, there's this sum that's greater than all the parts, and nobody knows what it is.

THE UNCONSCIOUS

'With writing songs, it is always a battle with my conscious mind, and yet when it comes down to it, it doesn't have much to do with my conscious mind. But I always put it there until I wear myself out with it, and then I surrender to what's going to come if I just do the footwork, if I just keep going towards it. And then when it comes, I have no idea what it is. It's not necessarily the greatest lyric or the greatest melody. There'll be this one song that actually crystallises; it takes on a life of its own. I wonder what it is that makes a song with relatively mediocre lyrics and a not so inventive melody just have a life of its own – and that's the thing you're always looking for. I have certain tools to work with, but what I'm really looking for is beyond anything I could consciously come up with using those tools. My best thinking is only going to get me so much. The reason I have to drag myself to writing is that I'm all too aware how I dig myself a hole by consciously trying to write a song. When I'm really looking for spontaneity, I can afford less and less to think about it and then write it down. Somehow the minute I start to apply my conscious mind to it, I'm altering it and probably not for the good. I just have to get out of my own way.'

Surrendering to the unconscious and getting the busy mind out of the way are necessary to allow the richness of the unconscious to come through the artist. Vocalist Patty Smyth told me what happens when she is able to leave her everyday, mundane thoughts behind during songwriting: 'It feels like the door opens and it's a stream of consciousness. I haven't experienced that with melody so much as with words. They flow right out of me – that's how it feels. I get out of my own way and it comes out fast and painlessly.'

The 'Visionary Mode'

Numerous musicians described the sensation of writing songs that tend to flow out in such a way that the artist is almost possessed by music that has a life of its own. Jung referred to this part of the creative process as the 'visionary mode', where the artist is in touch with primordial experiences that have recurred over generations. He explained: 'In the visionary mode, the creative person is more conscious of an "alien" will, or intention beyond his comprehension – a detached portion of the psyche that leads an independent life.' All of the musicians who spoke of this sensation seemed to hold it in awe, and many felt that the songs created in this way were very special.

'Songbird' was the result of such a process, according to Christine McVie. At so many Fleetwood Mac concerts over the years, I witnessed the effect 'Songbird' had on the audience. It would usually be the last song of the show, and it seemed to inspire in the crowd a feeling of reverence. To me, it always felt like a prayer. In our interview, Chris described this 'visionary mode' that sometimes occurs when she writes: 'Some songs I write I'm convinced don't come from just me. I'm not sure what it is. Many times it feels like it comes from some other source. It's amazing because half an hour ago you had nothing, then you've created something from nothing. Sometimes it flows so freely and it seems so effortless that there has to be something else charging your energy to do it, especially when you feel whatever you've written is good and "how on earth could it possibly have come from me". I think I felt that way with "Songbird". It was a powerful feeling because

I wrote it just like that. I wrote the chords and the words and the melody almost as if it was coming from someone else and not me.'

Billy Burnette took this idea a step further, by explaining how such songs are blessed with a certain universal appeal that other people instinctively recognise: 'With those special songs, you don't even know where they come from. I wrote one that we probably have 20 covers of by now – Ray Charles has done it – called "Do I Ever Cross Your Mind?" It's a song that's special to me, but I feel it was just handed to us one day. I feel like those are gifts. I know from my dad's experience when we were kids, he got out of his sleep and wrote some of his real big hits like "It's Late". He always told me that the best ones come real quick.'

Peter Frampton articulated how enduring songs like Chris and Billy described come from a wellspring with a life of its own: 'Sometimes, it's as if the song is writing itself. The songs that are written that way are usually the best because they happen quickly and your excitement builds as they do. One of the most prolific times I've had was when I wrote the *Frampton* album. In eight days I had written the whole thing, including "Show Me the Way" and "Baby I Love Your Way", which were written the same day. I wonder why – and can I have a few more weeks like that? Please!'

One reason the songs that emerge spontaneously from the unconscious are so meaningful to the artist is because they are sometimes made up of images or ideas from unresolved conflicts the artist has buried within. When manifested in the form of a song, they speak to and heal the artist. Sinéad O'Connor described such a song and its effect on her: 'It doesn't happen all the time [with writing]; it happens only occasionally, where it doesn't come from me, it comes from somebody else. It's really only happened with me on three songs, in particular a song called "My Special Child". We were recording this particular song after I'd been pregnant and had decided I wasn't going to have the baby, although I had really wanted to. I'd had an abortion, and I was very fucked up by this and really upset about it. But I was glad I had done it, and I wrote this song.

'We recorded the song, and when I was in doing the vocals, I really, really felt as if the child was there. I really felt its presence. I know that sounds mad, but I felt it was up there and it was coming from her. I was sure it was a girl and that it was coming out of me from her, because the song turned out to be something I wasn't expecting. It became a song that was basically saying, "Don't be upset because you've got your son, and your son loves you and he's really special, so don't worry." It was very moving. Any time we ever listened to the song afterwards, it was really shocking.'

The unconscious also holds the key to many personal problems that the artist, too busy to attend to, shoves to the back of his or her mind. Although these questions are left unheeded, the answers will often emerge in the form of a song. Kirsty MacColl described this phenomenon: 'I've written a whole song off the top of my head, which took two hours from start to finish. There was a lot of stuff that had been crammed in there that I hadn't been able to put down for three years [while having children]. After the first song, they seemed to come faster and faster. Sometimes I've written a song, and I've thought that's a bit silly or not really true to life, and then a week later something will happen and it's exactly like I said in the song – that's weird. Often

I've done lyrics and I haven't realised the full meaning of what I've written till a year later.'

Singer and songwriter Edie Brickell has had a similar experience: 'Sometimes you don't even know what [your songs] mean. They just come out, and it can be a year later, and you think, wow, I get it now, because you can look back on your life and see more clearly than at the time when you experienced it.'

Stephen Bishop told me that songs that seem to pour out have a louder ring of truth than those he struggles over: 'When I wrote the song "Separate Lives", I was so into it, so full of emotion from breaking up with someone. It all just came out. That's the best part, when you can hardly wait to write it down. It seems that lately a lot of my songs I've had to work on, I don't express what I really want to say. I try to be clever, and I say all these other things that sound cool. I don't really express as many of my feelings as I used to, which is not very good.'

As Stephen pointed out, songs that are consciously written may be forced to follow certain standards, and thereby not truly represent the artist's real feelings, rendering the song hollow and superficial. On the other hand, songs that come from deep within the artist's unconscious tend to be much more meaningful.

Julian Lennon also differentiated between those songs that rushed out of him and those that were forced: 'Something drives me, and I can't always explain it because I don't always have the urge to be creative. Sometimes I'll just stop and not even want to think about it, but then I'll just run to the piano, I'll play and have ideas, so maybe there's something going through me, I don't know. When

I'm writing – if I'm looking for a certain segment, like a bridge or something – in the past I used to spend a long time thinking about it; what I do is very much ad lib. But recently, over the last year or two, I've been able to sit down and hit one note and know exactly where I'm going next and have something written in a really short period of time. It's knowing what you're going to play without even knowing, which is very weird and very exciting when it happens. I can't explain it. Maybe it's a question of being more receptive.'

Submitting to the Creative Urge

I got the distinct feeling that Julian and most of the other musicians have a real reverence for this nameless 'thing' from the unconscious, which can seem nebulous one minute and powerful the next. Its presence can be so strong, in fact, that when the artist taps into it, everything else in his or her life must stop. He or she must drop everything and run to a pad and pencil, to piano or guitar. The impatient 'guest' can never wait, the artist being its humble slave. The unconscious is treated with the respect and awe it deserves. Rather than trying to tame the beast, the artist has no choice but to heed its voice as it forcefully crashes through from the unconscious. Billy Burnette alluded to this feeling: 'Once I get that little musical thing in my head, I've got to just give up what I'm doing to rush to a piano or a guitar and see if it's an idea. A phrase or a movie may put me into some feeling I want to write about. Or something somebody says could kick off that thing, which kicks off that other thing that gives the peak altogether.'

Keith Richards described his submission to the creative urge: '[The drive to create] is just something I obey. I hear something and I've got to learn how to play it. Once you know that, then you have no choice. You can't turn it off. This is a one-way tap; once it's on, it's on. You can try and ignore it, but it's far more powerful than you are. It's not a controllable thing; it just keeps coming from inside. You're a slave to it in a way.'

Rosanne Cash pointed to the destructive result of ignoring her artistic urges: '[The drive to create] is pretty intense to me. It's almost like a survival instinct; it's that primitive. If I ignore my work, I start having anxiety attacks, I can't really sleep well, my eating habits become erratic, I get irritable. It starts taking its toll in a very physical and mental way. So it's almost like the energy is there, and if I don't use it as it was intended, it turns toxic. It turns on me. It's very much a survival thing for me.'

Mike Rutherford, a member of Mike and the Mechanics and Genesis, said that being a prisoner to the muse is actually the greatest release: 'I've got no control over [the choice to create]. I'm like a man incontinent. I have a respect for whatever it is that enables me to do it. I try not to abuse it. The biggest high comes when you write something. By not abusing it, I mean I try not to force it; it's too precious. [If it won't come] I just leave it and do something else.'

Veteran musicians learn to recognise the signals that a song is waiting to be born, and so they heed its call. Stevie Nicks described the moment she realises a song is approaching: 'Sometimes I get a real serious idea for a song. I'll just be sitting there or looking at something, and it will come into my head. Something about those flowers over there will give me an idea. A name will come out, like "Rhiannon". Then, I'm instantly in tune that it's a song. I race to the piano. If I have an idea for the words first, I run to the typewriter. What I have is little flashes; I just see things. Without any speech at all, it just says something to me, and I'll quickly write that down.'

To capture those transient messages from the unconscious, Tony Williams told me that he readied himself to do so at the drop of a hat: 'I can be sitting around and a song will just come into my head. I have a couple of micro recorders, and I'll whip one out and sing the idea. If I don't record it immediately, I'll lose it.'

Ron Wood has found the urge to create equally strong in both his painting and songwriting: 'I have to be in a certain frame of mind to go and paint. Sometimes the urge is so irresistible if you're on an airplane or something, that's why I scribble a lot on notepaper or draw on little pads. When you want to do something like a big oil painting, it can be really off-putting if you're sitting there talking to somebody who's come to visit without phoning first. And you're wasting your time, thinking, Oh, I should be painting! When they go, you run down and do it. It's the same with a song. If I'm in the middle of a conversation and I get a song, I have to run off and play it into a recorder or something.'

Most musicians considered the songs that rush out like a waterfall of words and music their best. But songwriter Randy Newman claimed that his 'easy' songs are no better than those he agonises over: 'Sometimes your subconscious or something … it'll just be there, you can see the whole song. It's great, it's like getting a free ride. It happens often with this type of work. Those songs aren't necessarily better or worse, they're just different. You can see all the way to the end from the beginning. It's a real powerful feeling. You can wait for that forever. You've got to somehow make it happen, but I couldn't tell you how.'

Randy said that this happens most often with writing rather than playing because, 'I'm too conscious of my technical limitations as a player'. Stephen Stills, on the other hand, told me he finds this 'letting go' occurs easily while playing: 'I'm so far ahead of what I'm doing [when playing the guitar] that I'm very surprised when I haven't made a mistake. I'm really concentrating, and then all of a sudden it's so relaxed and so easy that I cannot make a mistake. All I'm doing is creating. You've got to give yourself to the music, give it all up so you can become one with it. There's so much going on at the same time – I'm at maximum output. It's to the point where I can be doing all that and daydreaming at the same time.'

Tapping into the Unconscious

Just as these musicians described getting the conscious mind out of the way when writing, others pointed to the equally powerful effect this process can have on performance. Only after the performer stops 'consciously' playing or singing, can he or she tap into the unconscious. Often what follows is the artist's ability to overcome technical constraints, which can result from the fear of making a mistake. Many artists described playing or singing with much more intensity and beauty when they stopped holding back. Numerous musicians described this exhilarating escape from normal consciousness during performance, which can feel like the music has taken on a life of its own.

The late Teddy Pendergrass explained why he tried to keep his singing on a higher plane: 'In my performances I don't consciously perform. I find when I consciously do it, I make mistakes. When I don't think and I just go for it, it all works out and it's basically flawless. When I second-guess it and think, well, what am I going to do here, or what note am I going to sing, or which place am I going to move to, ultimately I always mess up.'

Similarly, guitarist Albert Lee has learned to let go of his conscious mind during performance: 'I'll be playing something really fast, it'll just go by, because I play the guitar very fast and I don't have time to think of every move I'm making. It seems as if I'm skating over the fingerboards. I believe it's in the subconscious what's happening there, between my mind and my fingers. I might not be fully aware of what I'm doing. I could be thinking of something else, totally, but I'll be playing it.'

During improvisation, this letting go may occur more readily, since the musician doesn't have to think about a song's choruses, verses and structure. Guitarist Vernon Reid described the freedom inherent in this style of playing: 'There have been moments when I felt I really latched onto something. I've had those feelings when I've been improvising or playing and I feel like the music is playing me, rather than I'm playing the music. You're in the flow of something and you're not conscious, but you're aware. You're not making decisions on a conscious level; you're guiding it, but it's guiding you at the same time.'

Steve Jordan, who writes as well as playing drums and

bass, tries to keep himself open to receive 'energy' from the unconscious: 'I feel that we're all just receptacles, receivers, and if we keep ourselves clear and open, then we can receive all the things we're capable of receiving, all that energy. The clearer we are, the better we can transmit that, convey it.

'Some of the greatest things I've ever done – and amazing feelings – have come from things I didn't even know I was doing. And I can't take responsibility for them because that would be completely bogus. I know I didn't do that; it's written down that I did it, but I didn't do that. I have that feeling when I write and when I play. When you write that song and it just comes out automatically, especially if you've been slaving over a song for about a month and it doesn't seem to work, then all of a sudden a song comes out just like that, and it's the best thing you've ever done. It's the same thing when you play and you've been working on a lick and you just can't seem to get it and then that one time when you go for it in a situation where you wouldn't even try and then you just do it. Like on a recording session when you're a drummer, everybody else can overdub their stuff; if they make a mistake they can punch in their part, but with the drums you can't do that. A lot of the time you might have a tendency to play it safe, so when you go for something that you know you've been practising and that you can't do, and then you do it in a situation where you could blow a whole take that's been going quite well, you know you're not responsible for that.'

Songwriter and guitarist Bernie Larsen compared the release that occurs in writing with that brought on by performing: 'I feel that music goes through me. To just let go and play is second nature to me. It happens without much consciousness. To sit down and deliberately write or to create something, it doesn't happen. When I am writing I have a rhythm or a flow, and it's like speaking in tongues. The flow starts happening, and I believe it's connected to a rhythm of life. And it's going on subconsciously. You can relax and not try too hard, and something passes through you. The pre-destiny thing is beyond your control, although you can alter it slightly by going someplace else. Life has its own flow, and you get into that rhythm. Eight hours can go by just like that. You start moving as fast as time is going, and words and phrases will come out that relate to how I feel and what's going on around me. But there's no deliberate effort to do it. It's like opening a door and not looking and when you look back, it's come out.

'When you're playing, you go off into a grey sort of area and then you open your eyes and you're surprised where you are, you're just soaring with that. The writing thing is actual words. There will be phrases, and it's plugged into a motion, you get the gist of the feeling and it's connected to the rhythm, and from that point on you build around it. I will have a genuine emotion or feeling, I'll be empty, and a few lines will come out, and it's totally relative. It even answers questions that I have. Listening back to what I've done, things come out that definitely aren't mine – riffs, lines, melodies and feelings. They're mine – I guess you rent them or something. They come through me, so it's mine, but it sounds like someone else to me.'

The late singer-songwriter Phoebe Snow used the image of a vessel to express how she pictures herself as an artist: 'My feeling is that we are channels, basically, through which the creativity comes. It's not "Phoebe's music". Instead, Phoebe is a vessel that carries around some stuff, and if Phoebe chooses to open the vessel, then it will work. It's coming from this thing that is controlling the whole universe. "Poetry Man" took about five minutes to write. Some people ask me, "What were you thinking when you wrote this?" and I have to tell them I really don't know; it doesn't have anything to do with how my mind rationally works.'

Phoebe also described a similar process that occurred when she sang: 'It just comes out. If I think about what I'm going to be doing in a couple of hours or if I remember something somebody said to me yesterday, the flow is really broken and I can feel it. So I have to hurry back and get into my singing or I feel I'll lose it. I become someone else when I'm up there and yet I'm me.'

When writing music, Jefferson Airplane guitarist Paul Kantner explained how transitory and elusive he finds the material that flows from within. Therefore, he attempts to keep his conscious mind at bay until after the tapping into the unconscious has ceased. Although it can be helpful to utilise what has come from one's depths, the conscious mind can prematurely terminate the transcendence if brought back too soon. He observed: 'Stuff comes, and sometimes you can't write it fast enough. Sometimes the song is so good, and you're out somewhere and you start hearing this song. Your one instinct is to go write it down, but if you do that, the song is not the same as just sitting there and listening to it; it comes in and it goes out. And if you try to capture it, you can't. It's like a child's first birthday party. You could spend all your time taking videotapes and pictures, but you'd miss the whole party, 'cause you're wound up with all the buttons and machines instead of just sitting there and enjoying it. Other songs, you can catch. You have your tape recorder or you wake up in the middle of the night. It comes in a thousand different ways: sometimes a word, a line, a musical phrase, or an idea at a time. Other things come just full-blown. I used to try to capture them and you look back and they're gone. So I learned to just enjoy them. After it's done you try to capture it, but don't try to capture it in the middle.'

The Creative-Spiritual Link

For several musicians, the act of creating often verges on the spiritual. A link between creativity and spirituality was noted by psychologist Rollo May when he wrote: 'There is something in the act of creating which is like a religious revelation.'

In describing the unconscious, musicians have referred to that moment of connection – the midway point between conscious and unconscious – as a place of timelessness, a dream state, a feeling of awe and reverence, being given a gift, being used as a vessel, and at times the feeling of being in a trance. The prerequisite to achieving that state, said many musicians, was to surrender to the unconscious. This feeling recalls that spoken of by religious figures when they have described giving themselves up to a holy spirit.

Lindsey Buckingham told me that for him the creative process serves the same purpose that attending religious services might for some people: 'One of the reasons I enjoy working alone – and why that's when things will quite often come out well – is because it's very much akin to a religious [experience]. There is some tie between religion and art; I think there's a lot of crossover. What I do is get really centred and get into a space that I assume has religious connotations to it. Someone else's anchor could be going to church; the anchor for me is when I work on my own and I really get very close to something.'

Robert Burke Warren also feels that the creative act, particularly music, is connected to the spiritual: 'I believe there is a transcendent power, and anyone can get to it through the creative act. The outlet is the part of the brain that is more attuned to that which is not temporal. You can open up that receptor within you; you can tap into it through music. The part of the human spirit that music touches is deeper and more connected with that which is transcendent.

'I think music was a more important part of religion than it is now. My main memories from attending Catholic church as a child are of ringing bells and powerful singing. Once my mother took me to Ebenezer Baptist Church in Atlanta [where Martin Luther King Jr had once preached] and I'll never forget it as long as I live. It was an overwhelming sensory experience – the power of the music and the feeling that there was definitely something going on. There was incredible music, people were singing, and there was elation in the air. I firmly believe that music is connected to the spiritual.'

Keith Strickland pointed out the similarities between the creative process and meditation: 'When things are going really well onstage, it's almost like a meditation. You're very much in the present, and you're not concerned about its outcome or the past. It's sort of like you're right there – and that is a meditation. To get to that point, you have to work on it. It happens at different points in performance. Every night at certain times, I get into that state.

'Also, during writing, particularly in the beginning of writing a song, we try very hard to get into that state of mind, real open, non-judgmental about what it is we're doing, not even concerned about the outcome of it. And then just allowing anything to happen. It's very important to be open and allow the unexpected to occur and really let the song take on a life of its own. Then it becomes a part of the living process itself. It's truly a creative thing; it comes alive. It's like a novelist would have a character, and that character just takes on a life of its own. If you don't do that with songwriting, it's just too controlled and limited.

'It's spiritual in a sense in that it's starting out in the invisible realm of things. It's invisible to begin with, then you bring it into this three-dimensional world, and that's always a spiritual connection. All things – not just music, everything – first starts out as just a thought. Like the button on your shirt, someone just thought of that. At one point it never existed, and then somebody thought it up from the invisible realm, and it became physical. So I think the whole creative process is bringing the invisible into this reality.'

Drummer Robin Horn said of the spiritual nature of creating music: 'Sometimes something pops out that I've never heard before, and that's probably the closest thing to having a mystical experience. And when those come on, they are very strong and absolute. It just comes out in a few minutes. Other times I try to write and nothing happens. It seems like it will come when it's going to come.'

For Ravi Shankar, performing music was a part of his spiritual beliefs. He entered a near meditative state when he played sitar. Perhaps this helps to explain the transcendent effect his music had on his audiences and the ethereal feel of his concerts. He told me: 'It takes a lot of preparation before [the concert], meditating and praying, which is part of our music. I don't like to talk much with people before [the performance]. I try to be as pure outside as inside, so I have a bath and wear clean clothes. And then it's like trying to imagine what I'm going to play, which raga; I try to feel those ragas, and by the time I go onstage I'm so charged. Then sitting there after tuning, it's already in my head, and now it's physical, so with the first note I merge into that raga. And that is why it has that magical effect. Whether you understand or don't understand, it does have an effect. I'm not thinking what note I'm using; a raga at that time is like a person, like making love, in the sense that the whole raga merges with me and we become one.

'My first impulse that comes out is always the best. I have never been able to do better. The first gush that comes is it, then I can always work on that, elaborate it or shorten it, shape it up. Of course, being a performer with years of experience, one has to have the other consciousness, like being aware of time duration, not repeating [a raga], and depending on the audience, I let myself go in a different way; everywhere is different. I feel the vibration and it just comes out accordingly.

'As an Indian performing artist, I create spontaneously. Because we improvise all the time, we create on the spot, it's like an unfolding raga. It's a very strange thing; it's partly like being computerised. Our training is such that we've been programmed with the raga and all the ideas by our guru. There's a format that we follow. All that is there, but what we do there is really not something preconceived. Something [else] comes out of all this programming. It's a very strange thing: We have the structure that is so deeply ingrained that we don't say this is A and this is B. It just comes out, sometimes in long durations, sometimes in short durations, which we are also controlling.

'The second thing is that miraculous things sometimes happen: while we're doing that, something very new comes out which I have not done before or have not been taught before. When that happens, it's a great ecstasy. We try to put that somewhere in the future, it becomes an addition to the whole thing. Sometimes it comes, sometimes it's lost forever. If it's something really outstanding, we try to recapture it.'

Nancy Wilson also spoke of the importance of reaching a pure state in which to create: 'There are those magical times when it seems to pour right through you. That's the most incredible feeling I can imagine as far as songwriting. You're like the vessel or the instrument itself that somebody's playing – somebody or something. I don't have a specific name for it; there's a lot of names: Buddha, God, inspiration. I really do think that there is a lot of magic in it and a lot of greatness, which being an artistic person brings you a bit closer to. It can be the same [in playing], but in writing you're probably much more vulnerable because you're wide open and you're trying to push down all the voices that say, "Write a commercial song. Be competitive. You need a song that's more like this, more like someone else." What's hard is to be open enough to just be who you are, without all the other outside expectations. So if you can find a pretty pure state to write in, that's when it usually happens.

'I like to go out to the ocean. For me that's always a very religious experience. You go back to that almost like the womb, like going back to being connected to the ocean where it all started. All that power and all that "bigger than you" gives you a neat kind of feeling, and looking at the stars at night. Things like that really help you connect so much faster to that essence of where it all is and where it all comes from and, hopefully, what you can bring from it to the world. So that's a real source. Sometimes it just happens right when I'm at the edge of sleep. A lot of stuff will happen to me and I'll think, Oh, no! Do I really have to write this down? But I really do.'

A Nocturnal Glimpse of the Unconscious

Like Nancy Wilson, many musicians described getting creative bursts just before falling asleep. For most people, near slumber is the time when the veil between the unconscious and the conscious mind is most transparent. With the body and rational mind at rest, the inner self is freed. Rollo May wrote of this state as being conducive to creativeness: 'Obviously poetic and creative insights of all sorts come to us in moments of relaxation. They come not haphazardly, however, but come only in those areas in which we are intensively committed and on which we concentrate in our waking, conscious experience.'

Vocalist Dolette McDonald explained how she struggles to acquire the habit of writing down songs that occur to her late at night: 'The weirdest thing happens to me just when

I'm going to sleep at night. I hear the most incredible melodies, but I'm too lazy to get up. I'm learning to do that now, because my best stuff is at that time. That's when I think it's real – those times when I least expect it to happen. It's incredible. Nowadays I keep my tape recorder close to my bed and a pad and pencil just in case, because you never know. It's so ridiculous to just let these things go into the universe. It will come through me and I'll let it go into the universe, because I'm not smart enough to use it, so it will pass on to someone else. I'll hear it again and say to myself, "I know that; I've heard that song somewhere before. Of course you did, you dummy! It was yours and you gave it up." I believe that has happened to me.'

Red Hot Chili Pepper Anthony Kiedis told me how relentless the flow from the unconscious can be when he taps into it on the brink of sleep: 'There are some times when I sit down to write and it takes me hours and hours to hash out a few verses because I'm very meticulous and very much a perfectionist, and every syllable has to have a fluid connection with each other. Then there are other times when I can sit down and I can just start writing and writing and I will have written three or four verses or a complete song in half an hour or 15 minutes. I think some of the best songs I've ever written came out that way.

'There's also the thing that happens to me when I lie down to sleep at night. I start getting insomniatic energy, and one line will come into my mind and I say, "That's a beautiful line. I'm going to get up and I'm going to write it down." I write it down, and I'll go to lie down and try to fall asleep. And then another line will come to me and I say, "I better write this down", and it can happen for hours and hours. Then when I wake up in the morning, I've got a really beautiful poem.'

Ron Wood has successfully waited until morning to write down a song that popped into his head just before sleep: 'I wrote one of my greatest songs [which hadn't come out at that time], by just remembering it [after waking up]. I was lying in bed one night and I couldn't sleep; there was this song I just had to put down, and my wife Jo said, "Well, remember it." So I woke up the next morning and it was still there. I was going to punch her if it went! It just goes to show you can do it if you put your mind to it; you can picture a song in a visual way in your mind's eye, if you just have a basic structure to refer to.'

'Hidden Doors' of the Psyche

Dreams are often the ships that bring pieces of the unconscious to the harbour of consciousness. Throughout our lives, dreams give us a little peek into the mysteries of the unconscious. Jung poetically described the dream as 'a little hidden door in the innermost and most secret recesses of the psyche'. Kirsty MacColl told me: 'I've had dreams where I've written a really good line, and I have to quickly write it down in case I forget it.' Many musicians related getting bits of songs or entire pieces from their dream life, as is the case with Nancy Wilson: 'I have a lot of musical dreams. Melodies and songs will happen in a dream, and I'll wake up and try to recreate it. If you can ever catch that, you have the best music you've ever heard, but it's hard to catch. To me, that's probably the most spiritual experience, when you're dreaming and you hear this. For me, it's usually a lot of acoustic instruments with electric guitar, almost orchestra-type music with mandolins and acoustic keyboards.'

Legend has it that Rolling Stone Keith Richards got the idea for the main riff to '(I Can't Get No) Satisfaction' while dozing by a Hollywood motel swimming pool during an American tour. Sure enough, Keith admitted to 'dreaming up' many of his songs: 'Songs just come to me. I don't sit down and try and write songs. I wake up in the middle of the night, and I've dreamt half of it. I just need to pick up the guitar next to the bed and the tape recorder, push "record" and put it down. I'm not saying I write them all in my dreams – but that's the ideal way. You don't even have to get out of bed!'

For Don Henley, the elusive nature of his nocturnal songs can be frustrating: 'Over the years, since I was in my twenties, I've had dreams where I actually dream a song and I'm really excited about it, then I wake up and I've forgotten it. I've lost a couple of songs like that.'

Buddy Guy found his dream life to be an important part of his creative process. He recalled a dream from childhood in which he learned his very first song: 'The first thing I ever learned to play was John Lee Hooker's "Boogie Chillen", and I was lying down outside in Louisiana on a warm, sunny day. I was dozing off to sleep. I didn't even know I was tuning the guitar, but I knew what I wanted to hear. After dozing off, I woke up and I thought, this is not a dream – I'm playing "Boogie Chillen". The positions I had my fingers in, I thought, if I turn them loose, I'll never be able to do it again. And would you believe I played that tune for five hours so my fingers wouldn't forget it! I was afraid if I missed that I would never be able to play it again the next day, because I doubted myself as a self-taught musician at that time. It was no problem; it came again fine. I could play it the next day, because I never did put my guitar down until my mom and dad made me do the home chores. In fact, I sleep with it – that's what I do when I'm out of town now. I've got one I sleep with.'

The 'Feel,' or Unconscious Element, of Music

The unconscious is also the part of oneself that comes through in what musicians describe as the 'feel' in music, or as drummer Tony Williams called it, 'the spirit that touches people'. Technique is something different altogether. Obviously an important element to musicianship, technique is the actual craft of performing music that develops through years of practice. Its importance is analogous to the conscious mind's role in giving structure to images that flow from the unconscious.

Hank B Marvin, legendary guitarist from The Shadows and hero to many British guitarists, explained that technique is what gives a musician the ability to master his instrument so that he need not rely entirely on the conscious mind while playing. Thus, the musician is more likely to tap into the unconscious: 'I practise more now than I ever used to; I feel by improving a technique and by listening to a variety of kinds of music, not just guitar players, I'm putting more into my mind from which I can draw when I'm being creative. Obviously, the more technique you have, you can go for things you couldn't hope to if you didn't have the technique. So it does give you more options, more opportunity to be creative. The more you take in, the more you will absorb and, hopefully, the more of that you'll draw from, because I think creativity has a lot to do with drawing from other sources, using that as a foundation to build something different.'

Some musicians work hard at their craft and are technically brilliant, yet something is missing. One could call it 'the feel', or the intuitive quality of their musical expression. As important as technique, many of the musicians I interviewed valued this feel in playing even more. Some held the opinion that regardless of how technically brilliant a player may be, unless he or she has that feel, the music is almost meaningless. One can appreciate the technique, but at the same time not be moved at all by the playing. Technical playing appears to come from the conscious mind, whereas the feel springs from the unconscious. Phil Collins explained: 'You can have the feel for [playing music] and then cultivate it into something more; you can't buy it, or learn how to do it. Some of the most famous drummers – like, say, Carl Palmer – someone like that to me is a very unnatural drummer. He was taught, and it just sounds like it when I hear him play. There are other guys out there, you can tell, who just picked up a pair of sticks and started playing. Without putting down Carl Palmer, I've never heard anything from him that sounds convincing to me, and yet there are other drummers who can do far less but move me far more – like Ringo, for instance.'

Ringo confirmed Phil's comments about his own playing: 'If you ever watch me, I play with some sort of beat going on within me. It can be fast or slow; I just feel it.'

Drummer Tony Williams also emphasised the importance of feel: 'Some people are creative, but it's a self-conscious creativity. To me, [artist Salvador] Dali was very self-conscious. He lacked the spirit, though he was a great technician. You could say, "Wow, it's a nice image, but it's self-conscious." He did things just for effect.'

Again, the difference between feel and technique is similar to that between songs that come from the unconscious and those that are contrived. As Rick Vito pointed out, music with a certain emotional validity is more likely to communicate its message to others, regardless of its technical brilliance: 'I see a lot of technical musicians, and very few of them seem to have that feel that goes along with it. They're able to do technically a lot more than the next guy, but for some reason it doesn't communicate. So I guess not everyone has that.'

Vernon Reid distinguished between craftsmanship and inspired playing: 'Creativity on demand – I don't know if that's creativity or if that's craftsmanship. To make something happen that's creative, there's a level of craft where you can do that, but that's not really inspired creativity. That's sort of craftsman's creativity.'

Nancy Wilson believes that those musicians who put as much or more feel into their playing as they do technical brilliance have a longer-lasting effect on people's lives: 'I think with playing and singing, too – but especially as a guitar player – my philosophy has always been feel as opposed to technique. To me, having all the technique in the world means nothing. I think that's a great thing to know how to do. But it's more important that a musician play through her instrument like a human, in a human sense, the way Eric Clapton and David Gilmour do. Jimi Hendrix was really good at that. He spoke through his guitar; he wasn't just trying to impress you with how much he'd practised.'

Rather than just going through the motions, the musician who plays with feel is contacting the spirit within. British vocalist Graham Bell observed: 'I think what makes the difference between a good player and a great player is not always technique. It's that spirit in the person, being very open, wanting to improve and be very good. There are some people who can only play technically and don't have that feel. Technology that people have now, like drum machines, takes the feel away; it doesn't have much depth to it. I love to listen to people who move me!'

Mick Fleetwood spoke of his band's original guitarist, Peter Green, as a musician whose feel directed his playing, which was a perfect match for Mick's style of drumming: 'I rely completely on instinct as a player. Often, while I'm playing, there are certain moments when I disappear. Peter was absolutely oozing with feel, and I've never played with anyone who was that profound and so involved with that conviction. I think he saw that in me: there was an affiliation with this funny guy who was not such a great drummer but someone who was able to express himself without worrying how clever he was, and that really applied to what Peter represented as a player.'

It is no wonder that Lindsey Buckingham played so well with Mick in Fleetwood Mac, since he, too, greatly appreciates a musician with that intuitive feel: '[In music] you get into things beyond technique; you start to move into things intangible. I don't know what makes people have the quality that touches, but they must have taken something in their life that rings back true on the way out. Once I asked someone I respected, "Should I take music classes?" And he said, "Knowledge is always going to help, but you might stomp out something that is original about you; you'll start second-guessing things that you do that might not be by the book but which are you."

'Today, you've got such an influx of technology that you've got kids now who aren't musicians but computer programmers making music. But I think you're going to find that for every bit of high tech, people are going to need "high touch" on the other side to balance it out.'

The feel in music is so linked to the unconscious that 'computer programmers', as Lindsey described them, can sometimes produce music that lacks the expression of their soul. In the quest for perfection and with so much digital machinery available enabling a 'perfect' track, music can lose its spontaneity, or intuitive nature, in the studio. In extreme cases, musicians who rely totally on technical wizardry for performance can at times lose the raw, emotional contact with their audience. We have seen this happen when performers choose to lip-sync their material along with electronic backing tapes, rather than sing or play their compositions. Here, we have a one-dimensional spectacle rather than the give-and-take communication between audience and artist.

Rollo May wrote of the dangers of over-reliance on technology as 'put[ting] tools in between [oneself] and the unconscious world'. He explained, 'For if we are not open to the unconscious, irrational and transrational aspects of creativity, then our science and technology have helped to block us off from what I shall call "creativity of the spirit".'

Several musicians, some of whom originally embraced high-tech machinery, have reappraised the growing use of computerised technology in music. Christine McVie dislikes much of the results of modern recording techniques: 'Today the music is so diverse and quackish in a sense. There's a lot of wonderful music happening, a lot of really good creative stuff. There's also such a lot of trash. It's duping the public to go into the studio and use a bunch of electronics, which some people feel is equally valid. I couldn't argue with them, because they would say, "Well, that's my way of creating." To me, it takes all the spiritual out of it. To be going in with a bunch of gadgetry and creating a song on the computer is valid, but in a sense it takes the human soul out of it.'

Jeff Lynne, who has worked in some of the most high-tech studios in the world, has discovered through experience that music recorded in this way sometimes loses its spontaneity: 'I got into this electronic stuff several years ago. You end up sitting around the studio waiting for this guy to program all this shit into the computer. You end up saying, "What the hell am I doing this for? I could have played this, and I'd much rather play this." So I kicked it all out and that's how we did George [Harrison's] album [*Cloud Nine*], by just playing everything – real drummers, real guitar players, and no sequencers.'

Just as Jeff ultimately rejected technology in the studio, Steve Jordan predicts there will be an eventual backlash from audiences against 'canned' performances. 'There's very little music that's moving anyone. There's a lot of mindless garbage out there, and I think what we were doing on tour with Keith [Richards] was, we were people onstage actually playing, instead of having some machine play tape-recorded background vocals and having everything be the same every night. That's not music – but that's what's happening.'

Robin Horn stressed that musicians can use electronics as a tool, but in the end, it takes more than technology to reach an audience emotionally: 'There's a technical revolution going on right now in music. I think the musicians have to go through this and find out exactly what its place is and how much of it they want to employ, because it's only going to be a means to an end. What's going to touch anyone in the long run is going to be the human spirit that comes from the music. If the electronics are used to complement that, fine. But if they are used to create the music, you'll know, because it's cold. And it's devoid of any kind of emotion.'

Perhaps pressure from the music business forces some musicians to move towards technique over feel, to go for glitz rather than guts, in order to get a hit or follow up a successful album or fit into a certain trend. Keith Richards pointed out: 'Music represents the unconscious feelings of the people – of musicians and their audience. But at the same time it represents what the record companies think they can maximise their profits on. And so they'll stuff things down people's throats that they don't really want. A majority of what you hear is formula shit; it's what record companies find easiest and cheapest to produce and get the maximum profit. They like cats who go along with that, and now they've got the possibility with all the toys. They'd love to get rid of musicians entirely, those bothersome things that talk back and want to do it better.'

The 'unconscious feelings of the people' that Keith

mentioned is another important source of creativity. Artists are able to pull out of the ether and concretise sights and sounds, and by doing so bring harmony to our senses. Sinéad O'Connor told me: 'It's as if you're a prism; it just comes through you, out of your brain and out of your mouth. I think every person in one way or another is a vehicle through which certain information passes.'

Musicians can give form to that of which we might only dream. In so doing, they reach a part within us that speaks to us, by portraying a feeling that needs to be touched before it can be felt. Drummer Tony Williams told me that he believed that this drove him to create: 'Part of it comes from wanting to express a view of the universe, what you think life and the universe are about. It also comes from wanting to be connected with life and the universe, wanting to be connected with people, wanting to communicate with people and show your own humanity and your love for life.'

Musicians can express the hidden-away content within all of us, allowing us to feel what for most of us is concealed. This part of ourselves that we find in their music is representative of what Jung called the collective unconscious.

Chapter 4

THE COLLECTIVE UNCONCIOUS

'I ALWAYS RESORT BACK TO MUSIC BECAUSE IT
DOESN'T HAVE WORDS. IT'S JUST A VOICE THAT CAN
BE UNDERSTOOD BY ANYONE.'
ERIC CLAPTON

All creativity springs from the unconscious. Along with the part of the unconscious that is unique to each individual, known as the personal unconscious, there is another innate element that we all share. Carl Jung theorised that in addition to our personal unconscious, we have a collective, or group, unconscious. The collective unconscious (or world soul) is made up of elemental archetypes, or innate behaviour potentials, that actually influence us to behave or react instinctually to certain conditions, people, sounds and other stimuli. These archetypes are known to us consciously only through what Jung called 'archetypal ideas', which are manifested in specific symbols and images. 'The concept of the archetype is derived from the repeated observation that, for instance, the myths and fairy tales of world literature contain definitive motifs which crop up everywhere,' according to

Jung. 'These typical images and associations are what I call archetypal ideas ... They impress, influence and fascinate us. They have their origin in the archetype, which in itself is an irrepresentable, unconscious, pre-existent form that seems to be part of the inherited structure of the psyche and can therefore manifest itself spontaneously anywhere, at any time.'

Jung's hypothesis helps to explain how artists communicate the essence of our era, the spirit of our time, the zeitgeist. Musicians tune in to that thread which runs through all of us and, through their music, give it form. At their most creative, they are the mouthpieces for our age, reflecting the collective unconscious.

The way to see what is in the collective unconscious, according to Jung, is through these archetypal images and ideas. As Jung stressed in his writings, throughout time humanity has been empowered by archetypal ideas in myths, legends, fairy tales, ballads and personal dreams. Joseph Campbell, one of the world's foremost authorities on mythology, pointed out how part of the collective unconscious is given form by myths: 'A dream is a personal experience of the deep, dark ground that is the support of our conscious lives, and a myth is the society's dream.'

Musicians represent a type of archetypal idea from our collective unconscious. According to psychologist Erich Neumann, the 'form [of archetypal ideas] changes according to the time, the place, and the psychological constellation of the individual in whom they are manifested'. Through their creativeness, derived from the unconscious, artists have the potential to be a channel from the collective unconscious, or universal self. Rosanne Cash pointed out:

THE COLLECTIVE UNCONSCIOUS

'Music today taps into the collective unconscious, just like myths and fairy tales. These are new myths and new fairy tales. Music has to do this, because the collective unconscious is part of all of us. I think that's probably a huge part of the [creative] source.'

It is through exploring these symbolic expressions of the collective unconscious that we can recognise parts of ourselves reflected by the artist. As Peter Gabriel said, 'I put a lot of myself into my music and so I think people find echoes of themselves in it.'

The zeitgeist was greatly pronounced during the sixties, and musicians figured very prominently. 'The spirit of the times decides both the quantity and the character of the creative activity,' according to psychologist Dean Keith Simonton. During those years, 'love' was the message and musicians were its messengers. The songs they wrote were not so often about romantic love, as in times gone by; these songs were about universal love. There was an emphasis on a more meaningful and spiritual way of life.

The Beatles played a dynamic part during that age. Whatever they did, sang or spoke, people watched and listened. A confluence of events made the time ripe in the collective unconscious; there was a real hunger for change, and the musicians seemed totally plugged in to the essence of the time. During the sixties, there was a refusal to bend to the will of society as we had known it; there was an urge for a new kind of freedom, a need to break free from the old mould. This anti-establishment attitude was fostered by musicians. They became like gods, carrying that power which went along with the sense of an elevated idealism.

The feeling was, 'We can do anything; we can change anyone; and we can love everyone.' This attitude was reflected in Beatles songs, such as 'All You Need Is Love', as well as in those of many other bands, which all amplified powerful messages. There was an air of anticipation while people awaited the next Bob Dylan or Beatles record, so they could listen to the prophetic words that would carry the spirit of change.

A good description of the artist's role in our society, which also helps to illustrate the concept of the collective unconscious, was articulated by psychologist Rollo May: '[Artists] give us a distinct early warning of what is happening to our culture.' It is the spirit of the time that comes through artists; it is their job in life to impart whatever is coming through them. As Sinéad O'Connor said: 'I think the function of art is to reflect God and to try and remember all the knowledge that we had before we were born, of how powerful we are and what God is. I think that's the drive to create, to fill the space, to fill the emptiness, even for just two seconds, so as to achieve the sense of having reflected, of having opened up and connected, with whatever it is that is above us.'

Whatever it is that artists are tapping into, though, they are often unaware of it representing anything larger than their own self-expression. George Harrison told me that he found the Beatles' huge influence on society quite baffling at the time: 'I thought it was pretty strange why we made the enormous impact that we did – or have still. It's strange how the chemistry between the four of us made this big thing that went right through the world. There wasn't any country in the world, even the most obscure places, that didn't know about the Beatles – from grandparents to babies. It just blanketed everything, and that amazed me more than anything. We always felt that if we could get the right record contract, we'd be successful. But our tiny little concept of success that we had at the time was nothing compared to what happened. It was just enormous. It does make one think there's more to this than meets the eye.'

Ringo Starr concurred: 'I don't think we were actually there thinking we were tapping into this great God-given consciousness for everybody. I don't know if you think like that when you're a teenager or [in] your early twenties. You're just playing the best you can.' In the words of Erich Neumann: 'They are all moved in the same direction, though they follow an unknown impulse in themselves rather than any new road chartered in advance. This phenomenon is called simply zeitgeist.'

Music Reflecting Our Times

For me, the music of the sixties represented the changes I – along with many of my generation – was going through. I felt part of the big wave of it all. Today diverse forms of music continue to reflect the ever-changing attitudes of new generations of listeners. Graham Nash observed how varying musical styles mirror the times: 'In this world of turmoil and chaos, where the kids can't see a future, where people believe they can't get a job, you put that together with environmental pollution, where they can see the poisoning of the atmosphere and the earth and the water, and when you see the destruction of the family unit with so many divorces, and scatterings of people and family, it is reflected in popular music. It's chaotic, especially things like the punk movement – aggressive, rebellious. It's very interesting. I see the music of the popular culture totally reflective of what kids believe is happening in their lives.'

Mike Rutherford said he has 'felt' the mood portrayed by certain musical styles: 'I just sense moments, the feelings that are going on in young kids at certain stages; you hear a song, or you hear a mood or an atmosphere. It's there somewhere, you can feel it. I've always felt the strongest things are subconscious; a heavy lyric or a heavy sound is never as strong as some of those subconscious feelings. I think everyone inside is feeling it, even if not aware of it.'

Guitarist, singer and songwriter Bonnie Raitt remarked on the changes she has seen in society expressed by the music: 'For a while, especially in the so-called disco and Reagan era, there definitely was a turning away from moral and political content in pop music at least. Progressive radio all but disappeared, and even Jackson Browne had trouble getting his songs on the radio.

'Then the punk movement came along and blew the lid off all that cultural and moral complacency. Groups like The Clash, U2, Midnight Oil, artists such as Peter Gabriel, Sting, Springsteen, and especially the emergence of Tracy Chapman, all broke through with some great soul-inspiring music of conscience. People started to get sick of all the homogenous formula pop and began to appreciate the more homegrown sounds of folk, blues, reggae, world beat, and especially rap. Springsteen and U2 are the most unifying people I've seen since the Beatles.'

Nancy Wilson pointed to hip-hop as an indicator of what is on young people's minds: 'You can read a lot of what's happening in the music. You can keep your finger on the pulse of how they feel in the city when you listen to a lot of black music now.'

For Eric Clapton, pop music can be formulaic and superficial, but it can lead listeners to other forms of music that are more meaningful and more representative of this day and age: 'There's a lot of gloss, a lot of facade in music today. Fortunately, underneath the surface, there's good stuff going on, which supports the chrome up on top. People who are interested in music, or interested in what's being communicated, will always start out with the veneer and then dip down and find out what's underneath. They're the ones who will get the reward.'

The Power of Music

Many musicians concluded that they play a role in our culture. Paul Horn, an introspective person, described the very essence of the part musicians play in our society today. 'All music throughout the ages serves two purposes. [First] it's a reflection of the state of the world or a particular society of that time. [Second] in the hands of more aware musicians it has gotten past that, and the power of the music can uplift the spirit of man. In the hands of musicians like that, they are not just reflecting the collective unconscious but trying to change it and to push it in a higher direction. I've been to Russia quite a few times now and have seen that music is really a power to bring people together. It is the universal language, and it does have great power to connect people in the world. I think it is one of the most powerful "weapons", if you will, that we have for peace and understanding, and to communicate and begin to connect with each other.'

As Paul said, the musician has the ability to bring people together. Despite the dissension in the world, musicians have the capacity to unite us.

Several artists also discussed the idea that songs are all around us, 'in the air', so to speak. The musician's receptivity enables him or her to pick up the song and express it. Keith Richards elaborated on this idea, pointing to the extraordinary power of music to change society: 'Music goes through walls – it's like laser beams. The songs are all around us. It's just a matter of whether you're there to receive them. The idea that *I* created this piece of music is kind of pompous and the wrong end of the stick to me. Music is everywhere; all you're got to do is pick it up. It's just like being a receiver.

'As a musician, I just want to make some great records. Unwittingly and unknowingly, it can happen that what you're doing can be interpreted and you're taken to represent everybody – not just authorities or record companies – but the whole mass of the people. You can find yourself being involved without any real intention. In a way they write the songs for you. "Street Fighting Man" was just a mere comment, but all of that stuff turned us into – which was unbelievable to me – a threat to the British government. You'd think a couple of guitar players are really going to topple the Empire! That's the important thing about music, because it can. That's when you realise it has social and political overtones.

'You can get biblical about it: you have a power, but I don't suppose Joshua took his band and walked around Jericho and blew a few trumpets and the wall actually fell down from that. It was probably some cats inside Jericho who were saying, "Jesus, those guys are playing good! Open the back door and let them in!" That's how I think Jericho's wall crumbled. It's like the Iron Curtain – what happened in Russia is probably an analogy in the same way. The one thing they couldn't stop [was creativity], and it was the one channel that was always open when everything else was "no way".

'Music is very powerful; it's uncontrollable. Some people think you can lessen the power of music by trying to preach with it, but I think that it has its own power. If you want to write a great track and put it to music, that's alright too. But I think the real lasting power of music is on a far more subtle and indefinable level than what people say. It's the total thing.'

Like Keith, Don Henley feels that the role of the musician is to maintain the receptivity to pick up on universal 'songs' and then give them expression: 'I believe in the collective unconscious. I believe writing is tapping into that; I believe it's in the air. The good days are really spiritual; you feel that you have tapped into something universal. In a sense, you just give them back what they already know but can't express for themselves. That's what you're doing. You're expressing things for people in a very dramatic way, that they can't do for themselves. To paraphrase Emerson, if you look deep enough into one individual, truths about all individuals begin to emerge.'

Keith Strickland has experienced the sensation of tapping into the collective unconscious while writing and performing: 'Sometimes, particularly in performance, I feel as though I'm just really plugged into the cosmic channels, sort of like an antenna receiver just broadcasting from the centre. Also in writing, it's quite often like that: I feel as if I'm plugging into the collective unconscious. What's happening in music today is definitely an expression of that. The audience will identify with it; it rings true to their feelings.'

How music's sound and structure reflect certain societal changes has struck Mick Fleetwood: 'Music is definitely a barometer of social malady or wellness. Music causes something that either excites or calms down or instigates, without even a word being said. A verbal onslaught is part of music, but what music should represent ultimately is harmony. That's my real sense of what sound is, to bring harmony. That would be the whole point that people can express themselves through. And there is nothing without rhythm, no order, seasons – nothing.'

Another drummer, Steve Jordan, also views rhythm as a cosmic unifying force: 'Besides the voice box, the drum is the first instrument – it's natural: bark and skin – and the first mode of communication to pass messages from village to village, also for music. It's all about timing, rhythm – your heart is a drum – it's all that. If you're really good at drumming, then you're a little closer to what it is that makes it all special, the core. The more I play other instruments, the better drummer I become, and that [also] gets me closer to the core. And the better writer I become, the better drummer.

'Music is very powerful; it crashes down walls. It's the only universal language there is, and it can knock down barriers quicker than any UN meeting, any NATO meeting. That's why rock 'n' roll has been so powerful. I watched a band from Liverpool change the world. As far as I'm concerned, what else has done that!'

Robin Le Mesurier told me of a lesson he learned while touring with Rod Stewart: 'We were in Brussels several years ago, and staying in the same hotel were some high-ranking NATO officials. And quite often we'd have a chat with them in the bar; they would ask what it was like being on the road. One of them said, "You guys do much more for world peace and harmony than any of these guys here in the whole United Nations put together. You go around and you just play to everybody." And the first time we went to Thailand, it was run by the chief of police, but there was a sea of people with black hair, and every single one of them knew all the words but didn't know what they were singing. One song can unite millions of people; they all have something in common, the love for that song.'

Following in Musical Footsteps

From my conversations with so many musicians, I discovered that most were extremely receptive to the music that came before them. Indeed, they are part of a continuing cycle: They were deeply touched by a form of music or individual artists who stirred within them the longing to write and perform their own sound. They in turn go on to influence other fledgling artists. It was interesting talking to several generations of musicians and seeing a kind of chain. Bluesmen John Lee Hooker, B. B. King, Buddy Guy and Willie Dixon, for example, inspired the Beatles, the Rolling Stones and Eric Clapton, who then influenced Rosanne Cash, Vernon Reid, Anthony Kiedis, and so many others making music today. Eric Clapton expressed how he felt about his role in this cycle: 'I don't know why I chose to play the blues or rock 'n' roll. I don't know why it settled on me, in the middle of the countryside in England, to be a messenger. I've got no idea. I don't really like to analyse it, but maybe I've been handed something to lead on, to carry on in this generation. I often feel a very strong sense of responsibility toward that, as if it's something not really to do with me. It's like carrying a torch. It is more powerful than I am, and I have to be a servant to it. I always resort back to music because it doesn't have words. It's just a voice that can be understood by anyone.'

Bonnie Raitt recalled her formative years, when she was totally caught up in the civil rights movement and the music that represented it, blues and folk. The spirit of this time guided her and resulted in Bonnie's making music her lifelong career: 'While I was born and raised in Los Angeles, I spent my summers at a very progressive Quaker camp in upstate New York. It was co-ed and interdenominational with counsellors from all over the world. My introduction to being spiritually and socially conscious came primarily from there and my Quaker background. I lived from summer to summer, when I could spend those two-and-a-half months hanging out with people who were more into the peace and civil rights movement – the kids of UN people and liberal lawyers – instead of the beach-party, show-biz, politically conservative world L.A. was in the early sixties. The counsellors at my camp were very much into the folk music revival that was going on at that time: the Kingston Trio; The Weavers; Peter, Paul and Mary; Joan Baez; and later Bob Dylan. I naturally idolised my counsellors, who were all playing the guitar and learning folk ballads and protest songs. So I decided to trade the piano for the guitar. I didn't take lessons, I just taught myself.

'When I was about 14, I heard a record called *Blues at Newport '63* and immediately fell in love with the blues. I had always loved any kind of soul music – Ray Charles, Ike and Tina Turner, Motown, and Stax – all the stuff we lapped up from the radio. But now I had to choose whether to spend my allowance on the new Bob Dylan, Beatles or Muddy Waters record.

'Back in California the guitar became a sort of haven for me, a little safe place to go. I was longing to live back East and be a beatnik and a folk singer, but I was always too young. I wanted to go to Mississippi and march in the civil rights movement. I kind of lost my childhood at some point, being so alienated from the L.A. scene, and I became very serious in my dream of saving the world. I was so angered and frustrated over the plight of black people and the injustice and the horror of Hiroshima. I wanted to hurry up and get in the Peace Corps, so I could "fix" things, as if things were my fault. I think that attitude did a lot for misdirecting what would have been a more carefree adolescence – and less problematic adulthood, for that matter.

'Playing the guitar and singing alone in my room made me feel very much in touch with my spirituality. For me, creativity, music, spirituality and political conscience were all peripherally connected in me and [to] the times. Music was serving a political-social function of uniting people and questioning what had gone on before: "We Shall Overcome", "The Times They Are a-Changin'". There was a social movement ... reflected in the music.'

Paul Kantner, who founded the socially and politically influential Jefferson Airplane, described being swept up in that same zeitgeist: 'I was a California, late fifties, early sixties kid who got stimulated by the beatnik movement, early jazz John Coltrane kind of stuff. We came out of the fifties, which was really a suppressive time. It was a very Nancy Reagan kind of time, where everything was "perfect" in America and nothing was wrong, but all of us could see something was wrong and we didn't know what.

'It was like James Dean in *Rebel Without a Cause:* just these confused children running around, not having the slightest idea what the fuck was going on. The social movement, the folk music movement, came out of this fifties "white bread America". We were middle-class kids with no problems compared to other people in the world. We weren't rich but we weren't poor, [we were] comfortable, we went to college. We were just drifting without any idea of what we wanted to do. All these jobs looked tedious and dull and boring; nothing shined. Then you saw these people making music and social movements circling around them from the peace movement to the civil rights movement. American folk music, Pete Seeger, Kingston Trio, Joan Baez, Bob Dylan – that whole thing before [the return of] rock 'n' roll [in] '61, '62, '63.

'I had taken piano lessons in sixth grade to get out of math class, but it was real dreary and boring. I didn't go back to music till I was 21, when it meant something. It wasn't just music, but [it had to do] with the folk music and the civil rights movement in the United States, particularly in the late fifties and the early sixties, and just seeing people onstage get away with all this stuff, thinking, that looks good. It was as much social phenomenon as a music phenomenon. It's like John Lennon said, "There's a whole thing going on – and it's also a great way to meet girls." It was a great socialisation process – you're just thrown into this cauldron, very strange people. It attracts all sorts of interesting people, who have something to say, funny, witty, bright, searching, whatever. It seemed to be a better cauldron than my father's office for talking about interesting things and pursuing interesting ideas, just the draw of doing that.'

What is it about these particular social movements and musical heroes that Bonnie Raitt, Paul Kantner and others tapped into so strongly? Is it related to the fact that numerous musicians described being completely knocked out by a particular genre of music and/or its artists? I believe that in both cases it was the archetypal images manifested therein at work. Although the artists appreciated the music on a conscious level, its effect on the unconscious was even more powerful. For many, there was an intense identification with the music; it seemed to strike one's very soul.

Rick Vito, for example, explained the force with which he became attached to the guitar: 'When I was six I was given a guitar and also had some lessons. There was an identification I can't take credit for. There's just something about looking at the guitar, smelling inside the sound hole. There was a day that I connected how it is that you play chords underneath melodies, and I heard that connection of that whole thing. It's always been such a monumental thing, such a personal thing.'

Jung wrote of the feeling of being swept away by an image or idea: 'The archetype is a force. It has an autonomy, and it can suddenly seize you. It is like a seizure ... For instance, you get into a situation: you don't know what the situation is; you suddenly are seized by an emotion or by a spell; and you behave in a certain way you have not foreseen at all – you do something quite strange to yourself ... That archetype has now a suggestive effect upon you.'

Many artists recalled being struck with unforgettable force by a particular musician or type of music. It is my belief that the budding musicians were actually recognising symbols of the hero archetype, and that this allowed them to understand what is hidden in the collective unconscious. Their heroes played a symbolic role in getting them in touch with previously hidden parts of themselves, in a process similar to finding a missing piece of the puzzle of one's own psyche. The hero represented something magical, a touch of the divine, an entity larger than life. Among the musicians, the symbols and images that represented these heroes varied: a certain song, the shape or sound of a particular instrument, a specific feeling or attitude emanating from a particular musician. Any of these could evoke within the admirer an uncharted image, conjuring up a whole new way of viewing the world. Something about these particular heroes ignited an absolute need to be a part of whatever it was they represented. It was as if the admirer had been awakened through idolising his or her hero, and through this finding his or her own voice to continue the never-ending cycle of becoming the hero to others.

These musicians, many of whom are the archetypal heroes of today, enthusiastically described the heroes and musical styles that initially inspired them. For some it was the traditional folk musicians, for others it was blues, jazz and R&B artists. Pre-dating most other forms of popular music, the blues was singled out by several as being the force that hit them hardest.

Willie Dixon, who founded the Blues Heaven Foundation

to honour and sustain the blues tradition and its makers, formulated a very interesting theory about the role of blues music in our society: 'I feel like the blues is actually some kind of documentary of the past and the present and something to give people inspiration for the future. The blues is the greatest music on the face of the Earth. Everything likes music; everything that crawls, creeps, flies or swims likes music. They enjoy it; it attracts their attention. Most people like rhythm because they can dance to rhythm and it gives them an uplifting feeling. But blues has wisdom ... it's always been there. If it wasn't for the messages that the drum had in it years ago, we probably wouldn't have the type of communication that we have today. So the drum was giving a message, and even today in musical sound, you get a good sound, then you get drums that you know are trying to tell you something, but here comes the wisdom and they all wait together. This is why the blues has more than the rest, because it has an understanding [made with] words along with the good feeling and the message. And you can get this understanding and learn to communicate with it and have a good time.'

B. B. King also discussed the depth of the blues and his feeling that it lies at the root of all popular music: 'When I sing blues today I still get some of the spiritual feeling; it's a thin line between blues and gospel, in my opinion, and the roots of all music that I hear, especially in the Western world, seem to fit into the music that I play. So if I border the line of rock, or soul, country, or any other kind of music, I can incorporate it into the blues because there's a place there. [When I play] I seem to get the feeling of being in the village or the area where the character that I'm singing about is. Sometimes I become intertwined with that person, so I'm really living what's going on. I think that's the best part of being an entertainer, when that happens. Then you don't care what you look like, you don't care what people say about you, they can do all kinds of things to you at that time and you hardly notice because you're so into what you're doing. That is the beautiful, beautiful part of it.'

It was blues and jazz artists who kindled the fire that shot through singer and songwriter Eric Burdon, who co-founded The Animals, setting him on his career course. He recalled his childhood in the industrial city of Newcastle and how he was shaken by the music and its meaning: 'There's a John Lee Hooker song that sums it all up. It's called "Boogie Chillen". It goes something like, "Last night I was layin' in my bed, thinkin', at the bottom of the street there's this club where it's all happenin'," and then the mother says, "He's young and you've got to let him out," and the chorus is, "Boogie chillen, boogie chillen." As soon as I was allowed into jazz clubs, I would meet these players who were like the big boys. To me they were gods because they were jazz musicians. Jazzmen were and still are special people. It flows much more and lasts much longer.

'When I was 15, I went to see a jazz concert with Chris Barber's jazz band, a very traditional, organic band. Chris was the first guy to bring across American artists to England and have them perform within a jazz set, so jazz people could see what rhythm and blues was all about. Muddy Waters was one of the first people he brought across. At that point, an electric guitar was an oddity. They weren't a regular thing you'd see. So Muddy came – and at the level he was used to playing in Chicago clubs – he started to play onstage with this acoustic-sounding band on a summer's night, with all the doors open of the city hall where the show was. I could hear Muddy's guitar from about three blocks away. I just remember walking through the streets and hearing this guitar wailing, knowing it was something special.'

John Mayall, who has been called the father of the British blues movement, was also heavily influenced by jazz and R&B, in particular boogie-woogie. 'I was brought up listening to jazz, and Django Reinhardt, Eddie Lang, Lonnie Johnson, Louis Armstrong, Duke Ellington, people like that. I know I became *obsessed* with boogie-woogie, so anything that was going on with boogie-woogie piano, that's really what led me into my own exploration of American black music, and that drew me to the piano. I spent a laborious couple of years learning the left hand to do this, and then learning the right hand. That's how I did learn to play the piano, through trying to do boogie-woogie.'

Jackson Browne recalled how folk blues opened an inner door for him that led to Bob Dylan, all of which greatly influenced his own songwriting: 'When I was 15 years old, I started to play the guitar. Some of my friends were playing bluegrass. They turned me on to a whole bunch of really great folk artists – Sonny Terry, Brownie McGhee, Jack Elliott – there was a record called "Blues, Rags, and Hollers". Then I heard Bob Dylan. I thought he was cool, and I'd try to play some of the stuff he was playing. I was impressed by his wit and his attitude, which was a real carelessness like, "This is who I am and what I am and this is what I care about." He would talk about things that really mattered. There was this wisdom and passion in what he talked about.

The most appealing thing was he didn't give a fuck about what anybody else thought, and there was this wit and this comedy. They always called him Chaplinesque.

'As he began to make more records, he would change, but we were all changing too. By the time he came out with his third or fourth record, he was no longer folksy, he was writing these really interesting songs about experience. There's a great phrase in Dylan's "Subterranean Homesick Blues" in which he says "hanging 'round an inkwell". To me, it's one of those phrases that really meant *everything*, because you really can't stand around waiting for inspiration. You can try to be a disciplined person and be in shape to handle inspiration effectively when it happens. If you stand around looking for it, it never happens.'

Peter Frampton recalled his attempts to become his generation's version of his hero, British guitarist Hank Marvin. Peter, like many British guitarists, credited Hank with being a major influence on his playing. And just as Hank sparked Peter's desire to play, so did Peter pass along the musical torch to yet another generation of young musicians: 'I was about seven and a half when I started playing. At that time there was Adam Faith, Cliff Richard and The Shadows, Eddie Cochran and Gene Vincent. The Shadows were my heroes. More than the singers, it was the players. I don't know how many English guitarists don't quote Hank Marvin as their hero. He was the one who made you start playing, he and Buddy Holly, who I found out about later.

'Six months later I'd gotten "Tom Dooley" down and a few others I'd just picked up by ear off the radio – pre-record player. I begged and begged my parents for a new guitar. That Christmas, when I was eight, I got a plain old Plectrum guitar. And very soon after that my father came back with a record player, a Dansette, with an open top and two knobs in the front. He also had two LPs: the Shadows' first album for me, and the Hot Club de France, which was Django Reinhardt and Stephane Grappelli, for my mum and him. Of course, I thought that was absolute rubbish, but later I completely switched around. The Shadows, that was it for me. I ate on that record, I lived and slept on it. I learned every song, of course. They were all instrumentals except one, but that was it: that was the beginning. I became obsessive at a very early age. By the time I was 10, I formed a band. By the time I was 12, the band was called The True Beats and was a model of The Shadows. I was writing my own instrumentals then, and we were doing my material.'

Hank Marvin spoke of the musical influences and heroes that made as much impact on him as he later made on Peter: 'I started to develop an interest in traditional jazz when I was about 13, 14, which led to me wanting to play an instrument somewhere within that framework. The first desire was to play clarinet, it was such a fluid instrument. This didn't materialise; what in fact happened was I found out our French teacher in school had a banjo, which I bought from him for two pounds and 10 shillings. I learned a lot of chords.

'By 15, I started to play banjo with a couple of local trad [traditional] jazz bands, and I was singing terrible jazz vocals. I also started a skiffle group, trying to play what I thought was more purist skiffle, not the commercial Lonnie Donegan-type skiffle. We started to have this weird skiffle group, playing all these ethnic, real down-home, New Orleans folky things.

'When I was 16, my father bought me a guitar; by this time I was beginning to lean more towards the guitar than the banjo. From somewhere I acquired an amplifier; it was about the size of a large cornflakes box, and it sounded very similar. That really gave me such a thrill to hear this guitar and amplifier. I then was asked to join another skiffle group by a guy at school called Bruce Welch, who later became a colleague of mine in the Shadows. I was singing harmonies with Bruce and playing lead guitar.

'At one point we started to put on our own dances in small villages. One night the band didn't show up, so we all decided we'd play some rock 'n' roll. I didn't know any rock 'n' roll, but Bruce knew a few Elvis Presley songs and a couple of things like that, so we had a quick half-hour rehearsal and went on and played these rock' n' roll songs, and I really enjoyed it. This was late 1957; I heard a few rock 'n' roll things after that, like Buddy Holly and The Crickets and a couple by Elvis Presley. I was very inspired by the feel, and the sound was so different from anything I'd ever heard before.

'The guitar sound on the English records at that time was very bland, rather boring, and the reason was that the guitarists here were on to a different style of music; they were all jazz-influenced players. They all wanted to be jazz guitarists. A lot of them were session musicians; then along comes rock 'n' roll – they can't stand rock 'n' roll. It's got this very heavy off beat, which most of them don't like. It's based on a simple 12-bar blues; it's repetitive. They don't like it and here they are having to play it. The American rock 'n' roll guitarists were from places where country music was very strong, but there was also an exposure to black blues music. The difference was incredible. I was so inspired by that, and I wanted to try and copy it.'

Drummer Steve Gadd emphasised how artists can pass along the powerful musical message from generation to generation: 'When I was a young teenager, 14 or 15, my father used to take me to clubs to hear a lot of organ groups, where the groove got so intense. It was in Sunday afternoon matinees where the feeling in the club got beyond age, colour. The music was feeling so good you just couldn't sit still. That feeling made you want to be a part of what was creating it; it was so powerful. To be playing that way would be so much fun, to just be a part of that energy. Plus I heard a lot of jazz groups, like Dizzy [Gillespie], and Oscar Peterson, Max Roach, Gene Krupa, and I loved them all. I can remember listening to Tony Williams and Elvin Jones, listening to things over and over again. I was so impressed by some of the things they did; they touched me so much. You get something from everyone you hear; you try and take it and use it and pass it on.'

A Unifying Force

Musicians seem most acutely aware of their art form's power during live concerts. Back in the days when I attended so many Fleetwood Mac performances, I felt this intense communication between audience and artist. One particular night in 1970, when the band opened for the Grateful Dead in New Orleans, I had a realisation that their music was a language that could be understood by everyone in the audience with almost spiritual clarity. Everyone *felt* what the music was saying. The audience's instinctual attraction to that part of the collective unconscious manifested in the music is what makes this feeling so powerful. The musicians give form to instincts and emotions that are part of their generation's collective unconscious.

Several musicians discussed the intense link that can occur between themselves and the audience. Peter Frampton has felt such a connection not only when he was onstage but also when attending a U2 concert: 'In the case of U2, it's such a mood that is created. People have said to me it was more of a moving experience than just a regular show. Knowing how I feel onstage and when I communicate that feeling to the whole audience, it starts to become a sort of emotional feedback. I become totally uninhibited onstage. People in the audience are reacting to my actions and my mood as well as the music. I know that I can control the feeling in the audience.'

Robert Burke Warren pointed out how the audience can connect to the music and rhythm itself, regardless of whether they understand the words: 'When I was with the Fleshtones, we toured a lot of countries where people didn't speak much English. I remember in Spain, the audience didn't know what the words meant, but they would sing along. It was a real tribal type of thing. They would sing along with just the rhythm of the words; it was the rhythm of the language that got them. They had no idea what they were singing, but it didn't matter. Later it occurred to me that some of my favourite songs are ones where I don't really know what the words mean, but I like the way they make me feel.'

Michael McDonald stressed how his connection with the

audience is essential to his self-expression: 'The audience could easily be 50 per cent of the whole musical experience, probably more. Musicians can only respond to themselves so much; in many cases the show has been played so many times that it's only going to be so exciting. The real excitement for them is the rapport with the audience. What the audience feels overrides any element of boredom [from] having just rehearsed and played the same show many times. When you've played the same song for many years, the whole ball of wax is that night: that audience, that venue, and that experience unto itself. If the whole experience was going to be how well you played "What'd I Say" for the fifty-millionth time, you'd walk off the stage!'

Buddy Guy treasures the ability to communicate to his audience and is disturbed when he fails to do so: 'The feeling I get when I'm playing to an audience is "Am I reaching you?" Am I getting to these people through communication with my music? And I look out and I see a smile. Something tells me then, you've got it. But there are also days I don't get that smile. My message is not getting to you, so I've got to go back and figure how to get my message to you through my music – and that's what keeps me going with my music.'

The late Frank Foster, composer and bandleader of the Count Basie Orchestra, discussed his technique for ensuring that an almost mystical feeling emanates from the stage: 'Whenever I perform, especially standing in front of the Count Basie Orchestra, I mentally work a spell on the audience. In other words, I concentrate on the idea of hypnotising the audience, so they get the utmost enjoyment from the music. It's not about picking out a lady in the audience and hypnotising her for romantic reasons or for erotic reasons. It's about hypnotising the whole audience so they get a heightened appreciation of the music and go away feeling inspired and happy and have forgotten their troubles for these couple of hours, not actually understanding why they enjoyed the performance.

'While I'm performing, I will look directly at someone who is about [at] the midpoint of the auditorium; I can't see their face clearly, but I look directly at them while I'm playing, and I am actually hypnotising that person. I'm aware of some kind of movement, something is vibrating when I look directly at someone, and I imagine this to be some kind of power coming from or through me. It's concentrated on that one point where that individual is, then it vibrates; it spreads from that one point, and it's somewhat the same as a pebble being dropped in a lake. It expands outwards. It expands through the auditorium and spreads to everyone there.

'I think that no matter what type of music, it represents what's happening with the masses. I think the music has done that all through history. Every note of my music is crying out for freedom, is glorifying freedom of the spirit, especially in the area of making life happy or positive for others. That's what music is about. It's not about enslaving anybody; it's all about striving for the most positive conditions. Even the music that is angry sounding, that's anger against oppression and inhumane treatment from one person to another.'

The intensified feeling Frank articulated can also enable people in the audience to connect to one another. Keith Richards said: 'I think maybe the audience gets the same feeling that the people who are playing get. They feel connected to each other, and they can lose and forget themselves and realise how much they are connected to other people. All music does is enhance and illustrate the fact that we are all connected; we can't do without each other.'

The Musical Message

Many of the musicians are keenly aware of the opportunity to speak through their music about various political and social issues. They realise that people will listen because of who they are. I noticed that this position is held with respect and not regarded lightly. Several artists described how they have handled this role with their music. According to Mike Rutherford, message songs are meaningless unless they come directly from the heart. If written just for the sake of consciously making a statement, songs fail. He observed: 'For a while, I didn't like songs with messages; I didn't feel it was my place to tell people what I thought they ought to do. It wasn't my place to preach, and I didn't like it when people did that. I think it can very often be power misplaced and misused, but I'm changing a little bit.

'For a Genesis album, I wrote a protest lyric called "Land of Confusion", which shows how I've changed. As I get older, maybe I'm feeling more in a position to comment than I did before. I fight to not analyse it; everything I do is pure gut feeling. I let something inside tell me where I'm going. It's in your stomach, you know, it's just that feeling inside you. I found myself changing the way I write lyrics and being slightly more grown up, whether I felt older or wiser, I don't know.

'This particular song, "Land of Confusion", was a terribly simple message, which was really, we have a wonderful way of living and what a complete fucking mess we're making of it. It was a very direct lyric, but it was still done subtly. It's more a social comment, but I'm becoming more positive in my writing than I used to be. I think it's all to do with, we grow up, we change, and I like that movement. This creativity thing is affected one hundred per cent by that.

'I know a lot of people feel they owe it to themselves and to the world that if they're in a position to reach a lot of people, they ought to use it, but I'm very cautious of that. I haven't felt convinced of their genuineness a hundred per cent. The way I work, I do it for myself, it's purely for my satisfaction. And I'm obviously changing as a person because I'm looking at the world more than I used to and making more comments, but it's only because I want to do it. It feels right inside, not that I *ought* to. I can't ever feel I ought to do something and then channel my work in that way.'

Anthony Kiedis, like Mike, said he never calculates a message song, yet an overwhelming concern about certain issues carries over into his music: 'I don't really go into writing songs with the idea that I've got this purpose to educate or anything like that. But sometimes I'm overwhelmed with feelings strong enough on a political, social or environmental level, where I'll write something that ends up being purposeful.

'There was a time when I felt a great deal of anger towards the police and Ronald Reagan, just towards the whole structure of the American government spending too much money on war and so little money on education, paying so little attention to the minorities and the underprivileged, that I wrote a song called "Green Heaven". It was basically about the difference between life above land and life below the ocean, and how there's an incredibly spiritual and intellectual society of sea mammals, mainly dolphins and whales, that have such a harmonious way of life. Even though they have the capacity for anything, basically far superior to the knowledge of man, and their communication is much more advanced, they seem to live in a very beautiful, peaceful way. Then there's man who's above the land, just making a mess of the planet, making a mess of people, very inconsiderate, very selfish and greedy. So I wrote that song and that ended up as being fairly purposeful in terms of letting people know they didn't have to buy into the Reagan philosophy.'

Roger Waters' political and social concerns are often reflected in such works as "The Wall", which struck a chord in millions of people: 'I think I have an ability to see things in a way that other people feel but can't articulate or can't see. But if I see it for them, they recognise it. I do a sort of paring away of a lot of bullshit in the writing I've been doing recently. It's in a lot of the political situations that have to do with the way the globe is being run that seem self-evident to me, and that's what I write about, because they don't seem to be evident to the powers that be, that they're negative and they don't help people. Central to all of it, I feel a human being is more important than the rocks and the trees and the animals.'

Personal messages derived from the ups and downs of an artist's life can also have an impact when they are reflected in songs. John Mayall was driven to write about what he learned from his own experiences with alcohol: 'We are spokesmen through music. We do have a voice that people listen to, and you can get messages across. People do listen to words of songs. On the album *The Chicago Line*, I wrote a song about stopping drinking ["Give Me One More Day"], which is basically telling people, "Don't destroy your lives. It is hip not to drink." I think there are quite a few musicians who are also taking that stance, and it's great. People who admire you will listen to that, and you are an influence. If you can just reach a couple of people in the audience that one night, then you've accomplished something.'

Music as Healer-Teacher

Something is triggered in each of us when we listen to certain songs, a feeling so intangible that it might only whisper, yet be recognised. Appreciation can be a creative act in itself when music brings meaning to the sometimes deadening daily routine. For listeners who truly tap in, it adds depth to their lives and helps them see things and feel emotions more completely. Roger Waters explained how he thinks music does this: 'As an audience, we look at the painting or hear the music and recognise a truth of some kind that affects us deeply. It explains our universe to us in some way that is reassuring. It is that which makes me feel there may well be something to be in tune with.'

Michael McDonald seemed almost awestruck at music's ability to reach more people than any other medium: 'It's amazing how astute music is about the feelings of regular people. The media and politics are never in touch with how the people feel and think. With music, people who are totally illiterate can have a talent for musical expression that can be much more profound and much more in touch with what most people want to say or want to know. Often it comes from the most unusual corners of the music industry or from the street level. The most unlikely people have the most interesting things to say.'

Rosanne Cash has found that music can affect listeners by helping them see something hidden within: 'The essence of art, if it works, is it should reveal people to themselves. It shouldn't just tap into a vein that's already there and reflect back at them what they are. It should reveal something that's hidden to themselves. When that's working, it has power – power to heal and change.'

Richard Thompson agreed with Rosanne that music can help listeners look at painful issues, an important step towards healing: 'There are people who use music in a spiritual way in our world; it's absolutely their way of elevating. It does something to the human heart. This is the extraordinary thing about music, that whatever you're experiencing, it communicates to other people. It's not just this thing – "Oh, this is me having this great time musically" – that is communicated to the audience. It's a collective something or other. The way people respond to music when those exhilarating moments happen – it's a thing you remember all your life.

'When you inflict your creativity on other people, say an audience, you're very aware of what you can do to an audience, and there's a responsibility that goes with that. To some extent I find myself having to be moral. I express a morality in my music; there's a certain amount of propagandising in almost any kind of music, and that's okay. There's understanding that you don't want to feed people darkness or negativity. I write what's considered heavy-going kind of songs, but I don't see it as negative. I see it almost as a social necessity. Society is complex and strange and dark, and things happen. Being onstage you almost have to hold something up to the audience and say, "I know you don't want to look at this, but this is something we're all going to look at now, and after we've looked at it, we'll all feel better, won't we." It kind of works, it works for me and it works for the audience. Something's happened through singing it, through stating it, through letting it out in the room, and then sort of closing it up again. Mass catharsis!

'Not always the most popular music satisfies the collective unconscious of the most people. Popular music is basically crass and appeals at a crass level. It says something for people. There's a futuristic feeling with writing, where you're kind of dealing with what's about to happen. I think a lot of the less [commercially] successful writers are really tapping into the collective unconscious, but people won't realise it for another 10 years or so. The audience is slightly behind. I don't think someone like Madonna taps into the collective unconscious; I think she calculates, extremely cleverly, and she figures out her symbology and the right moves.'

Richard Thompson differentiated between musicians who tap into the collective unconscious and those who are simply aware of the cultural canon, or current trends, and jump on the bandwagon. The songs that result from the first group are ahead of their 'time' and have a life beyond that of the cultural canon. These are the songs that can trigger within us some basic truth that was previously hidden. This kind of art touches the world soul.

enny Boyd in 1963.
(© Eric Swayne)

Above: Jenny Boyd and Mick Fleetwood at Kiln House, 1970.

Below: The Maharishi's ashram at Rishikesh, north-western India, 1968.

Above: Jenny Boyd and George Harrison in his garden, 1991 . . .   *(© Pattie Boyd)*

Below: . . . and with Phil Collins in LA in the same year.

Roger Waters at home, 1987.

(© Pattie Boyd)

Ringo in his garden in 2003.
(© *Pattie Boyd*)

Above: Jenny Boyd and Mick Fleetwood on holiday in Corfu, 1970.

Below left: Robert Burke Warren.   *(© Franco Vog*

Below right: Mick Fleetwood performing at Day on the Green, Oakland Coliseun Stadium, California, 1977.
                                                      (© Sharon Weis)

Above: Eric Clapton at home in Surrey, 1985.

(© Pattie Boyd)

Below: Jenny Boyd and Mick Fleetwood, Malibu, 1977.

Above: Ravi Shankar. *(© Alan Kazlowsk)*

Below: Ronnie Wood at the premiere of Martin Scorsese's Rolling Stones documentary, *Shine a Light*, 2008. *(© Pattie Boyd)*

How Music Reflects Ourselves

As generations change, so does the music. Psychologist Dean Keith Simonton observed: 'Perhaps it is the spirit of the time – the zeitgeist – that determines how genius shall manifest itself.' Just as Michael McDonald mentioned, much of the music that is really in touch comes from the streets; hip-hop, for example, speaks for many young urban listeners like no other form of music. Several artists discussed the role of rap and hip-hop in our culture.

Vocalist Teddy Pendergrass agreed that rap is the genre most indicative of what young people feel and think today. 'Especially rap, but all kinds of music reflect what's going on, because it's what people write about. People write about what they experience, what they see. It reflects today's society. Rap music is one of those serious art forms. I must say I'm very glad that it's uniquely a black art form that also reflects what these kids are thinking. It's an expression, and I'm glad the expression exists, which gives me an opportunity to see what's going through these kids' minds.'

Ice-T discussed his role as one of rap's major progenitors: 'My drive to create is really to help my friends. I'm not driven like some artists who say they have to make this stuff; I'm really driven by the results. Creating music, or what I do, to me is not very hard. Rap is nothing hard for me to do because it's my life – it's easy. I didn't realise this is what people wanted to hear until one of my friends told me. I used to try to make stuff that I thought people would want to hear, and they'd say, "No, man, tell them that shit about the neighbourhood." I would think, nobody would want to hear that, that's depressing. And they would say, "People want to hear that; everybody don't live like you, they don't see what you see, you've got to wake people up," and I said, "Cool". So I did a record called "Six in the Morning", and everybody freaked. What I do is very easy for me to do, because all I do is absorb shit during the year and I just speak on it.'

To Sinéad O'Connor, hip-hop unifies people like no other contemporary musical genre. 'Hip-hop is the most powerful form of music and communication. It's the most honest; it reflects people's lives, and it encourages people to get together. It's the only form of music that has brought whole races together; it's brought young people together to have something in common. It's very spiritual. Any form of music that has come out of Africa – soul music, people like James Brown, hip-hop – are the biggest communicators. It's got so many messages within its rhythms, within the drumbeats, as well as its words. People don't realise how powerful hip-hop is musically.'

While Sinéad pointed to the spiritual nature of black music, Robert Burke Warren explained that because it taps into the collective unconscious, music in all its forms can bring out the spiritual within us: 'The creative force comes from the collective unconscious, which is the part of everyone that they're not acquainted with on a personal basis. Everyone has a side of their character that will always remain a mystery. That side is more in tune with the collective; it's sort of like a secret club that everyone belongs to, and the initiation into the secret club is the creative act. Everyone yearns for the experience of touching the common ground that they have with everyone else, and the creative act is the only way they can tap into that. When you hear certain music, it moves you, but it doesn't have anything to do with the physical structure of the music. It's *where* it touches you; it unites you with your inner self and thus with everyone else. When people become more in tune with their spiritual selves, music will play a great part in that – you can't have one without the other. I don't think there is any language that can get to the core of things the way music can.'

Bonnie Raitt agrees that the spiritual element to music can elevate humanity: 'I see a swing back to spirituality in music, because I think that there's a great sadness and emptiness today in people's lives. The despair and hopelessness has to be countered by hope and a throwing away of old models. The human spirit has always found a way to pull itself back together. We have to change our own lives first, internally and spiritually.'

Musicians as Role Models

Recognising their responsibility to their listeners, numerous musicians discussed the ultimate meaning behind what they do as artists. Jazz drummer Tony Williams elaborated on his own role as an African-American musician. 'I don't have to write a song about war or racism; that's not what music is to me. Music is above all that. Just me being here, being a jazz musician, is [in itself] a political statement. Because jazz comes out of the experience of being black in America – and that is a political statement.'

As one of the very few female drummers in the jazz world, Terri Lyne Carrington sees her role as that of encouraging others that they, too, can overcome hurdles: 'In the last few years I've come to feel like I encourage people – women and younger people – with my playing. And that's really what it's about for me. People come up to me, and I can see it in their eyes; they really feel encouraged, like it's something they always wanted to do but didn't. Or they see something in me that encourages them. I started seeing what a deep effect you can have on people, when they see you and admire you, that they can do something.'

Keyboardist Greg Phillinganes, who's played with numerous artists including Michael Jackson, pointed to the duty that musicians have because of their music's power: 'There's a responsibility because people are greatly affected by what you do. I know people don't want to believe in hidden powers or hidden messages behind music, but I believe that. I think it greatly affects people, and it's a responsibility. How can you account for the appeal that Michael [Jackson] had with the kids? I think it's positive; babies from six months to 16 love his stuff. He's got a serious thing with the babies. I think it's very powerful.'

Keith Strickland holds himself accountable for his part as a role model to youth: 'Particularly in rock music, there are young people listening, and I'm aware they sometimes will be listening to us more than, say, their parents. Fans look up to you, and in that sense, it's a big influence we have with what we're saying in our songs. I'm very concerned; it's a big responsibility there.'

Kirsty MacColl told me that she strongly believed songs should address political and social issues in their own unique way: 'Some people say art and politics shouldn't mix. But politics is everything. It's part of life. The only way you can change things is by changing governments or whatever. I think it's up to people who are creative to make a stand about those things they believe strongly in. But it's very boring if you hit people over the head with a message all the time. You can be subtle about it so people think they thought of it in the first place.'

As a songwriter, Sinéad O'Connor sees it as her role to give expression to difficult emotions, thereby enabling people whose feelings are buried the opportunity to get in touch with them: 'I have a specific function to perform, which is that I'm probably the only person around who communicates emotionally, who communicates very, very stark or turbulent emotions. My function is to get people to express themselves and get all the shit out. I express [emotions about] things that society doesn't want to hear about – like miscarriages, abortions, rape or child abuse. People never talk, for example, about whether they were abused when they were children. They're taught to squash it down, and as we're beginning to be aware, any emotion like that that's squashed down can make you sick. If somebody can come along into the world and encourage people to express very intense emotions about extremely deep issues that people have been taught never to talk about, it will help to heal people. So that's what I'm doing; I'm also healing myself because I've been through all of those things myself.'

The Artist as Hero

By looking within, discovering their own truths and voicing them, artists allow us to recognise some of the same truths within ourselves. Many have become spokespersons and are influential in pointing out and addressing social issues. It is part of their nature as an artist to witness and reflect. Psychologist Erich Neumann wrote of this role: 'Creative man is often deeply bound up with his group and its culture, more deeply than the common man who lives in the security of the cultural shell.'

There are millions of people who willingly put musicians on pedestals, who look up to them as heroes and follow their every word. But I often found in these artists a great reluctance to see themselves in this way. In their minds, they're only doing what they're supposed to do. Again, these musicians have become manifestations of the hero archetype from the collective unconscious.

Mythology scholar Joseph Campbell described the hero as: 'Someone who has given his or her life to something bigger than oneself ... The hero is someone who is sensitive to the needs of his time.' Campbell explained how the hero, after vanquishing all obstacles, undergoes a transformation of consciousness. The artist as hero travels a path into the unknown, and the obstacles he or she encounters are many. Unique to most of the musician-heroes included here are the disruptive, destructive trappings of the rock 'n' roll life-style. By overcoming these modern-day dragons the artist finds the jewel within: his or her own true self-expression.

David Crosby described the internal and external demons that lie in wait for many musicians and distract them from their purpose, that of creating music: 'The music is the central issue, and there are a number of peripheral issues that will pull you away from the music. One of them is, "Gee, I must be intelligent. Look how many people are listening to me." Or, "Gosh, I'm powerful. I can influence things this way or that way." Or, "Gee, I'm great. Look at all those people giving me all that adulation." Or, "I must be the sexiest thing on earth; look at all those girls wanting me." All of these are mistakes. They are all ways to mis-perceive ourselves.

'I have found the way to keep sane and focused on the central issue – which is creating the music – is not to look at myself in any of these ways. I do not think about whether I am powerful. I do not think whether I'm influencing people. I do not consider myself a hero or larger than life. Those are all mistakes. They are all ones that make you think you are bigger than life, and you're not.

'What you are, is incredibly lucky. You're a human being, regular and normal; you put your pants on one leg at a time, same as everyone else. You've been given a gift, and if you understand you've been given a gift, you work hard at it. You don't abuse it. I did abuse it, but I treasure it now and I work at it. I don't find it healthy to look at myself as powerful. I find it much healthier to look at myself as gifted and very lucky and grateful for it.'

Keith Richards acknowledged that musicians become heroes to their audiences, but he accentuated that the 'hero' is only human with his or her own foibles: 'People have the need to set people above themselves. The stage is the illustration of that – the demigods. The god thing is an illustration of that very need of a greater power. In lieu of finding out what that greater power is, people set up their own earthly version of it in order to express it. I stand on the stage and I'm thinking, what are you looking at me for, a damn old junkie hacking away at the guitar, what is this? This must be a primal need.'

Don Henley stressed that the hero's role can be problematic, especially if it entails one's lionisation: 'Because of my celebrity, I can accomplish a great many beneficial things that I might not otherwise be able to accomplish. I rather like to think that I can be a positive influence. My talent and my fame give me entrée into certain arenas. I can be influential to a degree in politics, and in various other causes, such as the environmental movement. I can raise money for these causes. I can influence my friends and colleagues to participate in charitable works. That part of celebrity is good, but it can also be very dangerous. It's a very fine line.

'Some people are very impressionable; they can be too much like sheep. Rather than think for themselves, people seem to prefer to follow heroes and icons. They worship demigods. We have become a nation of spectators, and I regret that. While I'm acutely aware of the need for role models in people's lives, I also believe that too much hero worship can be an unhealthy thing. I would hope that fans, followers and constituents of all stripes would see the importance of thinking for themselves and not blindly follow like sheep anyone who happens to wind up in a position of leadership.'

George Harrison agreed that musicians, with insights drawn from their own experiences, can help those who listen to their music. But he also cautioned, 'You have to be very careful, I suppose. In one way, we all have a duty to help each other, to help ourselves and then help each other in whatever way, whether it's just to get through the day. I think it's important to share experiences. For instance, if Dylan hadn't said some of the things he did, nobody else was going to say them. Can you imagine what a world it would be if we didn't have a Bob Dylan? It would be awful. There's that side of it. But then there's the other side, where you can start mistaking your own importance. I think I've been in both of those [positions] at various times. You suddenly think you're more groovy than you are and then usually something happens to slap you down a bit, so it all has to be tempered with discretion.'

Being courageous, as all heroes are, daring to look within regardless of what may be found, and expressing one's inner self to the outside world are all parts of the creative act. I got the feeling from Joni Mitchell, for example, that she has been on a lifelong quest for self-discovery and fulfilment. Through her music, the expression of her own exploration has enabled her to give others guidance and a chance to identify with what she has found: 'On a spiritual or a human level, I have felt that it was perhaps my role on occasion to pass on anything I learned that was helpful to me on the route to fulfilment or happy life. [That includes] anything that I discovered about myself, even if I had to reveal something unattractive about myself, like I'm selfish and I'm sad, which are unpopular things to say.

'By giving the listener an opportunity then to either identify, in which case if he sees that in himself he'll be richer for it, or if he doesn't have the courage to do that or the ability, then he can always say, "That's what she is." So I feel that the best of me and the most illuminating things I discover should go into the work. I feel a social responsibility to that; I think I know my role. I'm a witness. I'm to document my experiences in one way or another.'

Graham Nash is also aware of the greater meaning behind

his role as a musician: 'The power is for shaking people and waking them up. I use my music to reflect the times that I'm going through, to reflect some of the things that happen to me, to express outrage at some of the stuff that is unforgivable, to express the joy that I feel. That's a great power to me. It makes people less lonely; it brings people together; it can change the world.'

The Heroic Element Within Us All

Artists reflect the collective unconscious and thus give voice to the people. They are not self-professed heroes, but by the very nature of being artists, they are channels from the collective unconscious, and in their quest to create, heroes. David Crosby eloquently described what I feel is the hero living in each of us: 'The highest purpose we can aspire to is to call forth in people the best that human beings are capable of, the most exalted forms of the hero: the person who is willing to sacrifice to achieve; the person who has honesty and kindness, a sense of community; who has civilised himself and evolved above the level of combating animals. It can be called forth in human beings, and in that state can transcend all problems that we are faced with. The only way to improve it is to upgrade the consciousness; you can't legislate it.

'Every time that one of us does manage to slip into the mass media a nugget of truth that does in some fashion raise consciousness, we have performed a service, and it's to that I aspire. If I can do anything, I would love to bring joy to people's lives, bring people closer together, lessen the distance between people, let them see the sameness in each other, and let them share a moment. When you write about issues and events, like a Dylan, you can affect things in a wonderful way. John Lennon's "Imagine" is going to be running around this world for a very long time. There are things we can do that will affect our humanity, sometimes you are given the chance to make a difference, and that is something to be even more grateful for than anything else.'

By taking that journey within, finding out who we are, and coming to terms with the part we each can play in our world, we can all aspire to be the kind of hero David described. Although we may not have the musician's power and access to mass communication to affect society on a vast scale, each of us can make a difference in our own unique way. In addition to the empowerment that accompanies such self-discovery, there are other surprises that await those who tap into their creative selves.

Chapter 5

THE PEAK EXPERIENCE

'THE WHOLE POINT OF WRITING IS TO TRY
AND GET CLOSER TO YOUR CORE.'
SINÉAD O'CONNOR

There are times in life when one experiences moments of euphoria, moments when everything comes together, when all the fragmented parts of our being are fused into one. Many describe this experience as magical. It is a heightened state of awareness, and over the years has been given many names: inspiration, intuition, and more recently 'peak experience'. Psychologist Abraham Maslow, who first coined the term peak experience and has written extensively on it, described it as: 'A loss of self or of ego or sometimes as a transcendence of self. There is a fusion with the reality of being observed, a oneness where there was a twoness, an integration of some sort of the self with the non-self. There is universally reported a seeing of formerly hidden truth, a revelation in the strict sense, a stripping away of veils, and finally almost always the whole experience is experienced as bliss, ecstasy, rapture, exaltation.'

167

I can identify with Maslow's description of the peak experience, through having had my own spiritual awakening at the age of 18. During that flash of intuition, I felt calm and centred but at the same time tremendously excited and filled with energy. With a tingling sensation rippling through my body, everything appeared crystal clear. My realisation of life's being like a circle broke through in opposition to my childhood beliefs. I felt like a channel to a deeper part of myself, as if I were watching myself from above. I also experienced a feeling of unity with the universe, or existence itself. My search for enlightenment began. I was now on a path from which I would often swerve but never leave.

After this experience I longed for that same intensity again. I looked for and found it to a much lesser degree in a couple of expressions. Sometimes I could sense that feeling of oneness, as if there were no physical boundaries of separation, while talking to a very few people about anything to do with our spiritual realisations. My sister Pattie and I, for example, were definitely on the same wavelength. During the sixties, searching for awareness and self-knowledge, we would often get into that higher consciousness, where we wouldn't have to finish our sentences – we just knew what the other was thinking. The communication was on a different level. It felt euphoric. Other times, I've experienced this feeling while writing, either poetry or just finding words to express a deeper part of myself with which I was trying to get in touch. During these times words seemed to spring from nowhere and brought with them vibrance and clarity.

I found tremendous joy in listening to the musicians

describe their creative peaks or moments of euphoria while performing, composing or writing. It felt like our link: they articulated the peak experience, which had meant so much to me and had become the turning point in my life, and which for them occurs continually throughout their artistic lives. I hadn't realised before to what extent this was a part of their creative process. Throughout the years I had spent with musicians, no one had ever mentioned this magical phenomenon.

The only inkling I'd had was while observing Eric Clapton. I had this feeling that he'd touched the hem of God's garment while playing, that through his music he had a direct connection to something very spiritual. After only a few interviews, though, I realised that all musicians experience this creative peak in one way or another. Although they admitted it was very difficult to describe, most were happy to talk about it, the majority saying they'd never discussed it before. Many explained that it was not something they could make happen; there was no formula. The peak experience occurs of its own accord.

Why is it that artists are more likely to experience the peak, or experience it more often than the average person? According to Maslow, those people who have the clearest and strongest identity are exactly the ones who are most able to transcend the self. Indeed, musicians, because of their continual self-expression, are usually more sure of themselves, of who they really are. Also, as I have mentioned, creative people are courageous in that they are not as afraid of or overwhelmed by the psyche's unknown contents. They do not fear letting go. As Maslow wrote: 'The person who organises his life around the denying and the controlling of emotion, the fear of being overwhelmed by an emotion (which is interpreted as a loss of control) is enough for him to mobilise all his stamping-out and defensive activities against the peak experience.'

Judging from the musicians' descriptions, the peak experience seems to occur when the artist is totally in the 'here and now'. It is a time of complete concentration that overtakes the mundane, everyday way of thinking. Joseph Campbell spoke of the importance of the here and now: 'The experience of eternity right here and now, in all things … is the function of life.' Being in the here and now during a peak experience permits the artist to click into what I envision as an eternal wave that is the core of the universe, as well as the core of his or her self. Everything is in harmony both inside and out. It is the coming together of the conscious and the unconscious and one of the rare moments when the conscious mind is not fighting to keep the unconscious at bay.

By completely concentrating on the music they're playing or writing, musicians are able to open themselves up to a peak experience. It is as if an intense concentration can push the conscious mind away from 'self-consciousness' and the unconscious is allowed to filter through. The result can be songs that seem to come from nowhere, the ability to suddenly play a riff that had been too difficult before, or an onstage 'merging' with band mates. Indeed, musicians described a variety of circumstances in which the peak occurred: while writing, playing music alone, recording in the studio, rehearsing or jamming, and, perhaps most profound, performing before a particularly responsive audience.

Improvisational playing often can allow for the necessary

'letting go' during concentration that results in a peak experience. Jazz flutist Paul Horn remarked: 'When I was younger I didn't know such terms as peak experience, but I used to feel really high [at certain times while playing music]. When I started to improvise, I found I could get up and play music, with thoughts coming, and these thoughts could be translated into musical terms. I got an idea of what I could hear in my mind, and my inner ear would somehow find a connection [through] my arms and fingers to my instrument. That excitement is always with me. Any time you improvise it's exciting because you don't *know*; it's always new. Intellectually, by the time you've even thought about it, you're eight beats later.

'The jazz musician will play the melody, and from then on, new melodies are created over the same basic harmonies, and that's jazz; creating a logical, beautiful melody but it's your own. You could play that song night after night and never get bored because it will come out different each time. There's a creative excitement there, an energy. It's a spiritual thing. We learn about 'now' – the moment. When you improvise, you're totally in the moment. There's no time to think about it; it has to transcend the intellect; you just have to 'be'. So jazz comes as close as you can to the spiritual.

'Having now lived a while and followed the spiritual path, I can see the connection. It forces your mind to really be one-pointed. You have to be focused and, therefore, you're in the now; you're not aware of yourself. It's a transcendental experience in a way. In the true sense of the word "transcendental", there is no mental activity. We're in that place of stillness, which is the "absolute field", but in playing, what I have transcended is my self-consciousness, my mind drifting on to other things. I'm unaware of myself; I'm totally absorbed in the music. And as I get more absorbed in the music, then more can happen in the music. I turn out to be a channel. My mind doesn't say, "Me, I'm playing good tonight", or "I'm not playing good", It's not judgmental; it's a happening that's taking place, and that's enough. It's exciting to be caught up in that.'

The Transcendence of the Peak

Paul Horn's description of the peak experience reminded me of another written by Maslow: 'There is a tremendous concentration of a kind which does not normally occur. There is the truest and most total kind of visual perceiving or listening or feeling. Everything is equally important rather than a hierarchy from very important to quite important ... The peak experience seems to lift us to greater than normal heights so that we can see and perceive in a higher than usual way.' Different musicians articulated this intense feeling in various ways.

Vocalist Patty Smyth became very emotional as she described the peak experience, which she continually seeks while singing: 'One thing I strive for is to really let go. When I have had those experiences, I'm singing by myself. I've had those moments when I do feel the voice coming through me, and I know it's coming from out there. It's a certain tone in the voice that makes me feel that way. It chokes me up. It is very soothing; I enjoy the sound of it. There's something very familiar about it – it's weird. I guess that's when I feel so tuned in. I get self-conscious thinking about it; I don't ever speak about it that much. It's really special and it's not of me.'

Graham Bell explained how the peak experience lifts him above mundane daily life as he becomes one with his music: 'To me [the peak experience while singing] is like a journey. I am completely out of myself. For instance, I'm not thinking about what problems I have in daily living. When I'm playing onstage and I reach that flow, that's all I am – the music. It's very, very concentrated, and when the song ends, it'll take a few seconds to be aware of the audience again. As the music starts, you're travelling with it. I'm totally free of all pain. A lot of the time I'm singing, it's also like crying; I feel tremendously good, life is just so wonderful, it's an incredible feeling.'

Another vocalist, Cece Bullard, described the physical as well as emotional sensations that occur during a peak experience: 'It's like you leave your body. It's like you're dizzy and lightheaded and yet right there. My hands just seem to throb, like a pulse almost. It's the best feeling in the world, bar none. It took me a lot of singing lessons before I finally connected with that feeling. The first time it clicked and I connected, I nearly fell down, nearly fainted. I went white and had to sit down, and I started crying. It was such a release of emotion. It was more than physical; it was as if I'd been trying to put a round peg in a square hole and suddenly it just went, and it just shocked my whole system. It doesn't happen often.'

Keith Richards compared the peak experiences attained while writing to those experienced while playing guitar: 'With a sense of amazement, you can look down at your hands and say, "This isn't me playing." That is one of the things which leads you to believe there is some other energy going on, some other thing you're in touch with, because it's not you. Also when you're writing songs, it's a similar feeling except there's more adrenaline going when you're playing; it's more physical, and usually it's onstage, so there are other factors involved. You can have the same amazed feeling sitting in a room by yourself [as when] actually doing the job onstage. It's the moving hand that is writing.'

The most pronounced aspect of the peak is a sense of unity with the art form. Richard Thompson tried to pinpoint this transcendent feeling: 'It's very hard to talk about because you're not really there when it happens! It happens on most shows I play. You get inside the music to such an extent that you kind of *are* the music, or the music's you. You're thinking about it but you're not thinking about it. It's almost a flashing backwards and forwards of intellect and intuition: One minute you're thinking G flat, seven five, and then it's gone and you're doing something that you're not aware of. You're just sort of flying along, and then you have another conscious moment where you think, "Oh, yes, two bars left."

'The same thing happens with writing. It seems to go backwards and forwards. There are times where you're thinking logically what you're doing: okay, two more lines here, and that's got to rhyme with that. And then suddenly you've got six verses written, and you don't know how it happened. It's odd, and I wouldn't like to be writing a book about it myself! It's too hard to figure out. It's the time when you're not there that things happen. It's when your ego moves out of the way, when you create the space that the music can actually come in and through. It's what we musicians live for, those magical moments.'

Joseph Campbell said of this transcendence: 'You die to your flesh and are born into your spirit.' Mike Rutherford finds he is better able to lose himself while writing, rather than performing, and thus it is during the writing that he experiences the peak: 'It's an incredible high, a rush of energy. It's slightly hallucinogenic. I come back sort of a bit bleary-eyed and vague; I'm not quite sure where I am. I'm somewhere else for a while; it's like I come back to earth. Something breaks the moment and I'm back. You don't realise you're gone till something happens and you're back. It's a moment's magic that from time to time touches me, and I don't control it. Like Tinkerbelle, it just goes past.

'When I'm playing, though, I never get lost. I never lose myself in the same way. While playing, I get a different high: feedback from the audience. It lifts me somewhere but I always know where I am.'

Rosanne Cash has experienced the peak while writing, performing and painting: 'We all carry a divine spark in us. I think there is an access point in me, and if I can find it … Sometimes it's like reaching through fog trying to find it, and sometimes it's just there; it just presents itself. And if I can get to that access place, there's some kind of source that I draw on that works in writing and painting and music. When that's happening, when the gates are open and it's a free flow of information and inspiration, it's being in an altered state. It's very satisfying. Everything else disappears. It's like I'm part of a river and no matter what I did, I couldn't stop the current right then. It seems that sometimes it's easier to access when I'm writing. When I'm performing and I can access it, it's wonderful, and at the end [of the performance] it's like surfacing, like being part of this river and coming up.

It just feels so wonderful. It's impossible for me to contrive it, though. If I can get myself to the access point, then it works, but I can't make it up. I have a few tools that I use to try to get myself there. Sometimes they work, and sometimes they don't. It's elusive.

'I had an experience where I was painting in a warehouse in a friend's art studio one afternoon. Everybody had gone and I was painting. Then I looked around and it was dark and the whole building was empty. I had lost myself for four hours in this experience of painting. I got really frightened coming back to earth – it was a dark warehouse in a bad part of town. So I washed my hands and quickly got out of there. But during the time it was happening, it was pure essence and absolute accessing too. It was wonderful! There were no distractions, there's just nothing else. I don't think at any other time in life is there that kind of purity – purity of being.'

The physical effects of the peak can be overwhelming, Sinéad O'Connor said, as she transcends her surroundings: 'When I'm singing, what I'm aiming for is of not particularly being there, of just the sound being there, just the texture and the rhythm and the sound, and the sound of the words. It doesn't really matter what the words are; it's the sound of them and what they do to you. I believe very much in the internal massage. That's what it feels like and that's what I'm trying to achieve, which is why I sing with my eyes closed. When my eyes are open, I'm too aware of everything that's going on around me. I don't achieve this every time, but what I'm aiming for is to achieve it.

'A lot of times I shake uncontrollably. I can't control the shaking, and it's not because I'm nervous, it's because I'm singing. It's because it's coming out and it's making me shake. It feels like being drunk, it's like an out-of-body experience. There are times when I've done gigs – and it doesn't happen every time you do a show or every time you write something – but they've told me stuff I've done onstage that I'm not aware I've done. It's as if you've left and you've just come back.

'Whether you have a drink or not before you go on, by the time you get off, you feel really drunk. If I drink two bottles of beer before I go onstage just to loosen up, by the time I get offstage I'm completely drunk as if I'd drunk 10 bottles of beer, and I'm shaking and stuff. It's quite a physical experience, whatever it is that fills you up.'

Artists mentioned other physical effects experienced during the peak, including a complete disappearance of any kind of physical pain, even of body awareness itself. Paul Kantner, like Sinéad, prefers performing with his eyes closed to accelerate the onset of the state conducive to the peak: 'It's like if you've sprained your ankle that day or hurt your knee, all pain leaves your body and you focus on what you're doing onstage. You just focus in on it and you go into a zone, almost like voodoo. You just do stuff naturally. I like to play with my eyes closed. I have to force them open to know there's people out there!

'Generally, you just go outside of yourself. It's almost like astral travelling, although you don't get out and look down on yourself [but] it's just about at the bridge of that. You feel that you almost could.'

Phoebe Snow also mentioned how the peak can eliminate all distractions, physical and mental. After our interview, she took me to the New York City cathedral where she performed in a tribute to South Africa's Bishop Tutu. She wanted me to see the setting of what she considers one of her most extraordinary moments: 'The peak is sort of like a rapturous feeling; it's really wonderful. For a long time after my first album was out, I was not very well. I had some medical problems, but I had to slog it out, go on tour, and try to hang in there. The travelling would kill me, but for the hour and a half I was onstage nobody knew I was sick. I might be crawling on my hands and knees backstage, but I'd get out onstage and be transported. I think it comes in varying degrees; there's always a little of it there and sometimes a lot when you've got to almost reel yourself back in.

'Once I was called to come and sing "Amazing Grace" to welcome Bishop Desmond Tutu at the Cathedral of Saint John the Divine, in New York. The occasion was called The Harlem Welcome. There were African dancers, a parade of people playing percussion instruments and wearing wild costumes. There were 5,500 people in the room. I was to perform during the candle-lighting ceremony, where the whole cathedral was lit. The ceiling there is 152 feet high; every bay window has intricate stained glass. I was supposed to get up on a raised platform and sing.

'As I got up, they darkened the cathedral and so all you could see was the entire audience holding candles. It took me about a whole verse to get into it; by the second verse I was gone. I was doing it, but it wasn't me doing it; I was nuclear-powered at that point. It was like reflex action. I was so swept up in this thing that by the end of it I forgot who I was, what I was doing. I got lost. I was very disoriented when I finished, and there was Bishop Tutu standing on this pulpit opposite me. The eye contact was intense. I knew I had gotten transported.'

Maslow wrote of the 'ego-less, self-forgetful, ego-transcending' nature of the peak experience. Drummer Robin Horn described this facet of the peak, which he has experienced during certain performances: 'It becomes an almost selfless experience, where you're simply a vehicle and you're playing. It happened a few times on our Russian tour, and the keyboardist was very in tune with us too. We'd have these discussions right before going onstage: "Right, we're going to go on and not going to get in the way; we're going to be wide open, like a channel, and just respond to the music." From talking about it, I think we were more able to have that experience, because we were consciously aware of trying to experience that. So we had it about three times.

'I think my father is a master at this. He got used to getting out of his own way years ago. He takes it to that other level. When you're playing the kind of music that we were, which was jazz-rock, there's a lot of room for improvisation, and with a lot of the tunes we were free to improvise. With total complete freedom, everything comes out in the wash. It gives off a lot of energy: part of you is aware that this is happening, and the other part of you doesn't want to get in the way. When it did happen, I realised I didn't see anything. My eyes were open, yet I didn't see anything – the drums, the audience, nothing. So I'm wondering where I was, because visually I didn't see anything. I didn't remember my father's solos.

'On that level it happened at least once a night, where the music takes over, and it's like, "Where are you?" You're playing the music and you're thinking of all the technical parts so you're playing your best, but you're also listening intently to everyone around you, so you're playing your cues and you're being supportive. So much is going on in your mind, and yet there are points that it all becomes second nature, especially with the musicians on this last tour. It's a very strange experience. It takes a certain degree of mastery, because if you're thinking about the instrument and nothing else, that's where your mind's going to be. It's something that just happens. The more you're aware of the experience, the longer you live and play, the more you experience it.'

An important component of the peak experience that adds to its transcendent effect is the ability to see and feel one's own personal truth; in other words, how everything really is. The truth is powerful because it is the purest essence there is. It can make one cry or laugh with tremendous joy and a great sense of freedom, an inkling of how things are meant to be. During the peak experience, one also feels closest to one's own inner truth, an element described by Maslow: 'A tendency to move to his real self, to have become more of a real person.' Such an event can trigger an intense release. Stephen Stills explained how this sometimes happens to him while writing a song and described the emotional release following the experience. 'All of a sudden, it's all done. And I try to sing, but I can't, because I'm weeping, because I'm moved. Somehow, I've got it all right and I've said just what I wanted.'

Jazz drummer Peter Erskine described his peak experiences while composing as similar to a momentary departure: 'I'm not aware of it at the time. It's not like I close my eyes and put my head back in bliss. It's only when it's done and I listen back and think, wow, where did that come from?'

What the Peak Means to the Artist

As musicians described the peak experience, I was fascinated to discover the differences in what it meant to them. Most found it to be rare and 'magical', though a few accepted it without question as being almost commonplace in their creative lives. The late singer-songwriter Warren Zevon considered the peak to be just another facet of the creative process: 'Probably writing is more exhilarating, when words fall into place. I guess it's what they call, supposedly inaccurately, a quantum leap: a basketball leaves Magic Johnson's hand – supposedly when he's not looking – and it goes in the ring. Nobody knows exactly how. I remember sometimes trying to think of words and they just fall into place. I don't think it's magical or divine. I think it's more closely related to why a guy's particularly good at throwing a ball through a hoop. It has to do with mechanisms like rhyming and stuff: I've got this word and there's something blank in between it, and they click into place. When they just click into place, when it just fills in, this line to that line, then it's very exhilarating and you can be pretty sure that it's good.'

In contrast to Warren, Christine McVie feels that a peak experience is an almost mystical event: 'It's like magic, like a true elation that you can't really describe. You feel inspired; there's no other word for it. You just feel that you are electrically charged, something you have no real control over.'

In his description of the peak, Peter Erskine ascribed importance to ridding himself of his conscious mind while performing: 'When I've had it, I'd rather not be anywhere else in the world, or doing anything else. It feels like nothing can stop what's happening; it's perfect. It's very joyous and it's very dynamic. You're not dizzy from it; it's a heightened playing, but there's something very down to earth about it. We used to talk about it in Weather Report. [Keyboardist] Joe Zawinul would say his peak experience was that he was in the audience listening, and what that translated to me was, you were listening to the music and enjoying it and you weren't being self-conscious. You weren't auditing yourself. If you remove your ego, then I think you can reach that. If your ego is in a conscious state, then I think that door is closed.'

Guitarist Bernie Larsen tried to find comparable experiences in life with which to explain his peaks: 'It's one thing to experience this stuff, it's another thing to communicate it. I'd have to compare it to making love, very conscious and aware but unconscious and unaware at the same time. You're riding along with it and the momentum of the feeling. It is the *real* me.

'There will be times you wander from consciousness and then you'll be aware of where you're at, and other times it's downright startling to open my eyes. I will be flying; it's just like soaring. Probably it would be compared to the definition of astral projection; it's definitely up. It's entertaining; it must be like running the big touchdown, and your flow hasn't been stopped. It's a total letting go, because I don't think you can do it consciously. You can be sitting there with nothing much happening and you can hear just a drumbeat, the rhythm thing will start happening, and 20 minutes later you have a song sitting in front of you. And you didn't have that much to do with it.

'To me, it's the movement of life that's not physical. It's like a layer of information that comes through you. After a few incidents [like that] happened to me, I realised somebody else is driving and I'm in the backseat.'

Hank Marvin discussed another aspect of the peak: the innate knowledge that a certain creation could not have come about any other way, a sense that this is how it's meant to be. There is no questioning or uncertainty about it: 'We recorded a piece of music called "Cavatina". It was released under the title of "The Theme from *The Deer Hunter*" and we had a big hit from that at the end of the seventies. When we went to record it, we just set up the gear and laid everything down. I went to put my guitar work on and just played it. It was almost perfect; everyone went "Ooh, that's it!" and in fact it was it – virtually a one-take performance. It had such a lovely feel to it that it was just right. I knew it felt good when I played it.

'[During a peak experience, playing] has a magic; it just feels absolutely right, and you think, I couldn't have done it any other way. That's the way it should be. When it feels right, it creates an atmosphere: That's it; you've hit that lovely thing again. It doesn't happen as often as I'd like!'

Reaching the Peak in the Studio

Unlike many musicians, Jeff Lynne hasn't had peak experiences while writing or performing: 'The studio for me is the ultimate place to be. The only time I get near to something coming "through" me is when I'm playing in the studio and get a riff that's really good. It's spotting it that's the hard bit, because there are so many good riffs or so many possibilities. Some are just trash, some you'll get fed up with in half an hour, and some you'll go, "that's the one". And if it comes out, it feels very uplifting and satisfying and it's everything. Then it's like the best bit of your existence. I don't get that feeling anywhere else. It's when you get the right chords and the tune goes just right – it's very rare. There are times when it just hits you and you say, "That's it; I've made a musical statement that I really like."

Other musicians agreed with Jeff that their peak experiences occur most often while they are working intensely in the studio. Perhaps this is due to its timeless, womblike atmosphere, coupled with the artist's tremendous concentration. Lindsey Buckingham used the image of the painter and his canvas to describe his own sense of unity with the music he creates: 'There's no real defining what [a peak experience] is. It becomes magical; it's very uplifting. It can happen while playing an instrument. The process of my writing is so tied in with working on a 24-track or two 24-track machines and overdubbing. It becomes a painter and his canvas. You go in with certain preconceptions in mind, but when you have that intimate one-to-one with the canvas, you may impose a certain thing on it, but at some point it will start taking on a life of its own and speaking to you about what's needed. That kind of rapport on a one-to-one can provide very thrilling moments, euphoric moments.

'When you lock into a track you're playing, it's sort of a unidimensional thing. You may lock into a certain emotional tone, a sort of resonance of some kind. Two tangents meeting is usually one of the points that produces creativity; two things that don't necessarily relate [begin] co-relating and forming something else. That happens more tangibly in the studio, where you suddenly see that if you put this with that, you can visualise, almost see them as shapes, and that kind of thing can go on in multiples. It happens less on lyrics than it does with the form, the shape and the colour – the emotional tone of the music. The initial inspiration feels like it's coming through me. By the time I get it down, that is sometimes gone, but as things evolve, it happens [again]. It has to happen more than once in the process.'

Peter Gabriel explained how he uses certain techniques in the studio to prevent his concentration being broken and ensure the spontaneity required for a peak experience: 'I think you plug into this electricity – it's like a river in a way. No question when the magic's there, everyone in the room feels it. You're a bit like a radio aerial and you quiver when you're on to something. One of the things we try and get a lot more conscious about now is to make sure we record those moments in whatever form possible at *that* moment. You don't take an hour trying to get sounds right, trying to get all the bits and pieces operational and then find you've lost it. Immediately you put the red light on and catch whatever is around. And then even if it's only on two tracks of the 24, you can always pull them back up again, even if it's not usable in its own form. It will then speak in a language of magic to the musicians.'

Robert Burke Warren said his most exhilarating peak experience occurred in the studio. 'A while back I was in the studio playing guitar and singing a song I'd just written. It was a song that had come really fast; it had taken five minutes to write. The engineer said later that during the recording the atmosphere became charged with electricity. At the time I could just feel it. It was the most profound peak I'd ever had. There was nothing I had done to prepare for it in any way. I think maybe I subconsciously felt the song was worthy. So many times, you go for the nail and you don't hit it, and this time I felt I had. It was a one-take recording.

'It was wonderful, just incredible. There's no passage of time, there's no consciousness of anything except what you're singing about. It must have been the combination of having written the song, then singing it and playing it. It was a real breakthrough for me, because before that point I'd reached a peak only through playing music with other people. It was the first time I'd really tried to pursue singing as a means of getting there.'

Frequency of the Peak

As musicians passionately described their peak experiences, the unpredictability of the peak's occurrence became obvious. Many expressed the desire to identify the exact circumstances conducive to a peak experience. Drummer Ian Wallace, for example, described feeling that only when certain environmental factors are in sync can he relax and let go, thus allowing himself the possibility of the peak: 'Once I've managed to transcend such things as where I am, who I'm playing with, how I'm playing, what the temperature of the room is, how the audience is, who the rest of the band are, that's when the real playing happens. It's very seldom that it happens.

'Once you can stop thinking about [everything], then it's a trance kind of thing. You don't think about anything; that's the whole point: you don't think. Thinking is the thing that comes in the way of so much – that's the Zen thing. It's the thought that is the blockage. Once you stop thinking, instead of it being thought, it becomes existence. I suppose it's what you try and achieve in meditation. It's a feeling of going on to another state of existence. It's like white-water canoeing or something where you're really in control but you're being borne along at a tremendous rate by something that you only just have control of. It's almost like it's controlling you. It's that speed and yet at the same time it's complete tranquillity.

'It doesn't happen very often, though. You can get very close at times. Sound has a lot to do with it. It has to sound a certain way before you can feel comfortable enough to let it happen. I've played some gigs where the sound was so disruptive that there was no way that could happen, just by being so hung up on the sound.'

Another drummer, Steve Jordan, described how the re-emergence of the conscious mind will put an end to the peak experience: 'You zone out; a lot of the time you can actually watch yourself do things, almost like an out-of-body experience. Sometimes you're there but you don't know how you did that. It's all just this thing that happened, and then you go back and you listen to it and you go, "Holy cow, wow!" The classic is when you're doing something and you think, wow, this is incredible, and you look at yourself and try to figure out what the heck you're doing and then you blow it completely.'

Jazz bandleader Frank Foster said that he tried to pinpoint the conditions during performance that lend themselves to a peak experience: '[The peak experience] is really a great feeling. It has to be brought about by certain congruent conditions. For instance, you have to be feeling good and inspired yourself. And then you have to have a microphone in front of you, and a monitor that's working, and an audience that's very receptive, and a group behind you that seems to be particularly on, too.

'I've had moments like that, say, with the Elvin Jones Quartet or Quintet, when the inspiration just seems divine, and we could do no wrong. It's all about performance of the group and my own individual performance. I've had moments like that with the Count Basie Orchestra, and I've had moments like that with my own band at certain times in the seventies. And one thing I've noticed is that it was always when the moon was either waxing towards full or full.'

Hank Marvin, who has been performing for more than 50 years, is still baffled by the unpredictability of the peak experience: 'Some nights the feeling between the different musicians onstage is just incredible. We've got an amazing drummer, Brian Bennett, who's been with the band since 1961. He's very creative and just loves music in all its facets. Also, you can get a fantastic audience that creates a wonderful environment, but that doesn't necessarily mean you're going to play as well as you did the night before or the next night. But when all those factors come together, then it is magic. You feel absolutely elated, a tremendous feeling of joy, because it's all working so well. You can almost get high on it, a very good feeling, you go to the stage and you know you're not going to do anything wrong that night, everything is up, the band is so tight, it's just wonderful – and we get paid for it as well!

'There's no way of knowing beforehand. We've had nights

where we've felt terrific – a good sleep, a nice lunch, feeling very fit, very positively – and it's certainly not one of your better shows. And another night you've had two hours' sleep, a lot of travelling, you feel a bit under the weather, [but] you go onstage and it's wonderful. Now, why?'

Although for some artists, the peak experience occurs quite frequently, Branford Marsalis told me that he'd had such experiences while playing just three times in his life: 'High, you feel high. It's easy to do it physically, but it's hard to do it mentally. I feel that musicians who say it happens every time they play are full of shit. The sublime cannot be routine. Three times, and you never forget them. It's [with] a combination of musicians, it's never just me.'

Like Branford, guitarist Rick Vito said he'd experienced peaks only when playing with other musicians: 'It is probably one of the few and far between glimpses of paradise that anybody achieves here. When you get that thing going, the energy starts. You don't have to think, where are my fingers going? You've been playing so long that they go not only ... to that place but something special comes out. You don't create at all; you're an instrument of it, through here somewhere and out there. That is a very peak kind of experience – that's what makes it all worth it.

'I think it comes from playing with others. I haven't had it happen just by myself. The ultimate would be playing with a great band, with an audience that is tuned in with what you're doing. Just the whole place is joined in with the process; it all happens together. I think that's why people go out and hear live music a lot and have favourite artists. It's an exciting thing when that spontaneous thing happens. You never know when it's going to happen. You can't make it happen the same place two nights in a row. It may happen when you least expect it. I wish I could have on tape every single time that it happens, so I could relive [those moments], but you have to let them happen and then let them go, for the most part, into the ether, wherever. That's what keeps bringing you back for more of the same. And that's why musicians are special. It's the special high they get to have. I'm interested in other forms of creative expression: I've acted, I've painted and I've written, and I get satisfaction from all that stuff. But the greatest thing is playing music and letting that happen. If I had to think of never experiencing that feeling again, it's something I'd miss deeply.'

John Mayall explained that the improvisational nature of blues bands is conducive to a spontaneity in performance that cannot be found when playing alone: 'It's a very exhilarating thing when you play before a live audience or just between other musicians and yourself. The interplay you experience is something you can't really explain; it's just something that takes place. That's why I never play at home; I've never practised or picked up an instrument when I'm not playing on the road. So when I get together with this band – when we go out and do shows – [the peak] comes instantly. You're a part of something that you create as a band and individually. I like to savour the joy when we get together – that spark that happens. It's always a surprise. The blues is not a music you set down or play the same way any one time, it's always different – a creative process, an improvisation – something that takes place almost beyond your own control.'

Creative Communion

As Branford, Rick and John described, many artists have found that peak experiences come much more readily when they are performing with particular musicians. As they're playing, they not only transcend themselves but seem to merge with the other musicians. With this experience comes a feeling of unity. All the musicians on the stage or in the recording studio become one with each other and the music. Keith Richards said: 'When you're playing with the right bunch of guys, there's a joy and a very calm feeling, even though you might be doing the most frenetic stuff. At the same time there's this incredible thread to everybody else who is in there with you. If you're playing with five guys, you're thinking with five minds also, and it's all just going click-click, and you're not really aware that you're thinking.

'It's only sitting around now and later talking about it and trying to analyse it when I realise it. These things are incredibly difficult to explain. These questions are really great because it makes you think: the reason you have music is because if you could put it in words and write about it and explain it, then you wouldn't need music. That's the function of music. If you're a musician you can never really stop playing, even if you don't do any gigs, or you retire, you still in a way are inside yourself playing.

'[The peak experience occurs only with] certain people; that's an absolute requirement. There's no way I'm going to get a feeling like that if I'm not particularly happy. It's like working with these guys [the X-Pensive Winos] and working with the Stones. It doesn't matter what you get out of it in any material way; it's just that need to push it further, that incredible chemistry. You put them together and you get this other thing that's probably a small microcosm of what an audience is; that mass thing. What you can do on your own is okay, but what you can do with five other people – it goes up to the power of five, there's so much going on. You get to the point where you don't even have to look at somebody to know what they're going to do. The idea is we all transcend together.

'Obviously there's the odd technical hitch, but even so, the other lot can carry a guy through a problem. Just last night I screwed a song up. You wouldn't have known it because the band picked up on it straight away. They knew exactly how I was going to fix it, though I'd never been in that problem before with that particular song. They didn't have to think about it, they knew exactly what I was going to do.'

Steve Gadd described the unity from playing with a certain group of musicians, which enabled his performance to become transcendent: 'When I first moved to New York, Chick Corea went from an acoustic band to putting an electric band together. It was Stanley Clarke, Chick Corea, Bill Connors playing guitar, Mingo Lewis, who used to play with Santana, playing percussion, and myself. That band was burning. It wasn't like it was coming from me. It was coming from somewhere else, just coming through me. It was effortless.'

Without a doubt, there was a chemistry between George, John, Paul and Ringo, which resulted in the Beatles' experiencing many peaks. According to Ringo: 'It feels great; it's just a knowing. It's magic actually; it is pure magic.

Everyone who is playing at that time knows where everybody's going. We all feel like one; wherever you go, everyone feels that's where we should go. I would know if Paul was going to do something, or if George was going to raise it up a bit, or John would double, or we'd bring it down. I usually play with my eyes closed, so you would know when things like that were happening, but it took a lot of years of playing together till it got to that.

'First of all, you've got to get to trust each other, just trust each other in life – never mind as musicians – then you trust each other as players. There's really no words for the emotion you feel with it. You can play for hours and it's not working, so you have the downer. But when it works, when it clicks, there's really nothing like it I've ever experienced in my life.'

Greg Phillinganes shared a similar experience: 'Nate East, one of the top five bass players in the world, and I are so close personally and musically that when we're playing, many times we'll play the same thing and not even look at each other. That's happened many, many times. We haven't known each other that long – we met in the mid-eighties – but we play like we've known each other all our lives.

'Playing with Phil Collins, Eric [Clapton], or [drummer] Steve Ferroni, it's like that too. When you're playing with a certain calibre of people it brings out the best in you and wonderful things happen. All of the elements have to be on the same level. For instance, when I'm soloing I depend on the other players to set new directions for me, while at the same time I'm trying to set new directions for them, so it's a serious bouncing back and forth. It's a reflection, or mirroring, of ideas, and it all works together to create the

[peak] experience. There are times when it's really special and everything seems to gel and flow at the same time. The really special occasions don't happen as often, but they do happen.'

David Crosby spoke of that unity, particularly with his longtime collaborator Graham Nash: 'When I'm playing, what usually happens is that we achieve at its best a kind of gestalt between all the people on the stage, where we feel as if we are part of a larger thing and we are speaking with one voice. That's a wonderful experience, but it happens rarely. It happens more often the better the group is. It used to happen to us quite a lot when [Stephen] Stills, [Graham] Nash, and I were singing. We would sing and frequently hit where we knew what we were doing and it worked; we would feel like we were just singing with one voice, and it was magic. Really good bands can do that: I've done it with several people onstage – all of us playing and singing at the same time and we were on it. It felt ecstatic; it's a near telepathic union. I get it very frequently with Graham Nash. Nash and I get so linked up onstage that we'll both start a wrong verse together.'

I attended many performances of Crosby, Stills and Nash when my former husband Ian was playing drums with the band. Their transcendent vocal harmonies were very moving. One could sense the unity among the three musicians. Graham Nash discussed the intense link between them: 'I felt much more [connected] with David and Stephen than I did with the Hollies. Especially Crosby; I've felt so linked to him musically – which I guess is spiritually at the same time – that I know when he's going to make a certain mistake and I make the same mistake, so to people listening, we both sung the same thing. I knew it was a mistake, Crosby knew; we both smiled at each other. That's how closely linked I am with David.'

Stephen Stills, the third member of Crosby, Stills and Nash, values highly a musician's ability to become one with the music, to eliminate any self-conscious playing: '[The peak occurs] when everyone else is right there with me and totally concentrating on what I'm doing. I can just barely hint at something that I'm playing, and if everybody is concentrating on what I'm playing, then the rest of the band shifts with me, rather than being so self-involved. That hasn't happened for a while because the discipline in music has really gotten out of hand. Nobody pays attention to what people are playing so much; they're all into themselves. I'm from the jazz school, that's why I love playing with Ian [Wallace] so much, because he'll come right with me. And it's rare. The better the musician, that's all they'll do. They give themselves to the music, rather than showing off. You've got to give it all up; you've got to become at one with it. And the only thing that's important is that the noise you make is really good and fits.

'To experience that feeling, a band of any kind has to be paying attention to what I'm doing and vice versa. That's what made the Buffalo Springfield so special. Why this particular group of cats was so good live was that we would get that every night. It's turning yourself inside out and becoming a total player. I experienced it with [Jimi] Hendrix a number of times. The great players know that; they don't even consider themselves a player until they can do that. It really is a one-pointed focus with other musicians.'

Guitarist Albert Lee agreed with Stephen that peak

experiences occur during performance only when all the musicians merge themselves into the music: 'It works so much better when the band's in tune and it works as one. Then it really lifts what I'm doing, otherwise I'm just really going against the grain. I may be doing something dazzling, but it will sound stiff to me if I'm not playing over a perfect sound bed. It's exciting when you play with musicians and something comes about that you're not really expecting. If things aren't going well, no matter how well I play, it feels like I'm trying to push a car uphill, all bogged down. It can really take off when everybody is going in the same direction. There are those magic moments when the rhythm section has the perfect sound and groove, and you're able to just ride along, like riding along on the crest of a wave. It can lift you up.

'[It happened often with] Emmylou Harris and the Hot Band. It was a particularly good time for me, because I think I was really in tune with that band. It was my kind of music, and it was a band where everyone really listened to everyone else, which I rarely find. That band in particular was very sensitive to other musicians.'

Michael McDonald believes that during the peak a band takes on a life of its own, becoming more than just a congregation of musicians: 'Nobody knows why after a few months of playing together with the band, we break through into another level of communication musically that we could never achieve in a rehearsal. It seems to be honed in live performance; the rehearsal can only produce so much. That rapport in performance is magic; so much of it is done on a non-verbal level. There's a collective creativity, energy, and when it's interrupted by personnel changes, it's a shame. I know the band at a certain point would start to take on a musical expression of its own that had nothing to do with me telling everyone what to play. I didn't have to have the greatest drummer in Los Angeles or the hottest players. After about a year, you just know the band is performing at a level that would be hard to describe. You know there's a communication developed that's beyond conscious communication.'

Robert Burke Warren put it succinctly: 'When you're a musician, there's a single understated language you speak when you're playing. It's magic. You look and play off each other. It's an incredible feeling, very much like being high.'

Huey Lewis treasures a band that can transcend together: 'I find it more of a group experience for me. You look around and all of a sudden the song is playing and singing itself. It's just like a wave that you ride. It's tremendously exhilarating; it doesn't take any energy and you look around and say, "Yep, this is it!" It happens quite often but not for long periods of time. Almost at every gig that will happen somewhere for a fleeting moment. Some gigs it happens more often than others; and those are the good gigs. The object is to find that thing where you can completely relax and just ride.'

Mick Fleetwood found his most incredible peak experiences while playing with original Fleetwood Mac guitarist Peter Green: 'In terms of real high points, without any question it would be when I was playing drums with Peter Green. I'd be completely crying, weeping. It still happens, but it used to happen all the time. I was so devoted to that; it was very, very vivid, and I was sort of addicted to it. There were times I would be pulled into his situation, and it was the highest quotient of that happening. A lot of it was because of literally being there with him. The ride was just as good as driving.'

Bassist John McVie recounted with awe the many aspects of the peak experience he has encountered while playing with Fleetwood Mac: 'There's a presence coming at you. You can't deny that. You'd have to be dead to miss it. It hooks you in and engulfs you like a cloud. Everyone sits right in it for a couple of seconds or an hour. It's like being lifted; it's a physical sensation, and it doesn't happen a hundred per cent of the time. But when you're locked in, the band's locked in, I'm locked in with Mick [Fleetwood] and Chris [McVie], or whomever, and it's just riding along – that is incredible. It's almost as if you're going to levitate.

'When that happens, it makes all the bullshit, all the heartache, all the doubts, all the negative side of being a musician [worth it]. If I could bottle that feeling and sell it … Well, I'd bottle it and give it – I'd love everyone to experience it. It's the most incredible surge, it really is. I've got hot flashes just thinking about it now.

'It's really a oneness with these people, wrapped in with sound – you just float. It might not last for more than a couple of minutes, but when it happens, it's magic. It takes your breath away. It's almost like when you have a déjà vu experience and you don't want it to stop and you're scared that if you think about it, it will disappear and then, I'm thinking about thinking about it, so don't think about it and it starts trickling. But if it's riding right and you're just riding high, it's just such an incredible feeling and that's worth everything. All the dark side of [the music business], it negates all that completely. There, for me is a spiritual experience, right there, that's it. I think when people see visions or are filled with the spirit or whatever, maybe they feel like that.'

The Red Hot Chili Peppers' unity results in astounding peak experiences for each of them, said Anthony Kiedis: 'In our live shows there's some kind of miraculous energy that happens between the four of us that gives us a sort of superhuman energy to propel us through each show. It's fairly apparent to the viewer and the listener. Most of the shows that we play, it would seem as though it would be impossible to play like that night after night, but we continue to play with intensity. Just the very energetic, explosive nature of our band is consistent.

'People ask us how we keep it that way, and I think it's a combination of the chemistry created between these particular four people in the band. It's also a combination of the chemistry with the type of music that we write. The combination of those two things gives a very strong stage euphoria, something that I'm very grateful for and I live for. Sometimes it's such a great feeling it's hard to deal with when the show is over because it's almost like the downside of an artificial high.

'[When I'm onstage singing] I'm completely unaware of anything around me, except for [Chili Peppers] John [Frusciante] and Flea and Chad [Smith]. It seems as though I feel like I'm in some sort of psychedelic, swirling cauldron of hard-core funk when I'm singing. I just try to stay within that space throughout the show. It's always when I can make a complete connection with everybody in the band that our music sounds best, like when it's four people all aiming for the same musical point, and so I just really try to stay focused on the music and the band, and it feels great. It's not an egotistical sense of invincibility but I feel like nothing can harm me during that time; I have no anxiety or fear or worries really, for that moment while I'm playing, which is a nice thing. That's on a good night, of course.

'Every time I get together with the band and we write a song, there's usually so much love involved and so much happiness in the fact that we're creating something that we all desire so much, it all seems mystical to me. I get a sense of euphoria that I never experience any other time in my life. And since every song we've ever written seems to have held up over the course of time, I would say that it isn't a false feeling when it happens and that it's legitimate.'

Christine McVie also described the peak experience precipitated by an intense oneness among band members: '[When onstage, I feel] a sense of great unity, like my father would say when he was playing his one violin in a team of first violin, second violin, violas, horns, oboes and flutes. And then out of all those different mouths and arms and hands comes this amazing *one thing* – all these people doing the same thing together, which is so beautiful. That's what it's like when you're really tight onstage: you know everyone's thinking the same chord at the same time. You're playing as one thing. To all be playing that one thing is a tremendous feeling.'

The Link Between Artist and Audience

In addition to the oneness that occurs onstage, some musicians said that during a peak experience they feel a profound unity between themselves and the audience. As enrapt listeners concentrate all their attention on the performance, while the musicians are swept up in the music, a union of these elements transpires. The phenomenon seems related to psychologist Richard Guggenheimer's description of the peak experience: 'As absorption deepens, things happen which become explicable only in terms of increasing emotion. A sense of unutterable rightness glows around the entire structure.'

Billy Burnette sees the peak experience arising from a combination of band chemistry and audience involvement: '[The peak experience] is probably one of the most euphoric feelings I know. It's like a wave that runs through you. When it happens, I've said to myself, "This is incredible, why can't this last forever and be like this every night." It doesn't happen every night; it comes around once in a while. I think it's the band and the audience that make that thing happen. When it all gets matched up right, you all lift off. Fleetwood Mac [with whom Billy was then playing] is at the top of the list for getting that stuff happening. I suppose it's the magic they generate themselves.'

Nancy Wilson differentiated between the peak that occurs when she is jamming with her sister Ann and that which is precipitated by an audience. 'Usually [when I'm playing] I forget what I look like or who I am. Ann and I would sit and play a lot and just stare blankly into each other's face, and then one of us would say, "Oh my God, look at your face – your tongue's hanging out!" You kind of lose yourself.

'Onstage it's a little different because the audience is there and the energy level is so heightened. There's so much electricity – not just in the [guitar] cables. Usually what happens to me on those amazing nights is that you really feel truly larger than yourself, like you're 10 thousand feet high. You're kind of yourself, but you're also in the audience, so it's like some kind of circular reciprocity – it's all-inclusive. It's one of the best feelings. It can be so thrilling, especially if you feel like you're getting through and touching something deeper in the audience than just the animal instinct.'

To achieve the peak experience, Bonnie Raitt depends on the audience: 'This incredible exchange of energy goes on onstage, where you're almost transported. For me, the spark comes, very emotional, from the shared experience of what I'm singing about. It's the band when we really lock in and the audience knows you're locking in. I wish I could lose myself more when I play by myself. It's easy to do with an audience, but I tend to be too self-conscious and judgmental when I'm alone. The audience is more unconditional, as if the channel is more open.'

Peter Gabriel is very sensitive to the vibe given off by the audience and reacts to it accordingly: 'Performers feed off the audience; sometimes you can tell how a gig's going to go at the moment you walk on stage. You know what sort of electricity and energy is being put up towards the stage. I respond to that a lot. Sometimes you can generate that from nothing, but it is a lot harder.'

An audience's energy can transform a performance from mundane to supreme, said drummer Robin Horn: 'The audience can be a catalyst; it can evoke [a peak experience] a lot more strongly than if you are playing a jam session or a rehearsal. Being in front of the audience brings out an intensity, makes it that much stronger.'

Ringo Starr distinguished between those performances in which the band and audience connect and those where there is no unity: 'When you're on tour – and it doesn't happen all the time – sometimes you and the audience connect, just connect. Some nights, besides us [in the band] being connected – and we weren't connected every night either – we'd just go on and do the numbers, and we'd be the only ones who'd know if it had been good or not, but we'd still get the same applause. Sometimes, though, you would feel this presence together with the audience and the band, which was just such a mindblower. It felt better than the other gigs. You felt some sort of connection, where there was a whole wave of five or 10 thousand people coming at you; you felt that you and the audience were actually one.

'At [the Beatles' concert at] Shea Stadium there was no contact. We just happened to be playing; they were screaming, dancing, doing what they did, which they did in all the other places. So we didn't get it every night, but when you did, you just felt so ecstatic. That's what made me realise why all musicians keep playing.'

The Spiritual Element

For some artists, the intense connection to and unity with the audience and/or other musicians results in the peak becoming a spiritual experience. Indeed, most musicians described the peak almost reverently. Psychologist/philosopher William James said: '… Not conceptual speech, but music rather, is the element through which we are best spoken to by mystical truth. In the mystic states, we both become one with the absolute, and we become aware of our oneness'.

This sense of unity that the peak characterises, I believe, is absolutely connected to the spiritual. For those few moments, the artist is transported to a higher place. Maslow also described the spiritual feelings reported by those enrolled in his studies of this phenomenon: 'In peak experiences such emotions as wonder, awe, reverence, humility, surrender, and even worship, before the greatness of the experiences are often reported.'

These experiences are no doubt the most meaningful part of many musicians' unique spiritual life. Peter Gabriel spoke of the ethereal element that music brings to the artist's life: 'Music is spiritual and is a doorway into that world. Its power comes from the fact that it plugs directly into the soul, unlike a lot of visual art or text information that has to go through the more filtering processes of the brain.'

The reciprocal nature of the energy between audience and musician resembles the age-old fervour of religious celebrations. Paul Kantner observed: 'There's this big circle of something between you and the audience. If you play well, they really enjoy it and give something intangible back to you. That charges you up to play even better, which makes them get even more ecstatic. It's like a circle of energy. It's as close as I get to religion, and it's what religion should be about: much more exhilarating, much more unity with the people all around you, much more human touch going on. It's done just through people. It's been done around ancient bonfires at harvest festivals, among people who've worked all season picking crops, in ancient times, dancing and singing, and in voodoo rites, as well as among Christian fundamentalists, where they fall back and people have to catch them.'

For Eric Clapton it is essential that both artists and audience 'surrender' during a performance. He passionately described this concept: 'I can't really explain what it's like except in a physical sense. It's a massive rush of adrenaline which comes at a certain point. Usually it's a sharing experience; it's not something I could experience on my own. It has to be in the company of other musicians onstage, and of course with an audience. It's not even just the musicians; it's everyone that's involved in the whole transaction or experience. Everyone in that building or place seems to unify at one point. It's not necessarily me that's doing it; it may be another musician. But it's when you get that completely harmonic experience, where everyone is hearing exactly the same thing without any interpretation whatsoever or any kind of angle. They're all transported towards the same place. That's not very common, but it always seems to happen at least once a show. That's what you hope for; you start out with the framework of songs you're going to do and hope it's going to happen in this one, and if it doesn't you wait for the next one and see if it'll happen in that.

'You don't really know what it's composed of; it's just a point when everyone has got exactly the same momentum. There's a lot concerned with timing, but beyond that it's hard to describe. You could call it unity, which is a very spiritual word for me. Everyone is one at that point, at that specific point in time, not for very long. Of course, the defeating aspect is that the minute you become aware of that, it's gone. Music demands surrender; everyone there at some point is going to surrender at exactly the same time to the same thing – musicians and audience included.'

Joni Mitchell turned to a Jungian idea to help define the mystical nature of the peak experiences she has had while playing with other musicians, particularly in the studio: 'For me, the spiritual experiences are synchronicity. You can't beat it. For instance, in live performance the synchronicity is the beauty of everybody being really Zen – everybody not only hearing themselves while they're playing but hearing everybody else and creating spontaneously. This happens more on recording dates than in live performance, because by the time you get to live performance the music is somewhat composed. When you're in the studio, you're still in the searching mode, so you're dealing with the unknown. Therefore luck has to come into it, and synchronicity is good luck.'

Paul Horn articulated beautifully the unifying essence of music, which can result in a spiritual peak experience for audience and musician alike: 'When I was touring with Donovan, there was just the two of us with 25,000 people out there and you could hear a pin drop – that's power. The power is in the silence, that you got them to the point of being so still. The most powerful music is simple music; so often your intellect gets in the way of the whole thing. As human beings, we complicate things in life. The intuitive part of the brain, if left to be, will usually be very simple. Basic truths in life are so simple we can't talk about them. The power in music, I've learned, is in simplicity. It has nothing to do with technique, complexity – it's beyond that.

'There's a certain kind of magic there, and that magic is what I'm trying to verbalise. The magic is that people can be transformed through sound, simple sound. And also it's the person that's playing the music who is the channel for the music to come through. Ego will stop the magic. You have to surrender to be a channel, and surrender means to be absorbed in the music, lost in the music, and [to] become one with the music.'

'The world both inwardly and outwardly takes on an intensity that may be momentarily overwhelming,' wrote Rollo May of the peak experience. 'This is one aspect of what is called ecstasy – the uniting of unconscious experience with conscious – a dynamic immediate fusion.'

The ecstasy is so intense that some musicians attempt to prolong the feeling through chemical means. While talking to my then husband Ian Wallace about the peak experience, he remarked that one reason he used to drink heavily after a concert was because of his need to keep the high he had gained onstage. He didn't want to come down from it, and the drinking was a way of extending that euphoria. Bonnie Raitt confirmed, 'That's probably why a lot of people did use drugs after the show because it was just such an incredible high. When you come off stage, what else are you supposed to do? You can't just hug every one of the audience personally.'

Chapter 6

CHEMICALS AND CREATIVITY

'TO BEGIN WITH, DRINK IS VERY BAFFLING AND
CUNNING. IT'S GOT A PERSONALITY OF ITS OWN.'
ERIC CLAPTON

Drugs and alcohol have played a role in the lives of creative people for centuries. Consistently, people have used intoxicants as a means to change the body chemistry to enhance creativeness. More than a century ago, William James wrote: 'The sway of alcohol over mankind is unquestionably due to its power to stimulate the mystical faculties of human nature, usually crushed to earth by the cold facts and dry criticism of the sober hour.' As a tool to rid the mind of inhibitions and free the unconscious from the restrictions of the conscious mind, drugs and alcohol have been sought after by many to help trigger the creative flow.

Artists have also used chemical means to diminish the anxiety that can stall or prevent the creative process. Musicians and writers in particular have described taking psychoactive drugs to facilitate the flow of ideas, making it easier to overcome the boundaries of preconceived notions.

For example, a small amount of alcohol does tend to make people less inhibited, by getting the conscious mind out of the way and thus allowing the unconscious to emerge.

Drugs such as marijuana, LSD and mescaline became increasingly popular in the sixties and were often used in excess by those hoping to get more in touch with the inner self, wherein lies creativeness. For some people, LSD did provide a mystical experience, a feeling of oneness, as well as the disorientation of time and space associated with the peak experience. They found that the realisations they experienced during an acid trip could help open up their creative side. These illuminations convinced them they were capable of imaginative ideas. The blocks they had had in the past, such as a belief that they weren't creative, were eliminated – at least for a while.

Effective creative actions could not take place while under the influence of acid, however. The Swiss chemist who developed LSD, Albert Hoffmann, wrote of its effect on the creative process: 'Works of art are not created while the drug is in effect, but only afterward, the artist being inspired by these experiences. As long as the inebriated condition lasts, creative activity is impeded if not completely halted. The influx of images is too great and is increasing too rapidly to be portrayed and fashioned. An overwhelming vision paralyses activity.'

Obviously, the major problem with drugs and alcohol lies in the fine line that exists between use and abuse. For many, the 'tool' becomes the end rather than the means. In fact, numerous musicians I talked to have only recently reacquainted themselves with life minus alcohol and drugs. I could easily relate to them since I'm one of their number.

CHEMICALS AND CREATIVITY

My experiences made me wonder what it was like for those musicians I knew who had dabbled in drugs and alcohol throughout their creative lives. Some of them had used drugs and alcohol in moderation since their early days of creating; others had fallen into the trap of addiction. Did they use chemicals for the same reasons I had? I was curious as to how psychoactive drugs affected their creativeness. Did drugs and alcohol enhance creativity to a certain point, and then block it? Or are some people creative despite the effect drugs and alcohol has on them?

These are some of the questions we discussed in our interviews. Numerous musicians' experiences shed light on the whole phenomenon. Basically, I think the effect of drugs and alcohol is individual; no general statement can really apply to everyone. As Keith Richards told me: 'I think it's got a lot to do with knowing yourself. There's not a blanket thing of what's good for you; you know what it does to you. It's a matter of knowing how you react to things. It's a matter of being in touch with your metabolism.'

Kirsty MacColl said she believed that drugs affect all creative people differently: 'A lot of creative people have written great things when they've been out of it. I don't think they got more creative because they were taking drugs. They are creative people in the first place, and how they choose to go about it is up to them. There are a lot of people who wouldn't touch drugs with a barge pole but who are still very great artists. If you get to a point where you can't do your work because you're too far gone, it takes eight times longer [to create] than it would when you're straight. People who are really creative are going to be creative up to the point where they black out!'

Richard Thompson emphasised that although some creative people have used stimulants for inspiration, these substances impair the artist's ability to create: '[Drugs and alcohol] work differently for different people. I don't think they helped me at all, quite the opposite actually. There's a balance to writing, and any sort of drug upsets the balance – except coffee, of course! I can't remember having written a good song while under the influence of anything. I've written songs about being drunk, but only while I was sober. Different people have different tolerances, though. Some people have written great stuff; "The Rime of the Ancient Mariner" was written under laudanum [a tincture of opium popular in the nineteenth century].

'To be creative, you have to make illogical connections within your being. You have to pull strange elements together to create something new. You have to weave something new out of different strands of the world. Drugs can help you get into that frame of mind, but they don't give you the overall view. There are states of mind that you have to reach. Drugs can help you do this or they can destroy your ability to do it. I don't think I've taken any drug, alcohol, or anything for 15 years. I'm certainly much happier. I'm just trying to use what little brain I have left!'

A Change in Consciousness

Many musicians had reached a crossroads and decided to stop using any kind of intoxicant. Their comments were diverse, since their experiences had run the whole gamut from creative use to abuse. I had seen Eric Clapton struggle with these problems for a long time, so I was really interested in what he had to say about it: 'To begin with, drink is very baffling and cunning. It's got a personality of its own. Part of the trap [of drugs and alcohol] is that they open the doors to unreleased channels or rooms you hadn't explored before or allowed to be open. A lot of my creative things came out first of all through marijuana. I started smoking when I was about 18 or 19, and that would let out a whole string of humorous things as well as music. Then drink allowed me to be very self-piteous and opened up that whole kind of sorrowful musical side of myself. Unfortunately after that, the booze becomes more important than the doors it's opening, so that's the trap.

'I think in a lot of cases people do have an inhibition about expressing themselves. Most people are very shy and very neurotic and nervous about even meeting other people but are fine after having a couple of drinks, and that's the same with being creative. But anything that distorts your awareness or any mood-altering chemical will actually impair your thinking, because you tend to be just *wanting* rather than serving. You're not really in tune with anything at all other than your drug, and that works on your nervous system to a point where you are really at the mercy of it, so the only thing you can do is beg and ask all the time. This can happen with any kind of experience. At the beginning there can be an opening up and then you move on to the next phase where it all becomes confused, and then the final phase where the drug or whatever it is has actually got control of you and you've lost that original thing.'

David Crosby's addiction to cocaine landed him in prison. He eventually won his battle against drugs and has since reconsidered their impact on his creativity: 'What initially happens in the drug experience is that you feel the drugs are helping because they will throw your consciousness up for grabs. And sometimes, early on in the process, that worked for me. The problem with the drugs is that, as you become addicted to them, they become so debilitating that the creative process stops entirely. A whole other effect takes place. While I was an addict, for three years of my life, I didn't write anything. I didn't have the attention span or the will; it just shut down, as if it had atrophied. And then six months after I quit, I wrote lyric after lyric, and it's been that way ever since. So much for the drugs and hash creativity theory.'

Both Eric and David mentioned that the first allure of intoxicants was their 'mind-opening' ability. This seemed to be a major reason for many of those who have used drugs and alcohol to create. After all, as creative people, they are accustomed to taking risks and immersing themselves in chaos. They do it all the time when they tap into the unconscious. Being high is like being put into another world, one without form or structure, one similar to the unconscious. It perhaps makes it easier to dive down until it takes over completely, which then takes one on another path altogether.

Lindsey Buckingham now eschews alcohol and cocaine, but has found that marijuana can help put him into this other world, which he believes is beneficial to creativity: 'Cocaine is not part of my style: I certainly have done my share, but I don't buy it, I don't like it; it's not good for work. It might be good if you want to put yourself in the position of having to work 24 hours, but why do that? I work 14-hour days [in my studio] and I don't need cocaine to do that; I can just do it on natural energy.

'I do smoke pot. That's the one thing that seems to … it's not great for things like memory, but within the relative security of the studio, in the womblike atmosphere where I know what's going on in there, it's very helpful. It breaks down preconceptions you have about something; it allows you to hear it fresh. If you've been working on something for a few hours and you smoke a joint, it's like hearing it again for the first time. You walk away for 10 minutes and come back, and it allows you to keep coming back in for more and enjoy it. It seems to open a lot of the right-brain stuff. It seems to fire off a lot of things. For me, it's tied into a certain ability to visualise. It puts you way inside it. I would imagine if you smoke a strong joint, it's mildly psychedelic and it just puts you in touch with things. You journey inside. Things seem to come out of nowhere sometimes; it throws you a bit. You have to get unsure of yourself if you're going to break down preconceptions, if you're going to feel out of control. You're never going to do a good piece of work if you're just imposing your ego on something. But the other side of that, the alcohol, is something I've stopped doing. That and cocaine are not creative things.'

Joni Mitchell also described the importance of 'screwing on a different consciousness' while creating. Though she acknowledged that certain drugs can initially help in the process, she stressed the disastrous results of dependence: 'Writing is a more neurotic, a more dangerous art form, psychologically speaking [than performing music], because there you have to make the mind crazy. It's the opposite of Zen mind. That's why a lot of the great writers used stimulants – *Alice in Wonderland* was written on opium; all the great Welsh alcoholics – because writers need to screw on a different head. Sometimes they get lost in the different head, but with writing, you need to create the chaotic mind, insanity almost, overlapping thoughts. You have to plumb down if you want any depth to your writing.

'During the introductory period to a new drug, it can screw on a different consciousness. Any change of consciousness is refreshing, so is the contrast between going straight to whatever elixir, say pot; it tends to make you tactile, sensual. It warms the heart, for about the first 15 minutes. Then it starts to fog you over. You've got about 15 minutes of really concentrated creative thought and then it can flatten you. If you smoke that on a regular basis, you'd just be flattened, and it's anti-creative. But if you do it knowing, "I'm stuck here", take some pot and you'll swing into the opposite of where you are and ideas will open up. Cocaine can give you an intellectual, linear delusion of grandeur – makes you feel real smart. It can create great insanity very quickly. My definition of insanity is chaotic mind – too many thoughts in it, overlapping. For a writer, that's a lot of choices; epic thought can be very good, but if you do [too much], then it takes over and then it's anti-creative, almost immediately. For me, saki is a very warming elixir, but [with] all these things, you can't even do them two days in a row before they [begin to have] a deteriorating effect. They almost have to be done with a spiritual, ritualistic [feel], like a prayer.'

Though Edie Brickell concedes that chemicals can change one's creative perspective, she places a priority on being straight to create: 'If you think of your creativity as a pool of water, then drugs would be like throwing a rock in there. It creates ripples, and it gets a little bit out of focus. It changes it. Sometimes it's interesting and sometimes it's good, but sometimes it's not. I think too much of it will block up the water, will dry it up. You can have a balance, so I'm not against it, but I'm not for it all the time. I think you should be in touch with being straight, too. I don't think you need drugs to be creative.'

Bonnie Raitt described how she began using drink and drugs in the sixties as an act of rebellion but also to shut out painful thoughts: 'I was anaesthetised by drugs and alcohol and also the lifestyle. At an early age, I became "Bonnie Raitt" at a time when I was still very unformed. I had to crystallise this personality before I was really ready to do it. At that point, the schism between the young girl and the professional person made it very difficult and insulating for me. The responsibility for being rewarded for something I didn't feel I deserved made me hide behind the alcohol. I got sucked into the lifestyle of a "rock 'n' roll blues mama". It was also a very exciting, dangerous and rebellious thing to get involved in – celebrated by all the cultural heroes we in the Woodstock Nation looked up to, as rejecting all the violence, hypocrisy, greed and shallowness of the "straight" world. It was an affirmation of real human values to adopt the counterculture drug lifestyle. I couldn't wait to get out of school and drink and stay up playing music all night.

'But aside from having all that fun, I got out of touch with the person who's underneath all those layers. I built myself a personality. I think it worked in the beginning, but then as I got older, it didn't serve me as well. I think the lifestyle encouraged the music somewhat. I don't think it always got in the way. It's just that the drugs and alcohol part of it became physically and creatively debilitating and started running me at the end. I managed to put a halt to that and got in touch with why I'm here in the first place – a spiritual centre – and how important it is to be clear and to be able to open that up.'

Paul Kantner also recalled how drug use in the sixties related to creativity: 'In our generation, some drugs got out of control and were bad; some were quite good. It affects people differently. As it goes into artistry, it probably helps people achieve moments that they might not have otherwise achieved. I don't want to put this out as a prescription to indiscriminate drug use, hoping for the creative. You've got to be creative and work at that too. You can't just sit down and smoke a joint or drink a bottle of wine and expect creativity to just happen. You have to have something else before it. Some people use marijuana to loosen them up, some people use alcohol, some people use meditation, some people use jogging. Whatever gets you through the night, in moderation.

'Particularly in our generation, drugs presented a real problem with moderation, and they got out of control, as alcohol did with our parents' generation and some of our own generation as well. LSD was as close to God as I ever got – one step above the rock 'n' roll experience. It adds another element to it and drops a lot of doors that you normally keep closed. You just got close to people in ways our parents' generation wouldn't have even considered, would have been horrified by. [Someone] pointed out at one point that we took it upon ourselves to test ourselves with all these drugs, having no other tests to go through the fire.'

LSD's effect on Paul was an attribute of hallucinogens that drew many creative people to them. I, like Paul, took acid in the sixties for the same purpose. Abraham Maslow discussed the use of hallucinogens for mystical purposes: 'Certain drugs called psychedelics, especially LSD and psilocybin ... often produce peak experiences in the right people under the right circumstances.' However, as Paul mentioned, these drugs also carry their own unique side effects, including in some extreme cases a complete deterioration of the psyche.

Jazz bandleader Frank Foster found that certain drugs, particularly marijuana, could be useful to help open doors while creating, although their use could impair performance: 'I find that marijuana seems to particularly inspire me to want to create. I've found that some of my most meaningful or deepest ideas have come through inspiration gleaned from marijuana – not that I think it makes me perform better. It makes me feel I'm in touch with forces I'm not usually in touch with when I'm cold sober. I can get out of myself what the Creator has given me to produce whether I'm high or sober.

'I don't think I could do anything behind alcohol; alcohol generally interferes with the motor function. People who get drunk can't perform up to their ability, unless they've been doing it for years and years, like saxophone players who've been drinking all their lives and who can go on all night. Their systems have become sort of immune to the impairment caused by alcohol, although they are going to die from drinking it for so long.'

Sinéad O'Connor, like Frank, said that using marijuana opens herself up for writing music, but she finds it impedes performance and recording: 'I smoke dope quite a bit and that really does help – not when I'm onstage or in the studio performing [because] it sort of fucks you up – but when I'm actually writing, because it opens your mind up. I mean you mustn't do it all the time because then it has the opposite effect. You can't open yourself too much, because the human mind is only capable of receiving a certain amount of information. There are certain things you're not exposed to because you can't deal with it, so you shouldn't open yourself up too much. Look at all the poets – Blake or Yeats or Coleridge or Wordsworth – they were all opium addicts. Your life is so difficult; it's very hard to open yourself up. If you smoke a joint, you're much clearer, you realise what your thoughts are, but you've got to write it down really quickly before it all goes through your head.'

Jazz musician Paul Horn, who has seen addiction's devastating impact on many of his colleagues, gave a balanced appraisal: 'I've had some experience with drugs – not all drugs – and I've never really been heavy into it. Certain drugs with certain people can give experiences that, if you don't get dependent upon it, can be an opening of a door. In the early days, dope was just for jazz musicians. The drug then was simply pot; heroin came later. It seems that most people in show business are shy and that they need something to get past that to get to the music. And if you aren't strong enough spiritually and don't understand how to do that in a natural way, which most people don't, then they have a few drinks or a few tokes, to get past this self-consciousness and get into the music. I'm not saying it's necessary, but I can't block it out and say it's totally no good. There are great dangers in it, and we all know what they are.

If you get dependent upon it, you can't get past that and the dependency will destroy you. So it's really a tricky and dangerous ground to walk on, a thin line. If you're strong enough that you can have a taste of it at certain stages of your life and realise it's just a stage and [recognise] the dangers involved if you keep up with it, and then go on from there, it's alright. But if you go too far with it, then it can block your creativity and destroy you in the process.'

Paul's son, drummer Robin Horn, described how the negative factors of drugs outweigh their benefits: 'Drugs have the ability to bring out an experience that opens up your mind, that creates a larger vision, mind expansion. It's an artificial way of doing it. Pot opened up my mind; it gave me another experience. I don't know if I can attribute any effects from it towards the music, unless you want to say it does create a larger vision, and if that's the case, then it would apply to your instrument because the more you see, the more you can do. But I did it a couple of times before I played and I saw that was wrong within the first two bars. Some people can function, but not me. It's enough to get up there and play your best; you need all your marbles to begin with. When you bring the drug into it, you spend your whole time trying to overcome the restraints that the drug is putting on you. When you have to do something as pure as playing an instrument, then the drugs are going to come through. You may *think* you're playing wonderfully, because you're feeling great.'

By having what Robin called a 'larger vision' the artist may be able to use that new way of seeing things in the creative process. Overall, the musicians agreed that a different perspective on their creative endeavours can be helpful, but that the dangers of getting caught up in the escape from everyday life is enormous.

George Harrison agreed that initially, LSD and marijuana were beneficial, but that he discontinued using both: 'LSD did unlock something for me, and it released all this stuff. I used to spend time looking at myself in the mirror, and the face kept changing, from looking like a Mongolian and then to a Chinese man. I just kept looking, thinking, who are you? I think that pot definitely did something for the old ears, like suddenly I could hear more subtle things in the sound. But now I've found it's actually better not to do it while working. I need to be a bit more clear, because my mind is such a scramble at times, and all that does is scramble it more.'

Peter Gabriel disparages the use of drugs as giving a false sense of enlightenment: 'Mind-altering substances of one kind or another have been traditionally part of many cultures and have a place in shaping creativity. But I don't think it's something I would recommend to anyone, nor that it is necessary. I think it's possible to get to wherever you want to go without it. Perhaps sometimes it does short-circuit longer routes that maybe allow you to look through a window perhaps at a state that might be arrived at through spiritual work. I'm not sure you actually get there. It's a very dangerous road.'

Jackson Browne described how he used hallucinogens in the sixties as a creative tool, but only under the most controlled circumstances: 'I always thought [the drugs] enhanced [creativity] at the time, but you pay heavily. All these drugs have their effect; they change your perception about things. I used to smoke a lot of grass, when I was first starting to write songs. I didn't have the sense that I was using it for anything then. Out of all the drugs that I took, the experiences that I'm consciously aware of valuing are psychedelics. In the mid-sixties, when people began turning on to psychedelic drugs, it was revolutionary. It was something that had been talked about by Aldous Huxley. It was a scientific thing; it was a breakthrough. When I took it, I was real careful; I set up the whole experience. I've never been able to understand people who did it every day or took it casually, or do it and go to a concert or something.'

Huey Lewis articulated that, to a certain degree, drugs and alcohol can help artists leave everyday reality behind and delve into more meaningful introspection. He stressed, however, that the unpredictable nature of mind-altering chemicals renders them useless: 'For the artist or songwriter or writer, the object is to get away from society so you can reflect on society. There's a certain tendency to think drink and/or drugs help you do that. It may be correct initially, but the trouble is that it's very unreliable and doesn't work all the time, but half the time maybe. It can be effective; you can have a couple of drinks and maybe get a new perspective on something. The trouble is another time you may have a couple of drinks or a joint or whatever and write a bunch of crap, so it's unreliable initially and ultimately it's addictive and never works once it becomes addictive.'

Musicians frequently cited 'escaping the busy mind' as a prerequisite to being creative. The busy mind, or the conscious mind, is a sort of roadblock to that deeper, creative unconscious mind, on which artists rely to make music. Like a naughty, uncontrolled child that has just learned to walk, the busy mind is going here, there and everywhere, not allowing a moment's peace. It is forever working out things, analysing, criticising, moving all the time, as if afraid to stop for fear there will be nothing inside. Therefore, many musicians have used drugs or alcohol to sedate the busy mind to allow inspiration to come forth from the unconscious while the busy mind 'falls asleep'. By lulling or anaesthetising the busy, noisy, critical, conscious mind, there is more chance of creating.

Roger Waters pointed out: 'Alcohol in reasonable quantities has the same effect as lying in a bath: it deprives you of the jagged edges of your perceptions and senses. That's why I think it's such a popular drug, because it removes the nagging edge of life and consequently may well free the bits that are concerned with relating to the natural order. It may release your ability to confront your feelings on a more artistic level, because you stop worrying about, say, the mortgage. I know a lot of friends who are writers who use alcohol to write, just because it dulls the senses.'

Nancy Wilson of Heart told me she used stimulants in the past for the same reason – to cut herself off from the distractions of external influences: 'I used [drugs and alcohol] for a more direct way of shaking off the outside world and just getting into the more primal world quickly. Ultimately, it doesn't work, because you feel bad all the time. Also when you're in an altered state, especially with cocaine, you think every idea you have is just the greatest; there's no objectivity. Then when you see it the next day and it's like … We ended up by having a joke about it, we just called it 'blowatry' – big difference between that and poetry! [Cocaine] puts you in a heightened state of self-gratification.'

The False Promise

There does seem to be trickery involved when drugs come into play during creative times, and musicians talked about this problem. John McVie described how overindulgence in alcohol affected his creative process: 'At the time, it was incredible, being under the influence. I was incredible, I was amazing, I was unique. But the next day, while reading something [written under the influence] or listening [to something recorded while high], it was a bunch of bull.'

Robin Le Mesurier related to what John said: 'When the drug was white powder that went up your nose, and you used to work till two or three in the morning, thinking you're doing just great, then you'd walk in the next day and you'd realise there was nothing there worth keeping. On the other hand, alcohol – because of its qualities of making you less inhibited – in very small doses can be a little bit helpful up to a point. But only a very tiny amount, because if you go over the top, then it becomes the same old thing again: sounds great, but it's a mess the next day.' Steve Jordan pointed out, '[Some] drugs can make you feel like you're at the top of the world, until you come down and you see what you've done is terrible.'

So why continue to use drugs when they're so unreliable? Steve Jordan was among the musicians who spoke of the frustration of trying to write when nothing would come, and using drugs or alcohol as a shortcut: 'Out of frustration, you do drugs when you can't write and you think you need it. You've got to do something, so you hope for a different perspective. On occasion that might work, but usually what happens once you've had one drink, you just want another drink.'

Billy Burnette mentioned that he had seen this problem in both his life and his father's: 'Sometimes the songs don't come and you're so desperate and you're trying so hard, and you can't find that "thing" again. So you go to drugs or booze, try to find it there; then you end up really nuts.'

Joni Mitchell has also experienced this trap: 'Out of desperation, when you have no inspiration [you may try] to stimulate it with the addition of something artificial. But with the straight mind, the little shocks of daily existence can be enough. You go out the door of your house in one mood and you run into something that either elevates or depresses that mood; that change of mind could be the stimulation needed for the creative process. The straight mind is ultimately the best because it's the long-distance runner of them all. With the others, the road is too dangerous; it can burn you out, and kill your talent.'

Vocalist Patty Smyth agrees with Joni: 'I think it's been proven that [drugs and alcohol] lower your inhibitions and that they help a lot of people to get in touch with their creative side. But it's a limited 'in touch with'. A lot of [drug and alcohol use] is motivated by fear or being overly sensitive, or other things. I think you can really get to the place, the highest place without it, but that's the long row to hoe, and people want to get there and they want to get there fast.'

Guitarist Albert Lee told me how in the past he'd gone the stimulant route while trying to write: '[I've used drugs] to get me through that period where you're just slogging away at something and you really haven't got that initial excitement that you had at the beginning. I haven't taken any pills for ages, but when I've taken uppers I've been up half the night with them. I felt the nerve endings were raw and you are very in touch with your feelings; I know a lot of people who write like that, who stay up all night. Even without pills, though, just being up all night can get your nerves feeling like they wouldn't normally.'

Songwriter Randy Newman found that using stimulants as a shortcut had nasty repercussions. 'I used to take amphetamines to write years ago, and was very frightened not to take them. I figured any kind of edge I can get. As you can tell, it was obviously a traumatic formula. But all in all, it was one of the worst things I ever did; they weren't fun.'

Another reason drugs and alcohol so easily become a crutch is their ability to release inhibitions. Having drinks or smoking a joint to loosen up before going onstage seemed as necessary to many musicians as indulging in coke or drink at parties was to others at that time. In our interview, Mick Fleetwood confirmed that he has relied on alcohol for this reason: 'A few drinks is a helper to me. When I go onstage, I like to have a few drinks; it's not any fear of getting up and playing in public, which could very well be a reason for people drinking. When I first started playing professionally, we always had a few beers. It was part of the situation. You don't play blind drunk, but there have been moments when you're totally uninhibited about what you're doing and are completely unleashing your abilities into the lap of the gods. For better or worse, there's been a lot of liberated moments under the influence of the bottle, and there's certainly been those moments straight.'

Sinéad O'Connor also discussed how drink, in moderation, can 'soften the edges' during performance: 'I think alcohol comes in handy; like a couple of beers would help when you're going onstage and you want to just be yourself. Because if you're stone cold sober, it's all too clear, and you need to just soften the edges a bit.'

Keith Strickland doesn't make a habit of using alcohol, but it was a lethal cocktail and its effective inhibition-loosening power that resulted in the birth of the B-52s: 'How we got started as a band was we all went to this Chinese restaurant and we all drank this drink called the Flaming Volcano. It was this big alcoholic drink with a volcano in the middle and five straws. Then we all went to a friend's house and started jamming. Alcohol can make you very uninhibited; it has that effect and can help in that sense, I suppose. But I don't find it necessary.'

Intoxicants as Buffers

The very nature of creative people's childhoods – the feelings of being different and seeing things more complexly than others – no doubt inspired some to turn to drugs and alcohol during adolescence to cover up their specialness or even numb some of the intense feelings. Michael McDonald had seen this predicament in his own life: 'My experiences with drugs and alcohol were – having that kind of emotional liability as a kid – I used them as a crutch. It only became natural that the crutch permeated every aspect of my life after a while. I couldn't write unless I smoked pot; I couldn't go to the store unless I smoked pot. It was just a huge rationalising process that overtook me. I do think in some respect ... they saved my sanity, because I was so fearful without being able to admit it to myself, during puberty and high school, so unsure of who the hell I was, who I was supposed to be. I remember that first time I smoked a joint; I just sat back in a chair and felt I was in a big warm blanket. From that point I was always looking for that experience, that feeling of "I'm okay".

'That's what drugs did for me, and it made me feel that way when I wrote, when I tried to be creative. But quite frankly it wasn't too long before it just robbed me of so much ability to think straight, to function on any level. The only reason I believe I can be creative at all today is because I don't do any drugs or alcohol – not from a moral standpoint, but [a] purely physical [one].

'It was a lot like trying to build that superstructure for my creative process with drugs, that it became a part of the superstructure: "When I get high I will be creative and my mind will open up." I'd do something consciously to create this environment where I can write, much like the standards I'd set, "I'll make myself get it done by March." All those things, getting high, time restraints – none of it has worked over the years. Everything I came up with that I thought was going to help me be creative – my best thinking – would serve only to eventually destroy any creative process I had. As time goes on, you not only feel less and less responsible for it, you only hope you didn't destroy it [with] your own stupid ideas of it.'

The extreme sensitivity that Michael experienced during his youth stays with many artists throughout their lives, thus making them more likely to use substances to block out pain. Terri Lyne Carrington has recognised this vulnerability in some musicians: 'Everybody's life is different, as well as their capacity to deal with things. I think there's a lot of heartache in this industry, with very sensitive people, and they hurt a lot. Everybody's capacity to deal with pain is different. Some people turn to drugs to escape. I don't think you can criticise that. I know it's abusive, and it bugs me, but for the most part so many of the great musicians were drug addicts. Maybe they would have been better if they hadn't have been, maybe not. But who knows? I can't do drugs, because I'm pretty spaced without them. I have to have all my senses.'

Don Henley explained how he, too, had used intoxicants to buffer feelings that bothered him: 'I've been creative on alcohol and marijuana and cocaine. I've also had my creativity completely blocked by all three of those things. It depends on how often they're used and how much of them you use at a given time. Ultimately all the ability is there; the music is there inside. The only reason I ever used drugs was to overcome shyness or self-doubt, because writing sometimes requires spilling some of your innermost thoughts and feelings to somebody else, sometimes to somebody you don't even know very well.

'I think those substances were used merely as a little "instant courage", so to speak, to overcome those feelings of "Who am I to be doing this? Why do I deserve to get my feelings and opinions on this blank piece of vinyl that a million people are going to hear?" Some of the drug-taking was to overcome that feeling of un-deservedness, to blunt that somehow, because when you do coke, it makes you feel that everything you're saying is worthwhile and that everybody ought to listen. I didn't use drugs actually to create but simply to buffer those feelings of inadequacy, those feelings of "I don't deserve this".'

How Drugs Become Part of the Artist's Lifestyle

Don Henley said he'd also used drugs to deal with the demands of the music business: 'I sometimes used them to meet deadlines, to stay awake and get the job done – just simply to "do it", because the hours and the pressure were so gruelling. I don't recommend taking drugs to anybody, especially to be creative. All the stuff is in there, you just have to find ways to get it out naturally and take the time. I don't rely on drugs anymore.'

Billy Burnette told of the destructive effects of drugs, but also explained why they have remained part of the rock 'n' roll lifestyle since his father's days: 'My dad [Dorsey Burnette] and just about everyone he ran around with would take pills – diet pills, speed, whatever. It does open up that thing where you can go all night creating and writing. I know he wrote a lot of good songs on it, and a lot of people who I know have, too, and also without it, so I don't think it really matters. It's just something you get a dependency on where some entertainers feel that they've got to have it, whatever it is – drink, pills, toot – before they go on. It's all in their minds. In my dad's day, they would be on the road and not have any nights off, so that's where a lot of them got started, [being] on the road and you're feeling bad. They used every excuse in the world.

'Before I go on, I like to have a little shot of brandy to loosen me up. I don't like to get out there before I go on, but a little drink is nice to calm me down, because it is a kind of an atmosphere when you play for people. We've seen the abuse and what that's done to you. I think it was a big part of why I lost my dad in 1978. He was 46 and he had rocked pretty hard in this business, on top of the rollercoaster ride. I think [musicians] need that escape more than people in other professions. You're not really ever secure; when you've hit the big time, you want to keep that going. That rollercoaster effect is what drives people nuts. I started thinking I was doing damage to my body when I was in my early to mid-twenties. I always used to like to take a pill before I went on, because I felt I needed an upper. I knew it was wrong, but it made me feel good. But I finally got over that. And then when my dad died, I felt like, I want to be around a lot longer than my dad.'

Keith Richards, a former heroin addict, discussed the way drugs become part of a musician's life: 'I never took drugs with the idea that they were going to make me play better, and I think for most musicians the drug thing is a high-risk hazard of the game. If you're working 350 days a year and you're absolutely knackered and there's a little old guy on the show with you playing in the other group and you're thinking, I've got to drive 500 miles tonight and do two shows tomorrow, you look at him and say, "How do you do it, man?" "Well, you take a couple of these." And it starts off like that. Charlie Parker used to have to deal with guys who shoot up and were thinking how that's going to make them play better. And that always bothered him.

'That's also the thing I've had to deal with: "Hey man, you've got to take this." It's just the way I am that I can take a certain amount of stuff more than other people. The creative thing cuts through that, unless you waste yourself too much and too long and then you realise some of the contacts are not quite working, so then you give it up. It's just a matter of knowing yourself, which most people don't; they want to emulate somebody else.'

Just as young musicians often embrace the musical legacy of certain artists, some, as Keith pointed out, try to take on their heroes' self-destructiveness as well. These fledgling musicians mistakenly think they have to do the drugs their musical heroes did in order to play like them. Robert Burke Warren has seen this problem among players he has known: 'Some people think they have to take the same drugs as their favourite musician did, so they can be more like them. If they can't *play* like their idols, they can at least get the drug addiction right.'

Side Effects of Drug Use

Peter Erskine has seen how drugs and alcohol have stunted numerous musicians' creative potential: 'People who have gotten heavily into drugs and drinking definitely hit a plateau with their creativity. I can't think of anyone who's a heavy drug user who's gone beyond that great promise; they just crank out what they're doing. In the early part of a person's involvement with that stuff, maybe some marvellous creative demons can be unleashed, because of the inhibition factor, since it makes a lot of concerns, the ego, and pain [go away]. If the musician feels he's being freer or more creative, that can let out a lot of creativity. Shortly thereafter it doesn't go much further.'

Another physical and mental side effect some musicians mentioned is a total malaise in regard to creativity and just about everything else. Dolette McDonald said: 'Drugs make me lazy. When I was doing drugs and drinking, that's all I wanted to do. If I got a gig during that time, I'd do the gig and have a great time. I'd be real creative and involved in it, but if someone didn't call me for a gig, I wouldn't care. I'd just be stoned, nothing mattered.'

Tony Williams agreed that drug use creates inertia rather than art: 'At some point drugs and alcohol can loosen up a person and you can get ideas. But on a regular basis, no, I think that those things can be really destructive. You can have a drink and get loose and get funnier and get friendlier with people, and in music you can think of ideas. But I couldn't write music drunk; I couldn't play drunk. I have played after three or four glasses of wine and gone onstage, and I don't really like that. With drugs, too, there was a time when I used to smoke grass, and I thought grass put you in another head space and you have these wonderful inspirations, but a lot of it is self-indulgence. There's nothing wrong with self-indulgence if you know where to do it. So if you're always doing grass, then you lose perspective on where you are, and grass seems to take away drive and ambition. You become really complacent and self-absorbed.'

Robin Le Mesurier spoke of how insidious drug dependency can become: 'When I first started smoking dope, I used to think everything I did was wonderful. I used to talk to my mum about this, and she'd say, "One day, you'll realise that it's putting everything behind rose-coloured spectacles." I didn't believe her until I realised smoking dope took over so much. I couldn't go to sleep without a joint, I used to have a joint with my tea in the morning, and it just took over completely. I became so apathetic and lazy. I didn't write a song for nearly two years. I was just happy to let things go by. I then realised I was being an idiot; nothing was getting done; I wasn't being creative.'

Other physical problems related to alcohol and drugs are well known to all who've overindulged. Of course, musicians are not exempt. George Harrison told me about a particularly raucous Travelling Wilburys session that occurred the evening before our interview: 'It's like if you have a few beers and you get all excited – like last night. We had great fun and it sounded groovy, but at the same time, the next day you've got a hangover and you're all messed up.'

In the heyday of the seventies, cocaine became many musicians' drug of choice. To begin with, it appeared to stimulate the senses, but before long it actually had the opposite effect. In my experience, it numbed the emotions and took me further away from my feelings rather than putting me in touch with them. Perhaps even more destructive is the delusion of grandeur it gives its users. Jackson Browne discussed the drug's other detrimental effects: 'When I started doing coke, it was for fun and was always very casual. Then there was a time when I used it more and more. While I was doing a certain record, I would go and score my coke and try my best not to get involved in a conversation. Then the first thing that happens, you get loaded and begin to talk. I would think, I'm going to get home and play my piano. I was very young. Eventually you wind up years later, you're doing coke, and you have no such priorities. And you're sitting there remembering all the times you stayed up actually intending to write a song and you wound up solving the world's problems and feeling terrible at 11 o'clock in the morning and wrecking the next two days because you can't recover from it. It turns out I had to stop using any kind of drug at all to ever get any time to write.'

Phil Collins recalled a telling anecdote about the debilitating effect of drugs: 'It's so easy to get diminishing returns. I have [used drugs]; certain albums are a bit of a blur, not a blur that I don't remember anything; I just wish that I hadn't been so uptight. I know myself now, I know my capabilities, and I know I can't do it, so I don't do it. I haven't smoked for years. Coke and stuff, I just cannot function on that.

'An experience I had with smoking: It was about 1978 and we were playing in L.A., one of the Forum gigs and a guy came up to me and said, "I've got this Hawaiian stuff, just one puff, you don't need anymore." So of course we had two puffs, we went onstage, and there's a song we used to do – most of the Genesis songs were more story-oriented, so if you lost the thread, you lost it. So I started this song. I was standing there and the verse was coming at me and I thought, God, what am I going to sing? And just at the last possible second my mind took it away and I knew what to sing. I was in a cold sweat. So I vowed from that point, no more.'

Ian Wallace remembered his early experiences with drugs and described how he, like others, discovered their deadening effect on the creative drive: 'Hashish was so powerful at first; it opened up all kinds of things. I'd just lie there and fly. Listening to music was just absolutely amazing. You could get into the music so much – every note became a shape – it was really incredible, very influential. It enabled total concentration; it cut off all external influences. You would just get so totally into the sound that nothing else existed. But on the other hand, it took away the desire to do anything about it. After having stopped taking drugs completely, I've realised that for me being under the influence closed many of my creative doors.'

Creating Without Drugs and Alcohol

Guitarist Albert Lee stressed that his playing is much better when he is straight: 'It's taken me a long time to realise this, but I can play so much better without even one beer. I really can operate better if I'm totally straight. It is a lot of fun after having a few beers. It puts you in a different place than you would normally be in, but you're obviously sacrificing a lot of things by putting yourself under the influence of whatever you want to use. I haven't really done much coke over the years, I'm glad to say. I consider myself lucky that way; I don't really have an addictive personality. Like all musicians I've tried most things. I can take it or leave it. I think back to 10 years ago when I would occasionally have some coke before I went onstage; it was absolutely stupid. I'd get onstage and I'd be rigid. You could tell; I'd be playing really stiff and I'd think, what am I doing this for? I soon learned that was a mistake.'

Some musicians, such as Jeff Lynne, told me they'd either never taken drugs or had discovered from their first experiments that they had only an adverse effect on their creative process: 'I've never even tried cocaine, never wanted it. The first joint I ever had was in 1980. I never got into the drug thing at all. [When you create] you've got to be dead straight. I think the most creative part of the day for me is when I first get up and just start working on a keyboard, before [my] brain has had all the crap input. If I ever smoke dope now, I can't play anything. I can only listen back, but as far as performing goes, it just makes it worse.'

Branford Marsalis, like Jeff, has never allowed drugs to become part of his musical life: 'You can always tell when somebody's high; you can tell, you can hear it in their playing. It's not good for the body, it's not good for the mind. It's the real immature adolescent in everybody when they get caught up in that, find the romance in that shit. That's not part of my program. I'm too vain actually, to be honest, that's basically what it is.'

Graham Nash told me he'd tried them all, but he, like many others, has found that drugs deter his creativeness: 'Alcohol has never enhanced any creativity in me. LSD has opened up for me a gate, and there's a sign on the gate that says, "You already knew". Acid to me only reaffirmed basically what I already knew. I used to love to smoke grass, but I don't anymore; I haven't for years now. I used to think that it would put me into a space where I could dream, where I could space out, but I don't think it really enhanced the creative process. Cocaine absolutely did not. Coke blocks most things; it numbs you out to everything.'

Veteran rocker Hank Marvin explained that, in playing music, a clear head as well as unimpaired physical coordination are necessary: 'People were popping pills, even in the late fifties; it was fairly subtle, not all over the place. I never used anything. I drink alcohol, but even with alcohol there is the danger that it can become addictive. Rather than enhancing creativity – from what I've heard of experiments with people under the influence of various drugs in creative situations – their performance is well below par. I suspect that would be the case. I think it's far better if your brain is clear and it can work properly. Creativity is all bound up with things working properly and coordination inside – not only the mechanical aspect of the brain but also the more abstract, creative side – all working together.'

Buddy Guy, who said he has the occasional drink to lose his inhibitions onstage, also emphasised the importance of a strong mind: 'I've never experienced drugs, but I've drunk alcohol. I don't recommend drugs and alcohol to nobody, but I think if you're going to do it, you should use common sense. The strong mind is the most important thing that we can use against whatever we deal with in this short span of lifetime we have. When I learned how to play guitar, I didn't have drugs, alcohol or nothing else. I think I was at my best as being a natural person with nothing in me, with nothing in me telling me, "You're better or you're worse." My first drink made me get the nerve to turn my face around to the audience, to not have that shyness, which led me to have one – but only one – before I play. Some people have walked up to me through my lifetime and said, "You've gotta be doing drugs to play like you play", and I say, "My music is my drugs to me."'

Keith Strickland found that there are other means to achieve the effect many people seek through intoxicants: 'For me, personally, it's really not necessary to use alcohol for writing. I used to find whenever I'd be working on a piece of music for a long time, and I'd sort of got into a rut with it, that altering the way you hear it, the way you perceive it, can be very useful in getting past whatever obstacle is there. You can do that a number of ways; you don't have to use drugs. For example, when I listen back to something I've recorded, by just pitching the tape recorder faster or slower, I hear it differently. Or even a different environment can be effective. I've been known to work on something in the middle of the night, run it off onto cassette, then jump into my car and go driving down the road and listen to it. It's a different environment where you're slightly distracted but you're hearing it still – just altering the way you hear it slightly. Certainly the most reliable way is to let it rest and get a good night's sleep, a good cup of coffee first thing in the morning, then start back and hear it with fresh ears.'

What Keith described are natural ways of changing one's perception. These means can be just as effective as chemicals, without the side effects. For those who have become dependent on intoxicants, letting go of the artificial means can be daunting at first. Of those musicians who had decided to forgo drugs and/or alcohol, many recalled the fear of being unable to create without their crutch.

Christine McVie remarked: 'My experience is that [alcohol] doesn't block creativity; if it's there, it tends to make it come out easier. I used to do drugs, and I still drink wine when I'm writing, sometimes too much and then it really gets blown completely. There was a point when I stopped doing cocaine and I didn't know if I would be able to write without it. It was frightening, because you're lulled into a false sense of grandeur, a state of grace, when you do cocaine. You think you're invincible and everything you write is genius. I did write a lot of good songs on cocaine and a lot of bad ones, too. Then there was the period of coming to terms with not doing cocaine anymore. I didn't actually write for a long time. I was scared to. It's like looking at a virgin canvas and not knowing where to put the first stroke, without the aid of this drug.

'Then I got in tune with myself, with my head and my heart, so now I can write without even thinking about that naughty stuff anymore. It's a very destructive drug. I'm not saying I didn't have a lot of fun, and I would not change it, but I would not go back. I wouldn't do it again. So now all those fears are completely unfounded, because of course if you can write, you certainly don't need any artificial stimulus to bring out what's in there anyway.'

Rosanne Cash made a similar discovery when she ended her chemical dependency and began writing again. 'I used to think [drugs and alcohol] enhanced [the creative process] but now I think they blocked it. Once I got straight, I had a fear that I couldn't write, that being straight would numb out my work. I found that, in fact, drugs and alcohol blocked the access, made it far more elusive. It's not that it can never happen through that, but it makes it more difficult.'

Ironically, many performers who have stopped drinking or doing drugs have found that relaxing and overcoming any fear naturally occurs once you're onstage. Eric Clapton made this discovery: 'To play sober, to play straight, is like going to the dentist, I suppose. You're very, very nervous until the actual thing is taking place, then you call on some reserve inside you which is just waiting. Once you've got past the first couple of songs, you've broken the ice for yourself and for everyone else. I always relax after I've played my first solo.'

Stevie Nicks described how in the past she used drugs and alcohol to assuage her fears of performing. She, like Eric, has found that once onstage she can rid herself of fright simply through performance: 'In the beginning, [stimulants] made you brave. You're scared to walk onstage in front of a bunch of people. Last night [performing at a club] in front of only 200 people, my knees were knocking together. I was holding onto the microphone and my hand was shaking because I was so nervous. The old days to get away from that you have a drink, or whatever anybody does, and you got brave and so you don't have to experience that terrible fear. I get terrible stage fright ... where I'm very, very nervous. The last 10 minutes before I go on, my hands are really shaking to the point of having a lot of trouble working with my makeup or anything. It hits me about 15 minutes before we go on. I'm almost sick to my stomach and it's difficult for me. It used to be that you'd have a shot of vodka and tonic and you'd calm down.

'[But] the second I'm onstage [I realise that] I'm not nervous anymore. I think I'm going to be, I think I'm going to be nervous all the way through the song, but I'm not. The second I walk out, and the second I start to sing, it just goes away, and I'm totally confident. I know now that once I'm out there, I'm fine. That's probably why in the old days people did start doing drugs and stuff because they were simply afraid. Then that becomes a habit; you think you absolutely can't do it without it.

'A lot of us realise we're really lucky to be alive. The ones of us who did make it pretty much cherish the fact that we are alive. You have to learn if you can't depend on yourself without [chemicals], you might as well stop doing it and go to something else, because it isn't worth dying for.'

In the past Stevie used chemicals not only to get through performances, she said, but as a crutch for writing: 'As far as being creative, [chemicals] made you feel that you were braver, so you were more likely to say more, to write down more, to give away more of the secret or to maybe say too much, and that's the vicious circle of drugs and alcohol. You think it's making you better and in the long run it's not. It's taking away the actual essence of what you started out to do.'

Stevie also spoke of her difficulties adapting to a creative life without drugs: 'It's hard to adjust back; it's hard for everybody. Some people have and some haven't, and I wonder sometimes who will be the ones ... I know we will lose a few more and I think, thank God, it's not going to be me. Because I'm definitely going to be sitting in my rocking chair on my porch somewhere when I'm 80 years old, and I'm not going to be one of those people who they have a TV special on, and people sit around and cry. But it is difficult, and probably will always be difficult to accept this whole life in a different way. Because for so long it was lived under that dream cloud, dream child world of different kinds of drugs.'

Bonnie Raitt had recently stopped using drugs and alcohol and was on the brink of recording her hugely successful album *Nick of Time* when she discussed this change in her life: 'I am right on the precipice of being about to create something new, to come from this new being that I am. It's exciting but terrifying. I'm afraid of being mediocre, which, if you're a little bit loaded, you don't have to worry about. I think too much and judge too much, and alcohol suspended that for a while, so it actually freed me up. Now I have to tap into a wellspring I haven't seen yet.'

Bernie Larsen has found that his creative life is much

richer without drugs: 'I was never a regular drinker; it nullifed my creativity. With coke, I would get so withdrawn; I don't think I ever had a creative moment on cocaine. Now [without drugs] the writing is more consistent. I don't know if the drugs actually blocked that off or if they gave me less stamina. Like life, some days are like walking uphill, and if you do something to your body to make it even harder to deal with the challenges of everyday living, your will to progress is defeated. It's easier to have the understanding that it's not always there, because sometimes it's not there. There's nothing going on and it's fruitless to say, "I'm going to write a song right now." Drugs give some people the carefreeness to let stuff happen; some people think too much about things, and creativity requires a lack of thinking about a lot of things. I know when I took LSD, it changed my life. It literally changed how I thought about mankind and God. It can enlighten you, but the abuse of it is destructive.'

Graham Bell told me how his creativity has been enhanced by going straight: 'I feel I went backward by getting involved in drugs and alcohol. I know now I took away from this God-given talent to sing and write songs and create. I [mistakenly] thought, I'll get much more creative if I take cocaine. I started smoking dope and found that it put me on a different space or made me feel groovy or hip. I didn't see a lot of damage in those days.

'I think now to operate purely natural, I've found I'm singing much better and I'm playing much better. Everything's falling much more into place. I get up in the morning and play my guitar and get into that space. I used to think I'd have to smoke a joint or have a drink to get into that space; now I've found I don't. I just start playing and the music puts me there, and I'll feel very good, as if I've been uplifted out of my everyday trivia.'

Mike Rutherford, like Graham, has found that one's own natural state of being is more conducive to creating: 'For myself [drugs] have been a destructive force, without bringing any good. That's the main thing – writing and creating have always felt like such a natural thing. It's like you need to cleanse your body to do it. It's the feeling of purity I think.'

John Mayall cataloged the changes in his creative life since he stopped drinking: 'The only [drug] I've ever done is drink. I've had 17 years of drinking. I didn't start drinking until I was 35 and already established in the music business; it was something that was the thing to do. I had never had a drink before; it was the novelty of it. Everybody was drinking in the seventies so I joined in, and that took over for quite some years.

'I stopped drinking five years ago. I've never smoked a joint, never taken pills or cocaine. I don't think that any kind of stimulant can possibly be of any use to anyone. They can delude you. I've found after having the experience of using alcohol in the middle period of my musical career and seeing the contrast between the beginning and now, that now is a completely different focus. Everything is a lot clearer. You can actually get to the point and play better music because you know what you're doing. You're not getting blunted in any way.'

Anthony Kiedis has also found his creative power replenished and restored since he cut out drugs and alcohol: 'It's a strange thing. When I first began writing songs with this band, I was taking drugs and alcohol and it didn't really seem to bother me, depending on the combination of whatever kind of drug or alcohol I was on. Sometimes I would find a combination that I could work under those conditions, but then very quickly it got to the point where any time I was under the influence of any drug or alcohol, I had no inspiration to write an honest song. Anything I did attempt to write just seemed very empty and meaningless, and it basically went nowhere. I could sit down and be stumped for hours at a time trying to write something if I was under the influence, and so it became a very negative element of the band – the fact that any of us were taking drugs and alcohol. When we stopped, it was just like taking off the handcuffs and anything we've written since then has been the strongest stuff we've ever done. And it's much more fun this way as well.'

Ringo Starr gave up drink and drugs after using them for more than 20 years. Listening to him talk about his new life was very inspirational: 'I think that what you find is that you've spent so much time and energy, which you didn't realise at the time, getting drunk or stoned. I never realised it because it was a natural thing. As soon as I opened my eyes I was on a roll to eventually black out in the end – that's how bad it got for me – because I couldn't get high enough anymore. I couldn't get drunk enough anymore; and I couldn't cope enough to do anything, so I would just fold up and pass out. For me, I was caught solidly in the trap for 15 years. It started getting bad in 1975, and it was horrendously worse by '88.

'[When you stop drugs and alcohol] you have to learn to live with your emotions, because you're not putting them to sleep anymore. That's all drugs and alcohol do, they cut off all your emotions in the end; you don't have any, or the one major emotion you have is probably anger. Cocaine is fabulous for anger. You just get into a rage over nothing if things aren't going right in your drunken stupor. In the end, even grass stops your emotions. Grass was the one thing I always thought was safe and everybody should have, from the old hippiedom, because I'm an old hippie from the sixties. But grass is the same emotional blocker as alcohol or cocaine. It just takes you off into another land. For years, I quite liked that land; in fact I loved that land!

'In the end I wasn't a purist. I would take the full cocktail of anything – including the pills, the downers and uppers – without a care really. Just my brain told me I needed to have it bent out of shape, and I got caught in a terrifying trap that to be creative I had to be on some substance. And what happened to me was in the end there was no creativity at all coming from me, because I was too busy taking the shit. That was the most important thing in my life, as soon as my eyes opened, my brain started telling my body it needed something. I always thought I was having so much fun, but it was very painful even at the time. It's a sham you put on because you're lost; you're actually a lost soul for a while.

'What you find out now, which is great, is that you have so much time to live, so much more time to do anything, just getting up in the morning is a thrill – not staying up all night. The two reasons I stayed up mostly all night was, one, because I convinced myself I was an insomniac and [two] because I was frightened of the dark! Very shortly after I stopped drinking and taking drugs, I realised I wasn't frightened of the dark and I wasn't an insomniac. The best part of it for me, of what I've done, is after seven months I put a band together and went on tour, and I've done some sessions with people, and I'm just starting to work again. In the 22 months [I've been sober] the creativity is so exciting. I proved I could stand in front of an audience again; I can play. I had a few resentments because even friends weren't asking me to play anymore with them. And as a drunk, you get great resentments. Now I've signed up with a TV production company, and I've written some songs with another artist. I'm painting, taking watercolour and drawing lessons. It's such a beautiful life now, and it's only been 22 months. It's a wonderful life if you choose it.'

What is it in human nature that finds it so difficult to be in the 'here and now', to have that feeling of oneness? So much time is spent running away from ourselves and getting 'out of it'. Is it the search for our maker, looking for something out there rather than within? I have found that it is only in actually facing life that we transcend it and get to the core of our nature. I used to think I could get that feeling of oneness only when I drank alcohol or took certain drugs. Now I believe that we can find unity by expressing our inner selves, by being creative – something we all have the potential to do.

Chapter 7

THE CREATIVE POTENTIAL

'THE NET WITH WHICH YOU CAPTURE [CREATIVITY] IS
MADE UP OF THE THREADS OF YOUR ALERTNESS.'
JONI MITCHELL

Since researching the creative process in musicians and
witnessing their creativity, I have wondered whether
most people have the potential to be creative. Does
everyone have the capacity to experience that peak? I came
to the conclusion that each human being has his or her own
unique gift. Some have more of an obvious talent than
others, but everyone has some natural means of expression.
It is up to each of us to find our gift and to actualise it. This
leads me to believe that the most important question is not
whether we are creative, as in 'How do I get creative?' or
'Am I creative?' The question should really be, 'How do I get
more in touch with myself, my unconscious, my truth?'

Once the blockages from trauma and self-doubt are
released, we can start to get in touch with what our actual
gift is, our way of self-expression. It might not be something
that will have a tangible end result, like a painting or

sculpture, but it will be in tune with our inner nature. Creativity is the expression of what lies in the depths of our feelings. Psychologist Rollo May confirms: 'If you do not express your own original ideas, if you do not listen to your own being, you will have betrayed yourself.'

Finding One's Gift

Most of the musicians I interviewed had given thought to the universality of creative potential. The majority, in fact, believe that all people can express creativeness in one way or another. Some pointed out that they were fortunate to have found their own gift early in life and not had to struggle to discover it. Steve Winwood was one of those who mentioned this: 'Everybody has the potential to be creative; creativity manifests itself in different ways. Some people are lucky enough to be able to channel it directly into one field; probably other people have their talents diffused through lots of areas and can't immediately realise what their true talent is. Often people have a talent without knowing it.'

It is also important to accept one's gift once it is discovered, rather than be deluded by grandiose expectations. Christine McVie described the frustration inherent in pursuing a path that is not truly representative of one's natural gift: 'If I'm a brilliant songwriter but I'd rather be a gardener, and I'm out there slogging away trying to grow orchids, I'm never going to grow orchids very well. I should really be acknowledging my true gift. A lot of people aren't even aware what their true gift is until they've reached middle age. It's all a question of interpreting our gift and knowing how to use it.'

THE CREATIVE POTENTIAL

There is a difference between those who have a strong creative drive from childhood and those who find it later in life. As Steve Gadd said: 'In some cases it's hard for people to know what their gift is. In my case, I started [playing drums] as a child and it just sort of happened. I didn't have to go through that searching.' Those who find it later in life, as I did, have to take the journey within and release those emotional blocks to find their natural expression. Some never find it, tell themselves they are not creative, and then close the book.

Eric Clapton talked about the blocks to finding one's unique gift: 'Everyone has the capacity to be creative, but the gift comes in recognising it or being able to channel it. My gift is that I have 10 fingers that work. I have the capacity and that ability, but if I didn't have those 10 fingers, I wouldn't be able to play the guitar. Maybe I'd channel it somewhere else. Some people have the gift of being able to manifest it and others haven't. They are blocked in some way, maybe mentally or physically or spiritually.'

Bernie Larsen gave some good advice on becoming creative later in life: 'Everybody has the potential to be creative in their own way and in their own time. There are some people who write more complicated things at 15 than other people would at 30. But if the person at 30 had the determination and the support, they could achieve that. If you do something every day, one day is going to come along and you're not consciously trying to achieve it, and you're going to let go and get a little trickle of it accidentally. It's a gift that everybody has – it's just there. There is a rhythm to life and anybody can jump on that rhythm and then go with the flow.'

Many musicians feel that being creative is part of being human. Stephen Bishop said: 'Creativity is God-given. I believe everybody has the power to be creative and do creative things. Creativity goes in so many different areas, it's not just writing songs or plays or books.'

Nurturing One's Creative Impulse

After listening to so many musicians describe their lives, and through my own experiences, I truly believe nurturance plays a tremendously important part in having the courage to be creative. It takes fearlessness to actually be who you really are and to listen to that small voice within. By cutting through all the illusion, conformity and indoctrination, we can get closer to what we feel. On the other hand, by adhering to the status quo, one can often suppress what is felt inside. Jung speaks of the importance for us all to get in touch with our own truth; by being true to our inner being, we will automatically become more creative: 'Follow that will and that way which experience confirms to be your own, i.e., the true expression of your individuality.' Creativity is the expression of our truth, which can also be the universal truth.

Steve Jordan stressed how early encouragement is an important key to fostering creativity: 'It's a little easier for some people, but everyone has the potential to be creative. All you need is support. One day when I was 12 or 13, my mom gave me this little plaque that I still have in my kitchen. It says "Think Big". That changed my life. Everyone needs that to get to where they want to go.'

The importance of nurturing creativeness was also

touched on by Huey Lewis: 'Unless people are encouraged to be creative, they tend to be less creative. Creativity can be trained out of you. You need to be taught to just run with that sort of stuff.'

Lindsey Buckingham emphasised that societal structures are set up to discourage creativeness: 'All children are creative; it's just that 95 per cent get it capped off. The instincts go away, and people are channelled into certain ways of being, of thinking. I think it can be redeveloped, but I think most people's sense of creativity has been stomped out of them. Everyone can come up with something creative, but maybe they just dismiss it. A lot of being creative is being committed enough to what you're doing to follow through on it. The seed is only the beginning; it's the work that you put into it, and putting yourself on the line to actually follow through.'

Not all societies place emphasis on the material over the creative, however. Paul Kantner, who spent much time in Nicaragua under the Sandinista government, described how creativity was encouraged there culturally: 'Everyone has elements of creativity. Everybody isn't a great piano player or great singer. Some people have to study it, and some people can't get it after studying for a hundred years. But everybody has some capability of being creative. What does the word *creative* mean? Expressing yourself in some fashion beyond your normal workday.

'In Nicaragua they encouraged everyone to write poetry. It was a government programme to teach the people how to write, to express what they felt about their life, to examine it, and to see what could be done about it in tangible practical terms. I have books of poetry from Central America. It's some of the most beautiful and some of the most mundane, but the fact is that somebody who just picked corn all day and went to sleep and got up and picked corn all day for 30 years can all of a sudden write beautiful poetry.'

Nurturance Breeds Self-confidence

Encouragement can allow dormant creativeness to emerge, Phil Collins has discovered: 'There is probably something in most people that just never gets tapped, or they don't think about it, or they don't have the opportunity. For example, every year the Prince's Trust used to hold a holiday camp for a week in Norfolk. There were 400 kids there, between the ages of 15 and 20, from Liverpool, Manchester, Aberdeen, Edinburgh, and so on, all potential football gangs. The purpose was to encourage any natural talents they had. They were taught how to apply themselves, how to get on with other people, how to apply for a job. There were all kinds of different workshops they could go to throughout the week.

'I was a trustee, so I'd go up there on the last day. I'd get all the musicians together in the music workshop and form a band for that particular day. Some were musicians, but most of them had never touched an instrument before. They were encouraged to pick up something and play, and from there maybe they would take an interest in it. We learnt a couple of songs which we'd perform that night. There was one guy there, very introverted, and during the week he had plucked up enough courage to get up and sing in front of these 400 kids. He'd never done anything like that before. The reception this bloke got was absolutely fantastic because they'd seen him get strength through the week. They knew what he was going through, and they went mad.'

Jason Farrar, who has never allowed his blindness to deter him in any way, feels strongly that all people can be creative – if they learn to have self-confidence: 'Everyone has their own special ability and that's wonderful – whether they know it or not. Some people don't believe in themselves and so they can't see the special abilities that they have. It's a matter of really believing in yourself and knowing you can do it.'

Koko Taylor described the effect of self-confidence on the creative drive: 'People can do whatever they put their heart to; they can be creative. But there's a lot of people who don't have confidence and don't believe in themselves. You hear people say, "I wish I could sing", or "I just can't sing", or "I just can't write", or "I can't do this or that". But they really don't know that they can't do it, because they never tried. Sometimes when you think you can't do something and you go ahead and put your mind and heart to it and do it, you end up doing it better than a lot of people. You've got to have plenty of energy to hang in there. I feel really good about what I'm doing and that's what makes it come out right.'

Peter Gabriel gave several examples to show why he believes that anyone who gains confidence can be creative: 'I'm absolutely certain that everyone has the potential to be creative. The example I used to use, which isn't perfect, is that if I could convince someone in the street, anyone, that their survival was dependent on producing something very creative – whether it was music, painting, or whatever – if they took me seriously, then they would find they were creative. I'm sure music, poetry, painting, all of the arts, are languages – no more. Some people are more adept at speaking them, but no one is excluded or no one need be excluded. If a baby is dependent on drawing to get his milk, then he would become as talented as possible. I remember reading about some music students in Czechoslovakia who were hypnotised into thinking they were their favourite composers. They sat down at their instruments and didn't play new sonatas or whatever, but sat down with a self-assurance that they lacked left to their own devices, and that enabled them to really raise their standard. We put our own limitations on nine times out of 10.'

The Will to Create

The drive to create is the compelling force behind self-expression. As Peter Gabriel said, we invent our own limitations, and I believe that part of this is due to a lack of motivational drive, as well as self-assurance. Ron Wood says: 'Everyone has the potential but they don't all have the drive within themselves to realise they have something. I made Jagger do a drawing. He always said, "I can't draw." I told him, "Just do a drawing for me." He did one and it was the most fantastic drawing. He may never do a drawing again, but I wish he would. I think everyone's creative, but it's a gift that makes you keep turning the work out.'

Since society is not structured to help people find their creative gifts, it can prevent them from looking for them on their own. Keith Richards pointed out the difficulty of discovering artistic opportunities in one's life: 'Everybody has the potential to be creative. If I can do it, anybody can do it!

It's a matter of finding out how to tap into that creativity. A lot of people are not even given the chance to find out; they're not exposed to something that they could be innately brilliant at, they never come across the actual subject. The way things are set up, you do this, you go to school, you get out, and you go to work. If you're willing to accept that as it is, you're probably going to miss where your creativity lies. It's a lot to do with being in touch with yourself.'

As Keith said, it is that element within some people that allows them to break through the status quo rather than blindly follow society's rules and accept one's humdrum lot in life. John Mayall stressed the intrepidity required to follow a different path: 'Perhaps everybody has got a potential to contribute something. It's just a case of whether they will recognise it within themselves and have the courage to go out and say, 'I'll develop this and see if I can do something with it,' rather than just get nailed in a slot and get stuck with that for the rest of your life.'

In addition to the courage needed to find the creative path, an artist also must fearlessly face creative challenges throughout life. Tony Williams described his continual attempts to take his own creative expression a step further: 'I'm always reaching for something. That's what I think my mandate is, what my role is. I am supposed to be reaching for things; I'm not supposed to just be repeating what I've done. I can repeat things and I do, but it's no good unless I'm in the process of reaching.'

Vernon Reid remarked that some established musicians don't live up to their artistic promise: 'There are different levels and types of creativity. Everybody has the potential to be creative, but not everyone puts the time in, and so will be unable to fulfil that potential. That's the unfortunate thing. Some people don't allow themselves to dream beyond just the mundane, even some people who are artists don't allow themselves to dream and just do things. They are afraid of the avant-garde, doing something that will cost them their gig, cost them a regular pay cheque, or make their record fall off the chart. Creativity is not concerned with any of that, it really isn't.'

As Vernon Reid observed, even those who discovered their artistic gifts early in life need courage to be creative and to take creative risks. Eric Clapton said: 'It's like staring into the face of God sometimes. It's very frightening. You're kind of naked a lot of the time and afraid of exposing yourself. You're very vulnerable.'

Musicians must continually call on their inner strength to avoid the traps that society, or the recording industry, has set for them. Psychologist Eric Fromm wrote of this fearlessness: 'Every act of birth requires the courage to let go of something, to let go of the womb, to let go of the breast, to let go of the lap, to let go of the hand, to let go eventually of all certainties, and to rely only upon one thing: one's own powers to be aware and to respond – that is one's own creativity.'

Sinéad O'Connor described her continual struggle to buck the system. To remain 'pure' artistically, she has refused to be swept up in the opulent lifestyle that can sometimes deaden the risk-taking nature of the creative drive: 'The people in the recording industry are so materialistic that it's hard to actually try and do what you're doing. I'm so against the whole stardom thing – the limousines and all that bullshit – because it doesn't belong. It's not right. Artists fall into a trap very easily, then they stop doing their job [of being creative].

You get tempted by things like that, and it's very easy to fall into it. Why do you need to drive around in a big, flashy car? What are you saying to people by doing that? I've had huge fights with people over that. I'm severely disliked by a lot of people because of things like that – they think you're just being a bitch, which is really unfair.'

Lindsey Buckingham described feeling that his artistic ideals were compromised by Fleetwood Mac's massive commercial success. He insisted on following up the chart-topping pop album *Rumours* with the experimental and much less commercially successful *Tusk*. 'I had a problem with the [success of] *Rumours*. I thought it was good on some level, but I always thought there was a huge discrepancy between what the album was and how well it was selling. That's dangerous ground when you don't really think what's going on is all that great, that it's way out of proportion. Then you're caught in this machine, the great American axiom of, "If it works, run it into the ground." That's what my thing on the *Tusk* album was. The idea was to say there's no way I'm going to be involved in making a *Rumours II*. I've had mixed feelings about the whole Fleetwood Mac experience. If I was to do something that I really believed in, and it were to do that well, I would have a much stronger sense of having done something that I could get behind.'

The Many Faces of Creativity

Along with the willingness and courage to find one's creative potential should come the acceptance of the different forms it may take. As Queen Latifah said:

'Everyone has some type of creativity. They just have to discover it. Some people have a lot of different ways of being creative or a lot of different forms of creativity within them. Some people don't have many, but they have to find that one or those two things that they are really talented at.'

Frank Foster observed: 'Everyone has a mission. Everyone is here for a purpose, and not everyone has the same purpose. The person who has the ability to be a carpenter or has the ability to be a builder doesn't necessarily have what I have, and I don't have what they have. Each individual has something, some aptitude or some ability, with which they can serve humankind. I found mine as a musician.'

Creativeness can be manifested in many forms. The key is to find the means of expression that enables self-actualisation. Teddy Pendergrass said that he found self-expression through many aspects of his life: 'Being creative is part of me; I do it at every level of life. I do it with my home, I do it with clothes, I do it with singing, with writing, with decorating the home. That is just my thing.'

Ice-T explained how his rebellious outlook enabled him to reach that creative part of himself that no one else saw or encouraged: 'I was always the kind of person who could make it fit, who had ingenuity. Just because somebody told me something couldn't be done, I never accepted it. I had that kind of a creative ability. Not musically creative; that never crossed my mind, because I don't know how to play any instrument, so how was I going to be a musician? I couldn't sing. But poetry was something I had fun with, and I started out making rhymes. Being on the streets, I learned how to rap but not to play music; it was like street slang, and I could fascinate people. The more I fascinated people, the more I could keep people off me. I was in the army when "Rapper's Delight" [one of the first hip-hop singles] came out, and I thought, wow, that's kind of like what I'm doing. I've just got to learn how to do it to music. So I turned the record over and I started saying my rhymes.'

Realising the creative part within and expressing it any way possible can add to one's life, Roger Waters said: 'Everybody has capabilities to be creative at something on some level. Most of us don't realise our potential. I don't think it matters how creative you are or what, so long as you get the opportunity to have the good feeling that makes it satisfying for you.'

Although many non-musicians may feel intimidated by musical instruments, Keith Strickland believes that for them an emphasis should be on using musical means for self-expression rather than performing an accomplished piece of music: 'Anybody can write a song. You just state your intention, basically, say, "I'm going to write a song" and start at one point and end at one point and whatever you do in between. You've just got to have trust that something will occur. I think we're at a really good time now where everybody can do it. The tools are all there; everything's there for you. People are now more open to different forms of music.'

Tony Williams distinguished between the various roles of different creative levels: 'Everyone has creativity; it's just that some people have more of an opportunity for it to come out, or they have the upbringing that allows it to come out, [where] it's not squashed. A lot of people don't develop it or won't develop it. Everyone has talent, but it takes other things along with talent to really be creative, to make it into something. I know guys who play the drums; they have a lot of talent but they don't really play any music. Or people who can write songs but they don't write good songs or great songs. People have talent to pick up a brush and paint a picture, but whether it communicates anything to people is something else. People can be creative, but it's not necessarily anything that somebody wants to see or hear – something that touches people. So there's a difference between talent, creativity, and that other thing that's beyond creativity – the spirit that really touches people.'

The 'spirit' Tony described was something I felt myself when I watched him perform with his quintet. I was completely overwhelmed by the depth of feeling emanating from him. It was as if he were plugged directly into a musical tempo that was magnetised around him. The connection was very powerful. I believe this spirit was derived from his being so in touch with his own unique gift.

Taking Chances

Edie Brickell described an element necessary for finding one's self-expression that I, too, found to play a very important part in discovering my own creativeness: overcoming the fear of looking deep inside. By being too busy and protecting oneself from insecurities, there is no energy left for self-expression.

Edie eloquently remarked: 'Everybody has the potential to be creative. That's why there are so many unhappy people – because they won't do it, they won't let go.

Everyone has their own particular gift. You just have to accept it, "Okay, this is it", then let it take over. Trust it, believe in it. Once you believe in it, it's there for you and you're there for it. I was just lucky enough to stumble onto the path and stay on it and not be so scared. There is fear involved, but once you get over that, you realise what you're doing and your abilities, your potential in life, then it turns into excitement. Letting go of fear, that's what creativity is. It's just all possibilities, creative ways of overcoming fear. The more fear you can release, the more you can allow yourself to be creative and take steps in the direction of your heart. I think you have all the answers right there for you. There are so many means of being creative. Creative is just being yourself, really, letting go of that fear to be who you are.'

Robert Burke Warren also sees how fear can wipe out creativeness: 'Fear is society's tool to make people be like everybody else. Fear is the biggest obstacle to being creative. People with the drive to create don't have that fear, or they're able to surmount that fear and press on. They've been to the belly of the beast and instead of being devoured, they come back out.'

Cece Bullard maintains that fear is the most destructive enemy of the creative process: 'When I'm blocked, which is caused by tension and fear – fear of success, fear of rejection, and all those things tied into your creativity being involved in [the music] business – the flow seems to stop and I just jam up. That's when you have to meditate or something and have faith, which I can't live without, and release all that negative energy and try to let those feelings of creativity come through.'

Phil Collins told me what it was like, as an established musician, to overcome the fear involved in attempting new artistic challenges: 'You sort of push yourself to the edge to see if you can do it, because you want the challenge: if I can learn from it and see if I can pull it off. I had this terrible feeling after *Face Value*, the first album, that that was all I had. I thought, "Will I be able to do this, or will I get up there and nothing happens?" I'm scared as well, so I have to keep going to convince myself that it isn't all gone. It's a personal challenge each time.'

The qualities creative people need to cope with the feeling of being different as children can help them in later life to continually grow artistically. According to Joni Mitchell: 'You have to be able to go out on a limb. What keeps a lot of people from being creative is the fear of failure. In creativity, the accidents and the mistakes and the coincidences – that's what keeps some people from being creative. They're afraid to take chances. They might even be considered creative by some people, but at best they're just copycats. They hear that, they like it, they'll make something like it, they can do that. But to innovate, you have to have a certain kind of fearlessness. It helps if at an early age you got used to being shunned and you survived that. If you had to fight some things in your childhood, you now can stand alone.'

Patty Smyth has found techniques for conquering fear. 'If you just get out of your own way, be fearless about it and not so judgmental, then things happen. I will usually say a little meditation to turn my head off and get out of my way. For me, individually, that's a big part of my being able to let go of the fear and just take the actions and do it.'

Expressing One's True Self

As I discovered, being true to oneself and giving voice to the deepest part within is, in effect, being creative. Many musicians mentioned this in one way or another. Graham Nash said: 'There is an energy that one can tap and call upon. Every choice that I've made which has brought me to this point has been a very simple choice. To me, it is either right or it is wrong. It's a very personal choice, but every choice I've made has been based upon, "How do I feel inside, in my heart?" So I've followed my heart all my life; I've followed my instincts to do what feels good to me. I think my entire life is a song and my whole life is creation. I'm creating all the time. My emotional and physical eyes have to be opened. I feel haunted by things that need to be said. Very often those feelings get triggered by a phrase or something that I see or a feeling that I feel, and I'm haunted until the song gets out.'

Julian Lennon, like Graham, realises the value of being aware of one's true nature. '[Part of creativity] is the awareness of knowing you are being honest and true to yourself. A lot of people skip that fact and get on with life without really finding out what's inside. I have always listened to my inside, checked out my inside thoughts, before doing or saying anything.'

Peter Frampton also said that the key to self-expression lies in finding one's true voice: 'I have to feel in a confident mood. If I don't feel good about myself then how on earth am I going to be able to create something that comes from the heart – and that's the key for me. It has to come from the heart.'

It's a mistake to compare one's own worth or talent to

someone else's. That's what I did, of course, when I compared my own abilities to those of the musicians I knew. Dolette McDonald described feeling creatively inferior to the male superstars with whom she's sung: 'As far as writing, I'm getting better at it and feeling more comfortable doing it. I do have a lot of things to say. I was real intimidated by a lot of people I've sang with, because I've worked for some incredible writers, and my attitude was I could never do that. Then I stopped trying to compare myself to them and started to do what I do. I'm not going to know how good it is until I do it.'

Guitarist Rick Vito stressed the pointlessness of making comparisons: 'Everyone has the potential to be creative on their own level; I think that's what makes you human. Creativity is different for everybody. There are musicians who I listen to, and then I compare their playing to mine, and mine seems feeble, prehistoric. I don't know if I have the potential to play like them – probably not. But someone else might listen to his playing and think it's prehistoric next to mine, and think mine's wonderful. I'm sure that Eric Clapton went through a lot with regard to that very thing: people saying he's God, and yet he's aware he's just a man, he's reasonably good. But he might listen to someone like, say, Django Reinhardt, and think, I'll never be able to do that. And maybe Django Reinhardt was miserable because he got 10 bucks a night and didn't think he was anything special. So it's all relative.'

Ringo Starr discussed feeling overshadowed creatively by the writing team of John Lennon and Paul McCartney: 'The problem that people have is that they think they're not creative enough, or they compare themselves [to others]. I had a very hard time trying to present my songs to Lennon and McCartney. George did, too, before me, trying to present his songs. I had a real hard time. It's a bit off-putting when three guys are lying on the floor hysterically laughing as I'm trying to play my song!'

Willie Dixon viewed every attempt to create as a learning experience: 'People who try for *anything* can gain knowledge from it, and it all depends how much you try to think or try to involve yourself in something. If you involve yourself in something and think about it more, the more ideas can come to you. As these ideas come to you, you can understand them better.'

Conditions Conducive to Creating

I have found there are certain attitudes and conditions that are conducive to the creative process. One of these is ridding the mind of the mundane details of day-to-day life. It's important to find time alone, to just be, to daydream, without getting swept up by everyday existence. Huey Lewis stressed the need to keep one's mind free: 'I don't work best under pressure. For example, I think the real good stuff just comes to you, and those moments are when you have pretty much everything else out of your mind. You're not worried about the day-to-day stuff. A lot of people worry incessantly about the day-to-day stuff and never really try and forget about that. You really have to be empty, or open.'

George Harrison gave the perfect example of people's tendency to allow the mundane to take priority in life. He used the metaphor of 'beggars in a goldmine' to describe how human beings are so caught up in their existence that they fail to notice their inner richness. George recalled our sojourn in India and the number of people who dashed off to shop and flit about. He found it amusing that at the ashram, through meditation and stillness, they could find everything they needed, yet still they looked elsewhere: 'Although we have this divinity, or creativity, within us, it is covered with material energy, and a lot of the time our actions come from a mundane level. There is an expression "beggars in a goldmine", and that's what we are. We're like beggars in the goldmine, where everything has really enormous potential and perfection, but we're all so ignorant with the dust of desire on our mirrors. While we were in Rishikesh, I wrote a song called "Deradune". I never recorded the song, but it was about seeing people going along the road trying to head for this place called Deradune. Everyone was trying to go there for their day off from the meditation camp. I couldn't see any point in going to this town; I'd gone all the way to Rishikesh to be in meditation and I didn't want to go shopping for eggs in Deradune! The verse of the song said, "See them move along the road/ In search of life divine/ Unaware it's all around them/ Beggars in a goldmine".'

Don Henley has given much thought to the creative process. He described five different conditions that better enable one's creativeness to flow: 'I am constantly striving to uncomplicate and focus my life in order to get into a creative state of mind. I don't want to be totally caught up in the busywork or the "business" of making music. To be creative, I don't necessarily want to think about the paraphernalia; that is, I don't want to sit around thinking about drums and guitars and recording. I don't want to have to worry about hassling with the record company. I don't want to worry about touring or performing. To be creative, all those things have to be put into the background.

'A great many people who make popular music have a somewhat narrow focus. Music or the playing of it is their whole life. Consequently, their songs are often not very interesting. Form, these days, very often takes precedent over content. Personally, I try to maintain a broad scope of things that I think about and care about and do. I am involved in numerous things besides music. This sometimes creates conflict for me, but I am learning that the conflict is actually more in the way that I perceive the structure of my life. Often I become so involved in causes of various kinds – political, environmental – that I cannot find time to be quiet and let words and music come to me. I used to feel guilty about this, but I am realising more and more as time passes that these other seemingly unrelated involvements can be the stuff of good, meaningful songs.

'So my life, then, in terms of creativity is a constant struggle to achieve a balance between letting things flow in and letting things flow out. It is extremely important that I receive, process and regurgitate information and insights. The trick is the balance. The difficulty also lies in shutting out the world, in stemming the flow of incoming clutter. This sometimes requires a change of scenery, sometimes not.

'Solitude is also often required but not necessarily absolute solitude. It is not always pleasant to have nothing to listen to except one's own mind. It can be maddening. In Zen they call it "monkey mind". A more modern term for it is "brain chatter". I find that doing menial tasks – gardening, cooking or driving, for instance – can be very relaxing and cleansing. These things tend to clear away petty, worldly cares and allow creative thoughts to surface. Driving is especially good for me. I have written a lot of my material in the car with the cassette player blasting.

'The point is to be able to turn all the joy, sadness, yearning and turmoil that makes up one's daily existence into art, to see the wonder and the irony inherent in all levels of life and to use these things as stimuli. The creative process and daily living are so intertwined, so bound up in one another, that they cannot, for very long, be separated. Living and creating are parallel lines. The problem is how to allocate one's time and to control one's frame of mind. Control and discrimination are also quite necessary as far as what we allow to flow into us.

'[While creating] you feel very confident and calm in a way. It's sort of an excited calm, not beside yourself or you can't get anything done. You must be in tune. You are at one with everything around you, with the universe. It sounds corny, but that's the way you feel. Some days I feel, "This is a good day to write." I feel everything's in balance, everything's in tune, all is right with the world – I can do it. You just have a feeling of well-being. You feel insightful and in tune. When it all starts flowing, there is a sense of euphoria. But you sometimes must wait for those days. You can't force [it]. As Rainer Maria Rilke said, "Patience is everything"!'

One of the points Don mentioned as being very important to the creative process is solitude. It is through finding and accepting solitude that one is able to feel comfortable while delving into the rich material of the unconscious. Many people are afraid of solitude and continually avoid contact with it for fear of loneliness. In the classic volume *Letters to a Young Poet*, Rainer Maria Rilke gave this advice about being creative: 'What is necessary, after all, is only this: solitude, vast inner solitude. To walk inside yourself and meet no one for hours – that is what you must be able to attain.'

Robert Burke Warren explained that being alone is essential for his creative juices to flow. 'Solitude is very important to me. It's your own private ground. I wish I could impose it on myself whenever I want to. When I was a kid, I was never given a concrete rule of what is good and what is evil, so I take it all in and decide for myself. That's become, I think, an unconscious response to everything that goes on around me. I need solitude to do that, and I can't imagine being without it.' George Harrison said simply, 'I like quietness. I tend to write most of my songs in the night when the world goes to sleep for a bit and everything's quiet.'

Michael McDonald warned against building up too much of a structured process, which calls upon the busy mind, when trying to create. 'Lately I've been feeling like I actually have something to lose by involving myself in the process and not coming up with something up to my standards. You're always creating this fictitious superstructure around the creative process and putting on it stipulations, time restraints, standard expectations, attaching to it all this conscious garbage. But it is often itself just about the only conscious contact with that inner part of yourself that you make, where you find you have something to say that is surprising to you, whether it's musical or lyrical. It always has the feeling like you've said something, and somebody else says, "That was genius", and you didn't even remember what you said. So you think, "Oh, well, let me build this situation where I can constantly repeat this." And then all of a sudden you've built this monster for yourself that has nothing to do with the creative process.

'Creativity is not going to adhere to time restraints; it's not going to meet any specific standards you want to put on it. It's like trying to put those stipulations on a three-year-old child, because in a way it's coming from that part of you.'

Mike Rutherford agreed that forcing creativity doesn't work and described the euphoric state that occurs when he is able to open himself up to the muse: 'When I write, if I try too hard it's completely hopeless; nothing happens. It's like you have to free yourself up, and if I think about how it happens, the more I analyse it, the more it pushes it away. A perfect example: if I go in one morning to write with the idea that today I'm going to do something wonderful, nothing happens. If I don't try or think about it, with the attitude of "I'll give it 10 minutes", it all happens. It's frightening, because ideas come so fast. It's a wonderful feeling. You get these moments when you can do no wrong. Everything you play is wonderful.'

Steve Jordan has found a similar predicament when writing. 'Some creation, I don't even know where it comes from, it just happens. I just leave myself open and I'll create. Sometimes there's a drive to create that stifles your creation because you want to create so bad that you tense up and nothing happens. If you just stay open and clear, then you create. When you force things, it doesn't happen. When I just let it happen, being open to all the energy, the better writer I become.'

Joni Mitchell detailed the differing mindsets necessary – and detrimental to – creativity: 'Creativity comes from an urgency to communicate; the gift can be developed in people. Anybody can make something, in that way I think anybody can be creative. The net with which you capture [creativity] is made up of the threads of your alertness. If you could walk through the world with the same attentiveness as you played a video game, for instance, so nothing could bomb you, that's kind of Zen mind. If you're really playing well at a video game and you say, "Oh, I'm playing really well", that will get you, because that's the entrance of the ego. Up until then, you haven't had an ego, you've been no mind. And in no mind, time is huge; but [with] the entrance of one thought, then time is small. So making yourself attractive to creative inspiration, you have to train your ears to be as alert as possible and your eyes as alert as possible, it's a finer tuning.

'If you're too rational, you're not very well equipped [to create]. You need to be able to surrender to the mystic to be good, to be great, to have one foot in divinity, which is the only place that greatness comes from. You can be good, you can write a nice song; there's a lot of nice songs on the radio that don't have one foot in divinity. They can even be huge hits; it depends on your standards of creativity, what that means to you.

'If you're too reasonable, then creativity won't come around in you, because then you're not intuitive, and it requires a great deal of intuition. You need a bit of all of it: you need to be emotional, otherwise your work will be chilly. If you're too emotional, your work will be all over the place. You need to be rational for linear, architectural, orderly, structural work, but if you stay there too long, the stuff will be chilly. You need some clarity to make the thing pertinent. Dylan will write a song and it will have abstract passages and then it will have a direct phrase – like *bam* – directly communicate, and then he'll go back into something more surrealistic.'

Drawing on Emotions to Create

Some musicians described specific instances and techniques that had inspired or encouraged them to write songs. Indeed, many admitted to little tricks of the trade they had learned to entice the muse. One of the strongest motivations to create, according to several artists, is the need to express deeply felt emotions. Once these feelings are manifested in a song, they can touch a listener's heart. Graham Nash described an occasion that moved him and resulted in a song:

'I have to be moved before I write. Like, for instance, I wrote a song about the kids with cerebral palsy who were at the Bridge [School] Benefit that David [Crosby], Stephen [Stills], Neil [Young], Springsteen, Tom Petty, Don Henley and I did. We all got together and did an acoustic concert at Bill Graham's place in San Jose. Seeing the children in their wheelchairs, seeing a little girl cry because she wanted to get out of there and seeing another little guy in his wheelchair move his hand slowly over to hers and make her feel okay – feeling that emotion made me come back. And that same night lying in bed, internalising, thinking what a drag it must be in a prison like that – to have a mind that works inside a body that doesn't – and all of a sudden the words come and the music comes, and I go down to my piano and an hour later this beautiful song that came out of nowhere has been born.

'Physically I can be anywhere, because I have a pencil in my mind that is writing all the time. I thought I would need space and peace and quiet, but when you have three kids, that's a fallacy. So it's going on all the time, and I realised I can be anywhere writing.'

Eric Clapton said he no longer requires pathos to write but finds that other moods are just as valuable: 'I've always put it down in the past to emotional turmoil [that drives me to create]. That's more like a trigger; it sets off something that is actually dormant. It can be something that is triggered off by an outside stimulus like joy. A lot of people think it has to be from something particularly nasty or a problem of some kind, but it isn't necessary, I don't think. It's just something a little out of the ordinary in terms of a mental stimulus, something that makes or breaks your day.'

Certain sounds evoke particular emotions within, according to Jackson Browne. And in his songs, he can express very personal feelings through melody: 'Sound really means something, it suggests something to you. You have to find out what that is, and at the end you've got a song. Or you might think of a phrase that evokes all these feelings that suggest something to you. It really means something [to you personally] but it wouldn't mean that same thing to anybody else, unless you said it in the same context that would bring the feeling about.'

Don Henley has learned to trigger certain feelings to inspire his writing, but he stressed that a balanced emotional state is best: 'As I grow older, I'm learning how to draw on the sum of my past experiences and still maintain a healthy emotional distance. Sometimes, though, I still need to get out in the thick of it, so to speak, in order to trigger certain buried emotions. I sometimes have to work myself into a state whereby certain things that I have repressed can float to the surface. However, too much wallowing in emotion can ... backfire. Too many broken romances, too much pain and suffering, and some switch inside simply cuts off. One must remain open, not necessarily naive or innocent, but hopeful. Otherwise, after a while, nothing comes out.'

Kirsty MacColl said that she looked for a centre point in her emotional life from which to create: 'If I'm incredibly depressed, I can't write at all, and if I'm really happy, I wouldn't bother to write. I'd go out and do the gardening, so there has to be a kind of middle ground.'

Anthony Kiedis finds inspiration to write both within and without: 'By experiencing life to its fullest – the extreme spectrum, emotionally speaking – that's what gives me the creative impetus. That's what gives me feelings on the inside, just awareness of the world really. Sometimes I feel most creatively inspired when I'm outside. There was a time when Flea and I took a special trip to the south of Mexico just to write songs for an album we were about to do. I would go climb over these cliffs and sit in the rocks by the ocean. As I sat there, I had very little distraction from people or from cities or anything like that and I was able to just feel what it was that I feel about the world and write it down. I think other creative sources are just your emotional centres. When something happens in your life that really stimulates a specific emotion, I think you're inclined to write about it. If you're really feeling good about this or that, you might be inclined to write about it, or if something is a real bum-out in your life, then you'd write about that.'

Sinéad O'Connor uses her intense emotions to 'dictate' her songwriting. 'My life is very turbulent emotionally, and that's not necessarily bad, but things happen constantly from one end of the day to the other, so I'm constantly in the state of having to work things out and having to figure out what's going on, or what kind of thing I'm supposed to be getting from it, or what I am meant to learn from a specific situation. Usually it's when something turbulent is going on that you have to work it out in your head and then get it onto a piece of paper, so you can look at it and say, "Yeah, that's how I feel." You can look at it and it makes you feel aligned; you feel as if you've expressed yourself.'

Creative Tricks of the Trade

Michael McDonald described the process – or, rather, the 'non-process' – of invoking his muse: 'When you've worn yourself out with self-criticism until you can't stand to hear that voice in your head anymore, asking you why can't you do this, and all your fears have been exhausted about it, you go into a kind of trance. You finally relax into this endorphin state. You have that feeling you've got nothing to lose. Typically what I'll do is just mumble into a 90-minute cassette. I almost try to put myself in that trance state, which means putting down anything that comes through my mind musically or lyrically. More times than not, when I find something I really feel good about, I wasn't even aware of putting it down. I'll take that tape and drive around town listening to 90 minutes of garbage, picking out the gems. I believe that's where I'm going to find the best music I'm going to write – by accident.'

Vernon Reid finds it effective to 'relax' into a mind-set ripe for creativeness. 'I can put myself into a state where I can relax, and maybe I'll just wait. That's the thing about creativity; part of it is the waiting. You can exercise creativity, because it is an ability – it's an ability that can be honed and coaxed into happening.'

Stephen Bishop, as is his way, described his songwriting technique as a combination of fun and work: 'There are different stages: the fun stage is sitting around and goofing off and coming up with ideas. That's the fun part: no hassle, very relaxed. Then there's the organisation stage, which is also creative, where it's putting all our thoughts together into one cohesive unit and making it work. That's actual work; you've got to sit down and turn off the TV and get into it, which is hard for me. I'm a funster, I love to have fun. I go from one thing to another and say, "What can I do now that gives me fun?" It is fun to write once you're into it, but getting into it is not always fun.'

Stevie Nicks has her own unique system of songwriting, which she explained, along with her technique for tapping into the muse: 'I recently wrote six songs when I went home to Phoenix for about 15 days. I go from writing in my journal to typing out some ideas on the typewriter. I make it into a full-on stanza poem. It's really fun for me because I just put on music that I like that's got a good beat and makes me feel good and then I type along to the beat. I just read the words and put it into rhyme and then I'll take that paper to the piano and just start writing, and it either happens or it doesn't. Usually if I get it pretty complete on the paper before I get it to the piano, then it's usually real easy. If I go to the piano without anything, with just an empty piece of paper and a pencil, then it's harder. But I do that sometimes. I'll just sit down and I'll play a chord and I'll just write a line, like say, "the white-winged dove", then I'll play a chord, or a couple of chords and I'll start humming something.

'I have all my writing tapes, where you hear the very beginning, where I started with "Gold Dust Woman" or "Dreams", and you hear them evolve. All it is, is a trial-and-error thing, and if you're determined enough … I feel that you have to keep doing it and not give up. I tell people all the time that you should keep a journal, even if it's just, "I had a terrible day today and I don't want to talk about it, love Stevie", or "I dreamt last night …" Even if it's just three sentences, because at the end of five or six days, you would have created a habit and you will find that over a month that you have a whole story growing. Whether it's just for your own memories, so you can go back at any age, or if you are a writer or a singer, or some part of the creative business. You can be creative – anyone can be creative if they want to – you just have to want to.

'If I've done something that I thought was good that day, then I can relax. If I haven't done anything that I feel is very special, then I have a lot of trouble sleeping – I feel almost guilty. Sometimes I'll get out of bed in the middle of the night and go into my office and put the paper in the typewriter and get out my books that are inspirational to me – Oscar Wilde, Keats, Canadian poets, European poets – and I'll just open a page and read something, and I'll say, "Okay, this is my information for today, this is what is supposed to come through to me today", and I'll close the book, so I'll never be able to find that page again, and I'll think about it for a while, and then I'll probably write for one or two hours, then I'll be able to go back to bed. I'll take my writing to bed with me and put it right by my pillow so when I wake up the next morning I can read it. And everything will be alright.'

Phil Collins explained the group process that Genesis used to compose songs and emphasised the need for trust among band mates: 'When Tony, Mike and me – the guys in Genesis – go into the studio, we have nothing written. Nowadays we just keep all the songs we've written for ourselves and we go in and just turn everything on and start playing, and we improvise and improvise for days until something works. I'm taping everything and we'll listen back to it and say, "That sounds interesting. What happened there?" And we'll develop that into songs, so to do that, you have to have no inhibitions, to sit down and not be afraid to play badly, because if you're playing safe all the time, then nothing really new happens. You have to have the knowledge that the other people involved don't mind that I start to sing out of tune, if I'm going to try and sing a melody that isn't written. Just try and go for things that you might not be able to reach. We all know we've got to let our trousers down without worrying about it. And that's like a chemistry that you do get in certain bands, and that's what makes the band great, at least the experience of doing that. It's very enjoyable because you're creating something out of nothing.'

Peter Erskine said that a similar technique can open new doors when playing jazz: 'Some of the best creativity comes from imposing a set of limits; for example, jazz music improvisation is the most cherished part of what we do. A lot of jazz musicians – particularly the younger ones or the ones who are learning – learn certain notes or phrases, get them under their fingers so when they're improvising, they're really just recycling a lot of scales they've played before many, many times. So the guitarist John Abercrombie, when he teaches, he'll take a tune and only play half-notes so you can't play what your hands know. You have to be very creative then because every note has to be a good choice. It could be a bad choice, but you have to choose a note and compose, so that discipline opens all these creative doors.'

For some artists, environment can play an important role in affecting their ability to write. Steve Jordan said, 'Sometimes you have to be somewhere other than your home to create; sometimes you can't create at all unless you're at home. Sometimes your place needs to look a mess; sometimes you can't do anything unless it's completely clean.' Edie Brickell has one demand of her creative surroundings: 'Usually the house has to be clean, to have a nice environment [to create]. I can't stand a crowded, cluttered environment. I like sparse settings.' A change in atmosphere is beneficial to Peter Erskine: 'If I go for a walk, it's a great escape; instantly music comes to me. Or if I get very excited or very happy, it seems tunes that are long forgotten come back.'

Although their surroundings matter to some, others said it makes no difference as long as they have a pad and pencil close at hand. Richard Thompson's urge to write can strike anywhere, he said: 'I can sort of jot anytime. I take notes while I'm sitting on a plane or in an airport. I jot down observations, lines, hooks. I'm really happy if I can say, "This month I'm going to write from six to four, whatever it is, office hours." Three months is paradise. That's the most creative for me; not only do you get the tap turned on, tap's a bit creaky at first, you have to oil it and give it a good turn before it starts to flow, but once it's flowing and I'm doing it every day, it seems to have some cumulative effect and I can really get rolling. That for me is ideal, and I can only write when I'm well. If I'm ill, I can't write at all. I can write if I'm comfortable, even if I write uncomfortable songs. My last drug is coffee; I find coffee is a wonderful elixir. A cup of coffee and I'm ready.'

John Mayall sets goals for himself in order to create: 'Creativity for me starts with a desire to create something, and be inspired by something, or have a need to do something. For instance, when my house burned down, there was obviously work to be done, so something will always present itself where you have a challenge and you get inspired to meet it. That's where the creativity starts to come in, when you start using your imagination to what it can be and then see how close you can get to that. It starts off as a need. For example, when you get an opportunity to do an album, there's 10 songs that need to be done right there, so that starts you: "Okay, I need 10 songs, what are they going to be about?" Then you start breaking them down into sections and keys and stories, et cetera.

'Once you've got it mapped out like that, you can concentrate on any one specific song and, depending how your inspiration might go, you might work on just one song if you're in that particular mood. Sometimes, having got the subject, a couple of lines will just come to you and you build on that, before the music. The music might come first, but first of all comes the idea of what you're going to talk about – the story, the emotion – that needs to be put into words and music in its final entity. Get your subject first and that will lead you where you're going to go, certainly lead you into the musical mood, and then you just have to put the words together to express it in a story-like form.'

George Harrison told me he needed deadlines to write, but emphasised that creativeness never disappears completely: 'I find that, having just finished writing and recording an album, I tend to now work in spurts. At one point I think, "How do you write a tune?" I have just totally forgotten. But unlike some people who think they've dried up, I don't believe we dry up. Some people are really good at it; they'll set themselves an hour or two every day to go in there and write something. I don't do that. Somebody will say something or I'll see something, and I'll write it down on a piece of paper and later it will come into a tune. But the way I am at the moment I do have to force myself to do it; that's why deadlines are good. I never used to think I could write songs about specific things. I used to just write and the song would be whatever it became. Now somebody will ask me to write a song for a movie, and this is what's happening. I've done a bit of that lately and that's good too. You have to make yourself inspired.'

Looking Within

In the words of the musicians – and from my own experience – we've seen that there are several factors involved in actualising one's creativeness: recognising one's true gift, taking chances, developing the ability to concentrate, spending time alone to let the mind wander, and learning to have faith in oneself and one's true expression, which encouragement from others can help to nurture. How to get started doing this? Look within and find your real voice. When Bill Moyers asked Joseph Campbell in the acclaimed television series and book *The Power of Myth* how he would advise someone to tap into the spring of eternal life, or one's 'creative bliss', Campbell answered, 'We all have experiences all the time which may on occasion render some sense of this, a little intuition of where your bliss is. Grab it. No one can tell you what it is going to be. You have to learn to recognise your own depth.'

I've found there are tools that can help us do this. One way is through meditation. I continue to use this ancient technique to help me look inside, when mundane everyday activities are threatening to run my life. Keith Strickland, too, meditates on a regular basis to the benefit of his creativity: 'After having meditated for a while, I've discovered it's not necessarily a peaceful experience. Because when you do, certain thoughts arise; some really deep thoughts can arise that can be quite troubling, I find through meditation I am able to be more spontaneous. Just quietening your mind and your thoughts gets your mind very still and quiet, so that just a single sound can be so rich. It can be very inspiring. The sound becomes so much richer because you have so much more space. Through more meditation, it's like getting more to the core. Meditation enhances creativity. Ideas and thoughts can arise from almost nowhere.'

George Harrison, who became a proponent of meditation in the sixties, still found it effective in later life: 'Meditation is only a means to an end. In order to infuse energy and power and get it flowing through our bodies, we have to meditate. You infuse that energy into your being, and so when you are in activity, it rubs off onto that creatively. To really be in touch with creative energy, you will find that it lies within the stillness.'

In addition to the insights I've gained through meditation and psychotherapy, I have also found yoga helpful in reaching a deeper part of myself. This ancient practice combining relaxation, breathing and stretching exercises is yet another way of releasing the emotional blocks that can cloud one's self-perception. When the mind is harnessed through the concentration needed for yoga or meditation, there is space for intuition to come forth. It is easier to be receptive to self-expression when the mind has peace and space, or stillness, as George Harrison pointed out. Sinéad O'Connor said yoga had been effective for her, too, from time to time: 'Yoga is the thing that exercises all those points through which the universe – and music too – can communicate with you.'

I have found a few other tools useful for reaching that inner voice. Often I will just put pen to paper and see what will come out. One must not be afraid of what will emerge, however irrational or nonsensical it may seem. Writing down dreams can also help tap into the rich material of the unconscious. Very often I will find something there that is expressing some deep feeling.

Another key is to retrieve the childlike part of our nature, to regain that sense of awe, wonder and trust. To be creative, it is imperative to be flexible, open and receptive. As Rollo May wrote in his inspirational book *The Courage to Create:*

'If we are too rigid, dogmatic, or bound to previous conclusions, we will, of course, never let this new [creative] element come into our consciousness; we will never let ourselves be aware of the knowledge that exists on another level within us.'

To be creative, then, we have to get out of our own way, to allow the unconscious to come through. Again, in the words of Rollo May: 'The insight cannot be born until the conscious tension, the conscious application, is relaxed.' This point was made over and over again by the musicians.

We each have a gift – something we can do naturally – and it is up to us to find it. Our inspiration may come in a flash or it may need to germinate and develop gradually. In either case, it is something that is all our own. As Joseph Campbell said, 'I don't think there is any such thing as an ordinary mortal. Everybody has his own possibility of rapture in the experience of life. All he has to do is recognise it and then cultivate it and get going with it.' We can find this rapture, or bliss, as Campbell liked to call it, through the creative process. With self-expression comes the freedom to simply *be*.

Conclusion

FULL CIRCLE

'IF YOU ARE A MUSICIAN, YOU CAN NEVER REALLY STOP
PLAYING, EVEN IF YOU DON'T DO ANY GIGS OR YOU
RETIRE. YOU ARE STILL IN A WAY PLAYING INSIDE YOURSELF.'
KEITH RICHARDS

In describing the creative lives of musicians, it has brought to mind the story of finding my own creativity, a search that began many years ago and continues today. Although I often stumbled and fell dangerously close to the edge, I never abandoned the path. I look back and tend to think many years were wasted as the search went into darker corners, but maybe they weren't. Although painful, these lessons were to be learned too. What I did to myself is similar to the way metal can be bent only by putting it through fire. On the road to finding my own soul expression, the voice of my creativity, I never thought I would find it in exactly the same persona from which I struggled to escape: a musician. Musicians have played an important part in my life; they have symbolised both dragons and heroes.

After spending four years talking to musicians about their creative lives, mulling over our conversations, and writing about them, an integration has taken place within me. The two major opposing forces with which I grappled for 20 years have finally come together. For years my spiritual yearnings seemed diametrically opposed to the sensual world of musicians, drugs and rock 'n' roll. Among musicians, I was surrounded by intensive creative expression, which heightened my awareness of my own inadequacy in that area. Later, musicians represented my need to drink and so escape my shy, inhibited self, by opening up my extroverted side, which was normally well hidden from view. I found music exciting and I loved to dance, but my introverted side felt guilty for the frivolous lifestyle that went along with it. This more ethereal part of me enjoyed reading inspirational books, writing poetry and meditating – all without drinking or taking drugs. And so the battle had raged. Although both of these opposing personalities were part of me, I felt as if I were two different people. I swung from one to the other, never feeling whole.

Once I began my research, musicians became instrumental in my connection to my own creativity. They no longer represented one side of my continual battle. Instead, they became a catalyst to the liberation of my creativeness, which has culminated with this book. What I had labelled a spiritual quest, I realised, was actually the search for self-expression. By listening to musicians describe their creative lives, I became aware of a much deeper link to their inner world than I had ever experienced before. The musicians I interviewed taught me to trust and believe in my own creativeness. They have confirmed my recently acquired belief that all human beings have the potential to be creative in many different ways. Many have told me that they feel closer to their core, that they've tapped into the essence of who they really are, while they are creating. For most it appears to be the greatest feeling of integration they experience in life, where they feel more at peace with themselves, more complete.

It is when we are being true to our inner nature that we feel whole and the fragmented parts of ourselves come together. At these times one is aware of a sense of destiny, of being in the right place at the right time, a feeling of all is well in the world. Abraham Maslow, who has written extensively on the self-actualised person, said, 'A musician must make music if he is to be at peace with himself.' Indeed, Jeff Lynne told me, '[When writing], that's when you feel at peace with yourself for a bit, like, "I've done something really good." You feel elated for a while, it makes you feel more complete.' Similarly, Edie Brickell observed, 'Sometimes you get that locked-up feeling in your chest, where it's all blocked there, black. Creativity frees you, you feel like an open channel. I'm really lucky to do what I do – and grateful.' The late John Lee Hooker, in his seventies when we met, said that he still got an intense feeling when he performed: 'Sometimes when I'm playing the blues, tears come into my eyes. There's no limit to what I feel. It goes so deep.'

Michael McDonald explained that through creating he becomes who he really is: 'When I create, I give the child permission to speak, to be there. To stand up in front of a room full of people and have a perfectly good excuse to scream at the top of my lungs – which is what the vocal experience is all about. Playing rock 'n' roll music, I feel good inside. That is a big part of who I am. It is one chance in a world full of restraints to actually come out and be that.'

Robert Burke Warren also discovered his true self through

creativity: 'The drive to create is part of me. It's a spark that was fanned to a flame before I could walk. And it will always be there. When I'm playing, it's one of the only times I never feel self-conscious. I feel confident, like this is right, this is who I really am.'

Bonnie Raitt pointed out that as she becomes more aware of who she is, this self-knowledge is expressed through her music. 'I think if you're getting closer and closer to who you really are, who you really are has an awful lot to say.'

Some musicians described how living creative lives has enabled them to unify all the disparate parts of themselves. According to Robin Horn, 'Whatever I find out about drums, I'm finding out about myself. It just becomes expression – the ability to tune in and express yourself within the parameters of music.' This self-expression and wholeness is also important to Mick Fleetwood, who said: 'If I'm good at pulling feelings out of people who I play with and, hopefully, people that I'm with, I'm glad about that. It's a major thing to me. I want to be around people who really show themselves musically, don't let themselves be inhibited at all. I love to bring that out in fellow players; I need it. It has everything to do with attitude. It's letting yourself be who you are through your playing.' Bernie Larsen agreed, saying, 'I'm really lucky because I can satisfy myself with a lot of what I write – that's the reward. It's not monetary or approval from other people. I am fulfilled.'

Creativity, spirituality and wholeness go hand in hand, according to Dolette McDonald: 'I'm finding that the more spiritual I become, the more creative I become. I'm finding creative places in me that I didn't know existed. I'm becoming more focused and more centred and more secure about who I am, and other creative things are happening.'

Graham Nash also expressed the feeling that music has brought completeness to his life and that this, in return, has enabled him to make a positive impact on the world: 'I cannot separate myself and the way I live my life from my writing, or from my sculpture, or from my photography. I think life itself is the art piece, that the picture of my life will not be finished until I'm dead, and possibly not even then, because hopefully some of the music I've created will be affecting people's lives way after I'm dead. If I can make myself feel good, I can make other people feel good. If I can reach myself with some of the stuff I write, I know I stand a good chance of pleasing other people. I've started to realise I'm probably creating pieces to affect other people, to be remembered, to leave some mark on this planet.'

This mark of which Graham spoke was referred to by some musicians as their own sense of destiny to influence the world through their creativity: 'I believe I was definitely sent down here to take people away for a little while, to make them happy,' Stevie Nicks told me. 'When you come up with an idea you think is magnificent, or you sit down and play a piece of music that you know is going to turn into an incredible song, you walk away feeling worthwhile. Every day I feel I have to do something, whether it's [to] write a paragraph or sit at the piano for five minutes or go to the studio for a little while. If I don't feel I've done something worthwhile every day, then I feel worthless. I feel always that I have to hold up my end of the bargain, that I was given something by God, and He asks only that I give Him back something.'

Robin Le Mesurier told me a wonderful story about fulfilling the destiny he dreamed of as a young boy: 'I lived in a house in Earls Court for 25 years. At the back of the house you could see the Earls Court Exhibition building, and I'd seen the Stones play there and David Bowie and Slade – anybody that had played there. My mum used to make tea for all the kids who would line up outside the house to buy tickets in the middle of the night. So I used to see all this and think, I wonder if I'll ever play there.

'Then we came back when I was with Rod Stewart and did three nights there. I stood on the stage – it couldn't have been more than 300 yards from my old house – and my dad was there. My mum had died a couple of years before that, but I could feel her there; I just knew she was there. That, more than playing at Wembley Stadium, was one of the best highlights of my life.'

Through his creative experiences in Red Hot Chili Peppers, Anthony Kiedis has come to realise his own raison d'être: 'There are times when I think I have a very positive influence on the world through what I do. That makes me feel like I have a reason to be here, a purpose, to a certain extent. Having gone through what I've gone through in life and being able to put out a positive message in reference to, say, somebody on drugs, through my music, it may help somebody else who's dying a slow, agonising death, to give them hope and some encouragement. That makes me feel I have a purpose. Any time I can do something for somebody else, I feel like I have a reason to be here.'

Koko Taylor also said that she found fulfilment through uplifting people with her music: 'When I'm singing in front of an audience, I feel like I'm doing something to help someone, making people happy. People walk up and say, "You know that song you did, that really made my day." And that's the whole reason I'm out there in the first place – it's because of my fans. If I stayed home, I'd think to myself, somebody somewhere wants to hear me, wants to hear the blues. There are not a lot of women out there singing the blues – it's mostly men – so it's a must that I've got to hang in there.'

Singer Cece Bullard has a similar feeling about what she can do through music: 'I want people to benefit from what I've learned about not being negative, not letting this century bog us down. I want to make people feel better about themselves and that they can change the world – as corny as all that sounds. We can make a concerted effort just by being the best we can be. Each person can do something so important on an individual level, that's what I want to tell people. You affect everything around you. That's the kind of thing I would like to express in music.'

Rick Vito stressed the musician's role as a communicator of creative energy: 'It would be great to say something in a song [that] became popular to make people stop and think about some aspect of the human condition. A musician's responsibility is to say something that has never been said in quite that way before. The whole creative force is what most people probably refer to as God. It's almost incomprehensible; we're just little bits of that, little bits of the whole. It's all energy and communication of energy.'

Frank Foster saw himself as a messenger whose duty was to uplift the spirit of mankind: 'My music is out to proclaim the glory of God to everybody in the universe and to make everyone happy. Politically, every note is glorifying freedom, to make life positive. I'm trying to play notes that will make that ditch digger want to dig a better ditch. Socially, I think we should all come together and appreciate one another for our differences. Instead of fighting one another, let's love one another.'

Music for All Ages and Cultures

Since interviewing these musicians, talking to psychologists, and reading books on creativity, I have realised the special role musicians play in our society. By being a channel for the collective unconscious through their music, they reflect for us the spirit of our time. With music, they have the ability to touch the hearts of people and bring a feeling of unity and oneness to the masses. They can bring different people and cultures together.

Part of music's eternal nature is its constantly changing form, which enables it to continually touch different groups in our society. Yet as the music changes – and as outwardly people change – the inner essence remains the same. Albert Lee was one of several musicians who discussed this idea: 'I like old rock 'n' roll – that's as raucous as I like to get. Tastes change as you mature; you begin to appreciate other kinds of music. I love listening to thirties and forties music. Some of the music today leaves me wondering; it worries me when I hear heavy metal music. Are its listeners getting their aggressions out by listening to that? It puzzles me. I guess going through adolescence, you feel you have to make a statement.'

John McVie misses the connection he had with the sounds of the sixties and finds it difficult to relate to the new music popular today: 'All that very special stuff – the Beatles, Stones, Hendrix, The Who – that was such a phenomena, a lock-in of attitudes: social, spiritual, economic. The wheels just locked right. They pretty much defined the whole generation. We were lucky to be part of that. It doesn't happen today; there's nothing as special today. It's so diverse now; it's becoming a little bit less special; it doesn't have that warmth, that soul. As I'm saying that, I wonder if my dad would have said the same thing in his time about our music!'

Paul Kantner found the music of the nineties to be more representative of the stratified forces of that decade's culture, rather than the oneness of the sixties generation and its music: 'Today, various different musicians speak for various different groups [in society]. Before the Beatles – and even with the Beatles – it was like one large body. Then it fragmented, like a flower shooting pollen all over the place for new flowers to grow. Some of the new flowers are pretty ugly and some of them are quite beautiful. There's stuff to be had everywhere. There's just so much more of it, you're almost overloaded.'

Sinéad O'Connor stressed that a variety of musical styles permits a greater number of people to be reached: 'Music is the most powerful form of communication. There's nobody that doesn't listen to music. You have pop music, soul music, and you have people like Van Morrison. Not everybody is open to Van Morrison, so they'd have to get their information from Janet Jackson or Madonna. Pop music has just as much a function to perform as anything else. There are certain types of people that will only be able to receive information from that kind of medium. There's a person there for every section of society. We've got Janet Jackson, who's basically pop, but who is for some reason managing to communicate incredibly with people by the way she writes or the things she says in a pop format. Van Morrison would get another type of people; I would get another type; George Michael would get another type. There are different musicians for different mentalities.'

Although the sound of music changes, its purpose remains the same, according to Huey Lewis: 'Artists are meant to put their finger on something society hasn't figured out yet. In a way, artists are meant to be the enemies of society. Society is very structured, and our job is to rattle that cage for better or worse; generally we're supposed to be sort of outlawish.'

Sinéad O'Connor feels that music can bring harmony to our turbulent world: 'Music is very healing and balancing. Certain notes that are sung will balance things; they'll balance people; it balances you inside to hear it. That's why people are very into textural music because of the massage. It balances everybody and, therefore, it balances the universe.'

Don Henley described the cohesiveness music brings to humanity: 'Songs just keep you company, that's all. They make you feel less lonely; they make you feel like there's somebody else out there that feels the way you do. That's the effect a good song should have: to make a person feel a part of the world, a part of the human community.'

Chris McVie summed up beautifully music's timeless power: 'Music is the most gratifying of all sensory feelings that we have. Everybody gets something from music; not everybody gets something from looking at a painting. It's the passion, it's the spirit of the person; it moves people. And if they can't create it for themselves, they can enjoy the writings of another person and that is part of the pleasure of doing it. It's not to write and keep it all for yourself. I think you primarily write for yourself – that's the object of doing it initially. But then to lock it up in a cupboard and never to share it with anyone is totally pointless. One hopes one can give pleasure to people by playing it to them.'

Tony Williams described the power of music and how, by creating, it fulfils his inner essence: 'When I play the drums, I'm feeling music. I love the drums as an instrument; I love the physical and metaphysical connection, where they both touch each other. When I put my hands down, holding a pair of sticks and touch the drums, it's just a wonderful feeling, and things happen. And it's like they are my best friend, and I'm doing something with my best friend. We're doing this thing together and no one can come between us, no one – not my mother, my father, my girlfriend, the police, God – nothing can come between us. There's this thing that happens when I sit at the drums that is just me. Someone once told me if I lived my life like I played the drums, I wouldn't have any problems. It's a nice place to be and it's a place I've been all my life, ever since I started playing the drums. It's something that has given me the opportunity to be the person I am. Without that connection with the universe, I'd probably be a different person. So it's like the stream through my life that makes me want to be a better person, that makes me want to say something. This connection means [that] when I go out in life, I'm representing that. I'm a representative of that world, and that world is so wonderful [that] I have a responsibility to be wonderful.'

Steve Gadd agreed that through the creative process, he is able to tap into that higher element of himself that is also a component of the universal whole: 'I'm a part of something.

We're all a part of this thing. If I can live my life and try to get in tune with that, then it's great. The effortlessness that I feel when I'm playing certain music, if I could just take that feeling and live my life on that level, just be a part of that thing and flow with it. I think that the challenge is to try to live that way, to try and just flow with life.'

The artists' compelling drive to express themselves is that innate desire to be whole, to fulfil their destiny, to become in tune with themselves and the universe. Just as music's purpose is to give people's lives depth, so must individuals find their own purpose by discovering their inner truth through their own creative endeavours. As Joseph Campbell said, 'If you do follow your bliss, you put yourself on a kind of track that has been there all the while, waiting for you, and the life you ought to be living is the one you are living.'

It is up to those of us who are not musicians to find our own individual talents and, therefore, to find peace and a feeling of wholeness within ourselves. I truly hope the answers to which I have been led by so many wonderful musicians will give direction to others on the path to self-expression.

Acknowledgments

There are so many people I wish to thank for their help, support, and encouragement. First and foremost, I give my heartfelt thanks and appreciation to all the musicians who graciously agreed to be interviewed for this book. Every interview was unique and I felt honoured to have been invited into their world of creativity, where they shared their thoughts, memories, and their sense of humility towards the creative process.

I wish to give a fond farewell to those musicians I interviewed for the book who are no longer with us: John Lee Hooker, Ravi Shankar, Phoebe Snow, Koko Taylor, Frank Foster, Kirsty MacColl, Tony Williams, Ian Wallace, Willie Dixon, Teddy Pendergrass, Warren Zevon and George Harrison.

I give warm thanks to Sarah Lazin who recognised and wholeheartedly encouraged this book right from the very beginning. I also thank her for introducing me to my co-writer and friend Holly George-Warren, whose steadying influence and judgment were invaluable

I am grateful to our original editor at Fireside, Malaika Adero, and to our subsequent Fireside editor, David Dunton, for his commitment, enthusiasm and skilful editing.

I would like to thank all the photographers who generously gave photographs to be included in this book: Pattie Boyd, Alan Kozlowski, Neal Preston, Franco Vogt, Sharon Weisz and the estate of Eric Swayne.

I would like to thank the late professor Frank Barron for his willingness to share his knowledge and for putting his time and energy into our talks about creativity. I am deeply grateful and give thanks to Dr Ron Alexander for being such an inspirational teacher of psychology, a good friend, and for giving me his views on the creative process.

Special thanks to Martin Wyatt, Larry Vigon, Christine McVie, Mick Fleetwood, Graham Nash and Stevie Nicks for their contributions.

Lastly I would like to thank John Blake and all at Blake Publishing for recognising the importance of the timeless message contained in this book and providing the opportunity for it to be re-published.

APPENDIX ONE

Interview Questions

The interviews with musicians were based on the following questions:

1. What was your upbringing like? Any brothers and sisters? Did your parents raise you?
2. Would you describe yourself as outgoing or shy/introverted as a child?
3. Were either of your parents musical?
4. Was your creativity encouraged?
5. Who inspired you musically as a child?
6. Did you ever feel different from other children?
7. What age were you when you first became aware of your musical inclinations?
8. Did you have any idea what you were going to be when you grew up?

9. Did you have any unexplained or psychic experiences or significant recurring dreams as a child?

10. Do you believe in a greater power? Does it connect to your creativity?

11. Do you believe you're here for a reason?

12. What gave you the drive to go through the learning process of playing your instrument? What was it like for you?

13. Have you ever experienced a transcendent or peak experience while singing, playing or composing? Explain what that feels like.

14. Did you ever reflect, 'Why me?'

15. Are you aware of your creative abilities as a power?

16. Did any of your music ever feel mystically inspired?

17. What gives you the drive to create?

18. Do you feel everyone has the potential to be creative, or is it a gift?

19. Is there a connection to when you feel more or less creative to what's going on in your life?

20. Do you have a choice to create, or is it something that just happens?

21. Are you in touch with the child in you?

22. What part do drugs and alcohol play on the creative process? Do they enhance it or block it?

23. What do you feel when you're playing?

24. Did you ever feel spiritually connected to one group as a whole?

25. Do you think the music today represents the unconscious feelings of the masses?

26. When at the height of your creativeness, or during a peak experience, do you feel closer to who you really are?

INTERVIEW QUESTIONS

27. Have you any idea where the creative force comes from?

28. How do you feel at the verge of creating something?

29. Would you say the closest thing to a spiritual experience is when you're singing, playing your instrument or composing?

30. Have you ever felt there was a purpose or meaningfulness in your creativeness on a spiritual, political or social level?

APPENDIX TWO

Musicians interviewed for this book

Graham Bell is a singer and songwriter. Formerly a member of the British bands Skip Bifferty and Bell and Arc, he is currently a solo artist.

Stephen Bishop is a singer, songwriter and solo artist.

Edie Brickell is a singer and songwriter, who most recently collaborated on an album with Steve Martin.

Jackson Browne is a singer, songwriter and solo artist.

Lindsey Buckingham is a singer, songwriter and the lead guitarist of Fleetwood Mac.

Cece Bullard is a singer who has performed with such artists as Rita Coolidge.

Eric Burdon is a singer and songwriter, who originally formed The Animals.

MUSICIANS INTERVIEWED

Billy Burnette is a singer, songwriter and guitarist.

Rosanne Cash is a singer, songwriter and solo artist.

Eric Clapton is a guitarist, songwriter and singer, who before becoming a solo artist played in such bands as the Yardbirds, Cream, Blind Faith and Derek and the Dominos.

Terri Lyne Carrington is a jazz drummer and composer who has performed with such artists as Wayne Shorter. She currently leads her own band.

Phil Collins is a singer, songwriter and drummer who has performed as a solo artist and with the band Genesis.

David Crosby is a singer, songwriter and guitarist who was an original member of the Byrds and Crosby, Stills and Nash. He also performs as a solo artist.

Willie Dixon was a blues/R&B songwriter, singer and bassist.

Peter Erskine is a session drummer who has played with such jazz artists as Weather Report.

Jason Farrar is a singer, songwriter and pianist.

Mick Fleetwood is a drummer and founding member of Fleetwood Mac.

Frank Foster played saxophone and clarinet, among other instruments. He was a composer and arranger, played with the Elvin Jones Quintet, and was the bandleader of the Count Basie Orchestra.

Peter Frampton is a singer, songwriter, guitarist and solo artist and formerly a member of the British bands Humble Pie and Frampton's Camel.

Peter Gabriel is a singer, songwriter and solo artist who was a founding member of Genesis.

Steve Gadd is a session drummer who has played with such artists as Aretha Franklin, Chick Corea and Paul Simon.

Buddy Guy is a blues guitarist, singer and songwriter.

George Harrison, formerly of the Beatles, was a singer, songwriter, guitarist, solo artist and member of The Travelling Wilburys.

Don Henley is a singer, songwriter, drummer and solo artist, and a founding member of the Eagles.

John Lee Hooker was a blues guitarist, songwriter and singer.

Paul Horn is a jazz and new-age flautist and saxophonist who leads his own band.

Robin Horn is a session drummer who has played with Linda Ronstadt, Aaron Neville, and in his father Paul Horn's band.

Ice-T is a hip-hop artist and actor.

Steve Jordan is a musician who has played drums and bass with such artists as Neil Young and Keith Richards.

Paul Kantner, a founding member of the Jefferson Airplane and Jefferson Starship, is a singer, songwriter and guitarist.

Anthony Kiedis is a songwriter and lead singer of the Red Hot Chili Peppers.

B. B. King is a blues guitarist, singer and songwriter.

MUSICIANS INTERVIEWED

Bernie Larsen is a guitarist and songwriter who has played with David Lindley in the band El Rayo-X and with such artists as Melissa Etheridge and Rickie Lee Jones.

Albert Lee is a guitarist and songwriter who has played with the Everly Brothers, Eric Clapton, Emmylou Harris and many others.

Robin Le Mesurier is a guitarist and songwriter who played with Rod Stewart for many years and currently leads his own band.

Julian Lennon is a singer, songwriter, pianist and solo artist.

Huey Lewis is a singer, songwriter and harmonica player who leads his band, The News.

Jeff Lynne is a singer, songwriter, guitarist, keyboardist, producer and solo artist. He is a founding member of The Move, Electric Light Orchestra, and The Travelling Wilburys.

Kirsty MacColl was a singer, songwriter, and solo artist.

Dolette McDonald is a singer and songwriter who has performed with Sting, Don Henley, Talking Heads, Laurie Anderson, Steve Winwood, Peter Gabriel and the Rolling Stones.

Michael McDonald is a singer, songwriter, keyboardist and solo artist, and former member of the Doobie Brothers.

Christine McVie is a singer, songwriter, keyboardist, solo artist and a former member of Fleetwood Mac and Chicken Shack.

John McVie, a bassist, is a founding member of Fleetwood Mac.

Branford Marsalis is a jazz saxophonist who leads his own quartet, and has played with many artists, including his father Ellis Marsalis, his brother, Wynton Marsalis and Sting.

Hank B Marvin is a guitarist, songwriter and solo artist who led the instrumental band The Shadows.

John Mayall is a blues guitarist, singer, songwriter and solo artist who founded The Blues Breakers.

Joni Mitchell is a singer, songwriter, guitarist and solo artist.

Graham Nash is a singer, songwriter, guitarist and solo artist who was a founding member of Crosby, Stills and Nash and The Hollies.

Randy Newman is a singer, songwriter, pianist, soundtrack composer and solo artist.

Stevie Nicks is a singer, songwriter, solo artist and a member of Fleetwood Mac.

Sinéad O'Connor is a singer, songwriter, guitarist and solo artist.

Teddy Pendergrass was an R&B singer and songwriter and formerly a member of Harold Melvin and the Blue Notes.

Greg Phillinganes is a keyboardist who has played with such artists as Stevie Wonder, Eric Clapton and Michael Jackson. He is also a solo artist.

Queen Latifah is a singer, songwriter and actress.

Bonnie Raitt is a guitarist, singer, songwriter and solo artist.

Vernon Reid is a guitarist and songwriter for the band Living Colour, as well as a solo artist and producer.

Keith Richards is a guitarist, songwriter, singer and founding member of The Rolling Stones.

Mike Rutherford is a guitarist, bassist, songwriter, singer and member of Genesis and Mike and the Mechanics.

Ravi Shankar was a classical sitarist and composer.

Patty Smyth is a singer, songwriter and solo artist, formerly of the band Scandal.

Phoebe Snow was a singer, songwriter and solo artist.

Ringo Starr is a drummer, singer, songwriter, former Beatle and actor. He currently performs with his All-Starr Band.

Stephen Stills is a guitarist, songwriter, singer and solo artist. A member of Crosby, Stills and Nash, he co-founded Buffalo Springfield and Manassas.

Keith Strickland is songwriter and guitarist for the B-52s, in which he previously played drums.

Koko Taylor was a blues singer and songwriter.

Richard Thompson is a guitarist, songwriter, singer and solo artist. He was formerly a member of Fairport Convention.

Rick Vito is a guitarist, songwriter, singer and solo artist. He was formerly with Fleetwood Mac.

Ian Wallace, a former member of King Crimson, was a drummer who played with such artists as Bob Dylan, Don Henley, Jackson Browne, Bonnie Raitt and Crosby, Stills and Nash.

Robert Burke Warren is a bassist, guitarist, singer, songwriter and solo artist who has played with such bands as the Fleshtones and also starred in the West End as Buddy Holly in the musical *Buddy*.

Roger Waters is a singer, songwriter, bassist and solo artist who was a founding member of Pink Floyd.

Tony Williams was a jazz drummer who played with Miles Davis. A composer, he also founded the Tony Williams Lifetime and the Tony Williams Quintet.

Nancy Wilson is a singer, songwriter, guitarist and founding member of Heart.

Steve Winwood is a singer, songwriter, multi-instrumentalist and solo artist who was formerly with the Spencer Davis Group, Blind Faith, and Traffic.

Ron Wood is a guitarist, singer, songwriter, Rolling Stone and former member of the Faces.

Warren Zevon was a singer, songwriter, guitarist, keyboardist and solo artist.

APPENDIX THREE

Recommended Reading

I found the following volumes to be very helpful in understanding creativity and other psychological concepts discussed in this book.

Arieti, Silvano. *Creativity: The Magic Synthesis.* New York: Basic Books, 1976. (The different aspects of the creative process are covered thoroughly in this book. Arieti provides many examples and studies conducted by himself, Frank Barron and others who have researched creativeness.)

Barron, Frank. *Creativity and Personal Freedom.* New York: D. Van Nostrand & Company, 1968. (Psychologist Frank Barron has spent many years researching the creative process. Here he describes characteristics of the creative person and such concepts as creative motivation.)

Campbell, Joseph, with Bill Moyers. *The Power of Myth*. New York: Doubleday, 1988. (Based on conversations between Bill Moyers and mythology scholar Joseph Campbell conducted for the television series of the same name, this book is one of my favourites. It explores the part myths play in our society. Within its pages are many inspirational words about our innate creative potential and the beauty of fulfilling it.)

Evans, Richard I. *Jung on Elemental Psychology*. New York: E P Dutton and Company, 1976. (Compiled from conversations between psychologists Richard I Evans and C G Jung, this book offers detailed yet informal descriptions and examples of some of Jung's most difficult concepts.)

James, William. *The Varieties of Religious Experience*. Foreword by Jacques Barzun. New York: New American Library, 1958. (This classic gives wonderful examples of the peak experience and its spiritual connection through the ages.)

Jung, C. G. *Memories, Dreams, Reflections*. Recorded and edited by Aniela Jaffe; translated by Richard and Clara Winston. New York: Random House, 1961; New York: Vintage, 1989. (In Jung's scintillating words, this book tells the story of the great thinker's life and discovery of his own inner world through dreams and images.)

RECOMMENDED READING

Maslow, Abraham, H. *Religions, Values, and Peak-Experiences.* New York: Viking Penguin, 1970; 1987. (This little book contains the quintessential discussion of the peak experience, as formulated by Maslow.) *Toward a Psychology of Being.* 3d ed. New York: Van Nostrand Reinhold Company, 1968. (Another one of the greats, this volume is dense with information about the self-actualised person and his or her qualities. Maslow describes in detail the course required to fulfil one's creative potential.)

May, Rollo. *The Courage to Create.* New York: W W Norton & Company, 1975; New York: Bantam, 1985. (This is an easy-to-read and exceptionally inspirational book on the creative process. Rollo May emphasises the importance of expressing ourselves and also speaks of the significant role artists play in our society today.)

Neumann, Erich. *Art and the Creative Unconscious.* Princeton: Princeton University Press, 1959; 1974. (Although this book requires a great deal of concentration, it contains some of the most fascinating information on the collective unconscious I've read anywhere. It requires time to assimilate and digest.)

Rilke, Rainer Maria. *Letters to a Young Poet.* Translated and foreword by Stephen Mitchell. New York: Random House, 1984; New York: Vintage, 1986. (Inspiring letters written by turn-of-the-century poet Rilke to a hopeful student are collected in this volume. I found this to be a particularly good translation.)

Serrano, Miguel. *Jung and Hesse: A Record of Two Friendships.* New York: Schocken Books, 1966. (This beautiful book gives insight into the great minds of psychologist C. G. Jung and writer Hermann Hesse through their correspondence and meetings.)

Simonton, Dean Keith. *Genius, Creativity and Leadership.* Cambridge, Massachusetts: Harvard University Press, 1984. (Another leader in the study of creativity, Simonton gives his views on the creative person based on his research).

Wilmer, Harry A. *Practical Jung: Nuts and Bolts of Jungian Psychotherapy.* Chiron Publications, 1987. (This overview of the basics of Jungian theory is a good choice for beginners. Wilmer uses layman's terms and ample illustrations to explain such concepts as archetypes, dreams and symbols.)

INDEX

INDEX

INDEX

INDEX